KATHLEEN W. NATALINO

JUVENILE DELINQUENCY
Causes, Control, and Prevention

JUVENILE DELINQUENCY
Causes, Control, and Prevention

Harjit S. Sandhu, Ph.D.
Professor of Sociology
Oklahoma State University
Stillwater, Oklahoma

Gregg Division/McGraw-Hill Book Company

New York   St. Louis   Dallas   San Francisco   Auckland   Bogotá
Düsseldorf   Johannesburg   London   Madrid   Mexico   Montreal
New Delhi   Panama   Paris   São Paulo   Singapore   Sydney
Tokyo   Toronto

Library of Congress Cataloging in Publication Data

Sandhu, Harjit S
  Juvenile delinquency.

  Includes bibliographical references and index.
  1. Juvenile delinquency—United States. 2. Juvenile justice, Administration of—United States.
  3. Juvenile delinquency—United States—Prevention.
  I. Title.
  HV9104.S3155   364.36′0973   76-50138
  ISBN 0-07-054650-9

JUVENILE DELINQUENCY—CAUSES, CONTROL, AND PREVENTION

Copyright © 1977 by McGraw-Hill, Inc. All rights reserved. Printed in the United States of America. No part of this publication may be reproduced, stored in a retrieval system, or transmitted, in any form or by any means, electronic, mechanical, photocopying, recording, or otherwise, without the prior written permission of the publisher.

1234567890 DODO 7832109 87

The editors for this book were Susan H. Munger and Susan Berkowitz, the designer was Tracy A. Glasner, and the production supervisor was Kathleen Morrissey.
It was set in Primer by Kingsport Press, Inc.
Printed and bound by R. R. Donnelley & Sons Company

To members of my family—Roop, Sara, Ken, and Teji—
who taught me to live with different lifestyles

Contents

PREFACE ix

CHAPTER

1. **The Nature and Extent of Delinquency** 1
   Legal Definition   Historical Perspective   Incidence   Trends   International Perspective

2. **The Making of a Delinquent** 33
   Delinquency-Generating Sources in the Society   Delinquency-Generating Sources in the Individual   Delinquency-Provoking Sources in the Interaction of the Individual and the Society

3. **The Diversity of Delinquent Expression** 71
   Rebellious and Fun-oriented Delinquency: Vandalism   Middle-Class Delinquency   Gang Delinquency   Drugs and Delinquency   Female Delinquency   Psychopathic Expression

4. **Delinquents: Types and Characteristics** 105
   The Violent Offender   The Property Offender   The Authority Offender

5. **Delinquents, Police, and Detention** 135
   Police-Juvenile Encounters   Juvenile Investigation Units   Police-Juvenile Relations   Temporary Detention

6. **The Juvenile Court** 157
   Development of the Idea of a Juvenile Court   Philosophy of the Juvenile Court   The Juvenile Court in Operation   Supreme Court Decisions   The Juvenile Court after the Gault Decision   The Court's Vulnerability: Externally   The Court's Vulnerability: Internally   The Future of the Juvenile Courts

7. **Juvenile Probation and Aftercare** 187
   Historical Development   Goals and Functions   Organization of Probation Services   Probation Officers   Referees   Case Load Size   Supporting Services   Diversion and Civil Commitment   Juvenile Aftercare   Parolees' Return to Their Communities   Support from Parents   Who Succeeds

or Fails?   Effectiveness Studies   Juvenile Justice: International Perspective

8. Juvenile Institutions   219
History of Institutions: An Unfulfilled Promise of Reform   Present Status of Institutions   The Inmates   Working Philosophy   Treatment Programs   Links with the Community   The Inmate in a Total Institution   Custodial versus Treatment Institutions: Differential Impact   The Therapeutic Community   Effectiveness of Institutional Programs

9. Community Corrections   245
Community-based Corrections: An Alternative to Confinement   Youth Services Bureau   Residential Centers   Nonresidential Programs   Interaction between Corrections and Community: A Two-way Process   Volunteers

10. Delinquency Prevention   273
The Assumptions   Citizen Action   Delivery of Government and Social Services   Youth Services Bureaus   Practical Programs for Delinquency Prevention   Programs for Drug Abuse Treatment and Prevention   Programs for Employment   Programs for Education   Programs for Recreation   Programs for Religion   Critique

11. Final Impressions   299
Status Offenders   Inappropriate Intervention   Federal Efforts: New Legislation   Work Force   Treatment Trends

APPENDIX   309

INDEX   315

Preface

The problem of juvenile delinquency has been with us for a long time, and its causes and cures have been deliberated upon by various persons and in various ways. Despite all the efforts, the problem has not abated; rather, it has grown to serious proportions. The seriousness of the problem has caused deep concern, leading to new thoughts, experimentation, innovations, national commissions, Supreme Court decisions, and federal legislation. As a result, the amount of literature on juvenile delinquency and youth crime has increased. The President's Commission on Law Enforcement and Administration of Justice with its several task forces appointed in the middle 1960s and the National Advisory Commission on Criminal Justice Standards and Goals of the early 1970s have made a number of recommendations. Even though these recommendations may be accepted only partially, they are bound to influence the policies and practices of the juvenile justice system profoundly. Since a student does not have time to go through the various commission reports and Supreme Court decisions, this text presents the important recommendations, as well as standards and goals.

Obviously, these recommendations are based on previous experience, tested theories, and the knowledge accumulated over several decades. This background is important for the student and so has been represented in the text. By including both theoretical and practical outlooks, this book should appeal to both the scholar and the field worker. An added dimension of the text is the frequent reference to delinquency in other societies, and the different reactions of those societies. Delinquency in affluent societies is compared with that of poor societies.

In the first chapter, lengthy tables illustrate a discussion of the arrest trends and incidence of specific offenses according to the age, sex, and race of the offender. There is also a historical account of the reaction of Americans to their delinquent youth. The theories of causation, which often are difficult to grasp, are neatly encapsulated in Chapter 2. Delinquency expresses itself through fun, destruction, gang activity, drugs, sex, and psychopathy. These diverse delinquent expressions are dealt with in Chapter 3. The next chapter deals with different types of delinquents, including status offenders (authority offenders). Chapters 5 to 9 discuss the juvenile agencies that generally process and serve the delinquent. The historic Supreme Court decisions are discussed at some length to give students an idea of their impact on juvenile courts. Current evaluations of the effectiveness of different kinds of juvenile institutions and their practices are discussed. The Youth Services Bureau, a promising new organization, is given a proper place. The Appendix contains useful information on juvenile service agencies and publications as well as suggestions for applying for educational loans and grants and employment.

The author must acknowledge his son, Tejindar who, despite his heavy preoccupation with medical and psychiatric pursuits, willingly took time to make several suggestions. Gratitude is also due to the staff of McGraw-Hill Book Company. They not only gave greatly needed encouragement to the author from time to time, but put in a lot of imagination and work to help bring the author's manuscript to its present status.

Harjit S. Sandhu

JUVENILE DELINQUENCY
Causes, Control, and Prevention

The Nature and Extent of Delinquency

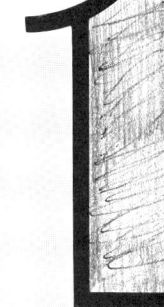

Each society has defined delinquent behavior in its own way. Large industrial societies generally seem to have very little tolerance for juvenile mischief. In these societies, social relationships are relatively impersonal. In such an impersonal society, or *gesellschaft*, an offender is usually someone not known by the community. The unknown always evokes fear, so the industrial society is fearful of the offender. Because of this fear, the industrial society takes steps to ensure its safety—mainly by enacting laws against the delinquent. Industrial societies seem to overreact in fear of the delinquent. They restrain the individual, for example, under curfew laws and drinking laws. They get unduly concerned about the orderliness and obedience of young persons. So they enact laws against wayward conduct, unmanageable behavior, and disobedience by youth. Repressive enforcement of these laws leads to conflict, distrust, and hostility between the children and the authorities.

On the other hand, an agricultural society or other *gemeinschaft* community is more likely to know its delinquents. And, knowing them, it fears them less. With less fear, there is a relaxed relationship between the society and its offenders. Very few laws govern the behavior of youth. As a result, there is relatively less delinquency in agricultural societies. These societies can put up more easily with whatever delinquency they have.

LEGAL DEFINITION

There are multiple jurisdictions within any society. Each jurisdiction has its own statutes defining delinquent conduct. Every violation of federal, state, or municipal laws committed by a youth under a particular age (usually 18, 17, or 16 years) constitutes delinquency. The same violation committed by an adult above the age limit is considered crime. However, society generates far more delinquency than crime by imposing more restrictions on juveniles than on adults. For example, juvenile laws prohibit running away from home, absenting oneself from school, wandering about railroad yards, using obscene language in public places, visiting places where liquor is used, indulging in sexual promiscuity, associating with criminals or other deviants, and smoking cigarettes. These laws also take note of disobedience and ungovernable behavior.

At the same time, juvenile laws provide protection for dependent and neglected children. Clauses in the statutes provide supervision for children who are exposed to physical (including sexual), social, and moral hazards. Children may face these risks at the hands of their families, friends, or other persons who exploit them for personal benefits. A girl whose mother is a prostitute, father an alcoholic, brother in a mental institution, and boyfriend a pimp could be in a situation of both hazard and neglect. In these circumstances, the girl could easily be considered a potential delinquent. Juvenile delinquency is, therefore, what the laws describe it to be. Tappan uses the following definition:

> *Delinquency is any act, course of conduct, or situation which might be brought before court and adjudicated* whether in fact it comes to be treated there or by some other resource or indeed remains untreated. . . . *The juvenile delinquent is a person who has been adjudicated as such by a court of proper jurisdiction* though he may be no different, up until the time of court contact and adjudication, at any rate, from masses of children who are not delinquent.[1]

The Children's Bureau, a former federal agency, defines legal juvenile delinquency in the following words:

> Juvenile delinquency cases are those referred to courts for acts defined in the statutes of the state as the violation of a state law or municipal ordinance by children or youth of juvenile court age, or for conduct so seriously antisocial as to interfere with the rights of others or to menace the welfare of the delinquent himself or of the community. This broad definition

of delinquency includes conduct which violates the law only when committed by children, e.g., truancy, ungovernable behavior and running away.[2]

Neglect cases generally concern children whose parents have abandoned them. Also included are children whose parents neglect or refuse to provide the proper care (including medical care), education, or environment. There are, annually, a great number of such cases. There were as many as 157,000 dependency and neglect cases in 1965. It is estimated that more than half of all neglect proceedings involve children under 6 years old; and 90 percent involve children under 12 years old.

Dependency usually means either complete absence of a legal custodian or lack of proper care. This is not the result of a refusal to provide, but rather because of physical, mental, or financial inability.[3] There is a feeling that dependency cases involving financial inability should be "dealt with administratively under Social Welfare Law rather than judicially under the Family Court Act."[4]

Legal Age of Delinquent Children

Who is a juvenile usually depends on state law. The age at which a person can no longer be charged as a delinquent in a juvenile court varies from state to state. In most states, an individual becomes an adult in the eyes of the juvenile court at age 18. A few states also have a *minimum* age below which a child cannot be formally charged with delinquency. However, in such cases, a child below the minimum age can appear before the juvenile court, usually as a "neglected child" or a "child in need of supervision."

It is not uncommon to find individuals between 18 and 21 years of age in juvenile correctional facilities. These people may have been sent to juvenile facilities when they were still legally juveniles. Or, on occasion, they may have been sentenced by a criminal (adult) court but committed to a juvenile institution. In isolated cases, a young offender who is legally an adult, but who is physically or psychologically immature, will be assigned to a juvenile facility. Furthermore, *youthful offender* statutes exist in a few states such as New York and California. These statutes provide for the special handling of certain suspected or adjudicated offenders. Such offenders are beyond the age jurisdiction of juvenile court but are still relatively young, usually under 24 years old. Youthful offender statutes attempt to allow more flexibility in the judicial processing of the young adult. They stress treatment-oriented sentencing.[5]

It is not easy to explain this variation in age limits for delinquents. The young have, at times, questioned the arbitrary age limits placed on them for quitting high school, taking a job, marrying without the consent of their parents, or drinking beer. They have also challenged the authority of the state to call them for the draft at age 18, but to prohibit them from entering into or signing certain contracts until age 21. The upper age limit for juvenile delinquency and youth crime should have some logical relationship to other age limitations. Middle-class values seem to influence the age boundaries for delinquency. When middle-class youth were involved in drug offenses extensively, the age limit was raised to 18 years to save them from adult courts. In California, the juvenile court and the adult court have had jurisdiction over persons aged 18 through 21. Youthful offenders in this age bracket have been handled by both juvenile and adult courts. For the most part, the choice depends on the circumstances of the case and the offender's characteristics. More recently, the trend has been to try to lower the age limit—which is down to 14 years in Illinois and New York.[6] This may reflect the middle class's growing fear as crime and delinquency invade suburbia.

Changes in the age limit for youth crime affect the jobs, work, jurisdiction, and responsibilities of juvenile police units, courts, and other juvenile agencies. Changes in the age limit also affect adult corrections and penology in general. The 11- to 17-year-old age group represents 13.2 percent of the population. According to the report of the President's Commission on Crime, this group was responsible for half the arrests for serious property offenses (burglary, larceny, and auto theft) in 1965. The arrest rate for these offenses is highest for 15- to 17-year-olds.[7] The 18- to 25-year-old age group shows more arrests for violent crime than any other age group.

If the juvenile-status age limit were raised, more offenders between the ages 11 and 25 could be handled in an informal and rehabilitative manner by juvenile agencies. On the other hand, when the age limit is lowered, it seems to be motivated by an increasing fear of juvenile offenders. This fear leads to a desire for harsher (adult) penalties against them.

HISTORICAL PERSPECTIVE

The term *juvenile delinquency* may be new, but the problems of children are as old in history as the children themselves. Every society has treated its children in accordance with its religious, social, and political beliefs. Several rapid socioeconomic changes, such as the breakdown of feudalism, rise of industrialism, colonization, migration, and urbanization, have influenced societies' attitudes to children. These attitudes were also shaped by catastrophic events such as epidemics, wars, depressions, and a breakdown of the family system.

The early Americans brought with them the welfare norms of their old countries. In England, people who were helpless and needy through no fault of their own were helped, but the criminal was punished. The delinquent or criminal was sent to a house of correction and put to work. The adults and children were kept together. The punishments were harsh. "The vagrant, including drifters, strangers, squatters, and beggars were ostracized."[8] In America, the colonists inflicted severe punishments on children. Whipping was quite common. Repetition of offenses could bring the death sentence. Rothman has listed cases of young girls who were hanged for their "sins of disobedience."

> One Boston minister told a young girl about to be hanged that her sins were the direct result of "your pride, your disobedience to your parents, your impatience of family government." . . . Early lessons in religion and obedience could protect the child from the fate of the gallows.[9]

With this emphasis on proper disciplining of children, it was the essential duty of the family to raise children to respect law and authority. According to Rothman, "Ministers instructed their congregates not only to raise children to be God-fearing, but to make them 'serviceable in their generation.' And statutes sought to enforce the command."[10] Though the punishments were severe, the colonists were not much inclined to put children in almshouses or jails. They kept the child in the home and held the family responsible for resocialization. The almshouse and jail, if and when used, closely resembled the household in structure and routine.[11] It should be remembered that there was little or no use of the penal institution for punishment during the eighteenth century.

Reliance on Institutions

There was a shift in penological thinking in the nineteenth century. The social and religious leaders of America started blaming evil influences in the community environment for provoking delinquent behavior. They connected delinquent behavior with parental neglect, criminal models among companions, and drinking by the youth. These were the days of rapid industrialization, when many Americans were lured to big cities in search of jobs. In large, impersonal cities the young roamed about in the "streets of vice," visiting prostitutes, night clubs, and theaters. The puritan critics thought that the society was going to ruin itself without family and community discipline. This sensitivity to growing indiscipline in the society brought about the rise of a penitentiary.

The Quakers built the first penitentiary at Cherry Hill, Pennsylvania, in 1829. The philosophy behind the Pennsylvania Penitentiary System was that the prisoners should be made to penitate to reform themselves. The Quakers thought very highly of their penitentiary system, both as an instrument of inmate reform and as a means of reforming society. They considered the penitentiary as a model of discipline, orderliness, and reform which could be transposed to society. Thus, according to the founders of the Pennsylvania Penitentiary System, their model institution was intended to bring order to the disordered republic.

Much the same philosophy was behind the founding of the first House of Refuge for delinquent children in New York in 1825. This was soon followed by two other schools, in Boston and Philadelphia. All these new institutions, designed for the correction of children and youth, indicated a strong belief in the effectiveness of the asylum. The House of Refuge was considered capable of weaning children away from the corrupting influence of the taverns, gambling halls, and brothels. The house was supposed to train and rehabilitate its charges and spark the reform of the whole society by example.[12] The managers of the House of Refuge were very optimistic that "no habit can be rooted so firmly as to refuse a cure; and that the minds of young children, naturally pliant, can, by early instruction, be formed and molded to our wishes."[13] This was to be achieved through strict and steady discipline, continuous supervision, and mild but certain punishments.[14]

According to Rothman, there was a new flood of child-guidance books. These books conveyed a clear sense of crisis for the family and the community. "All feared for the cohesion of the community, finding in the swelling number of deviants and dependents dreadful confirmation of the dimensions of crisis. Here was dramatic evidence that the very foundations of the republic were in imminent danger of collapse."[15]

Most of these books were written for mothers, telling them of better practices for raising children. The child-rearing texts were ventures in reform. The authors "hoped to secure social stability through individual rehabilitation. They traced the origins of the problem to the decline of the community life and the weakness of family government, and found in their diagnosis a solution."[16]

Amidst all this furor for the institution, history took a fortunate turn somewhat away from institutions around 1841. John Augustus, a Boston shoemaker, requested the court to release a particular offender under his supervision. This was the beginning of probation. He gave supervision to about 2,000 persons, a good number of whom were juveniles. Augustus was assisted in probation work by a large number of clergy and other interested citizens. This involvement of the community led to the formation of children's aid societies in several large cities. Thus, around the middle of the nineteenth century, foster-home care started for those children who either had no home or whose homes were a harmful influence. The societies arranged for the placement of the child in a suitable home, but the board was paid from public funds.

Juvenile Court

Juvenile legislation took a giant step when Illinois enacted the first juvenile court law in July 1899. The fundamental premise of this pioneering legislation was "that the care, custody, and discipline of the children brought before the court shall approximate as nearly as possible that which they should receive from their parents, and that as far as practicable they shall be treated not as criminals but as children in need of aid, encouragement, and guidance."[17]

Federal Involvement

The present century has seen a series of White House Conferences on Children. The first conference gave birth to the Children's Bureau in the Department of Labor in 1912. The purpose of the Children's Bureau was to "have a central office where facts of child life may be collected, reviewed, and interpreted to individual and organized groups thus making possible intelligent action and reducing needless experimentation."[18] The bureau provided technical assistance, arranged research studies, and distributed information to the agencies dealing with juvenile delinquents.

The Juvenile Delinquency Prevention and Control Act of 1968 was, in part, a concerned nation's response to the continuing problem of juvenile delinquency. It was administered by the Office of Juvenile Delinquency and Youth, in the Social and Rehabilitative Service of the U.S. Department of Health, Education, and Welfare. The Act was designed to help states, local communities, and public and private nonprofit agencies to develop their capabilities in delinquency prevention and control programs. Help was made available through grants and technical assistance.[19]

In 1972, a separation took place between the delinquency preventional programs outside the juvenile justice system and delinquency control activities within the juvenile justice system. The former were funded by the Department of Health, Education, and Welfare (HEW) and the latter were entrusted to the Law Enforcement Assistance Administration (LEAA). In 1974, the Juvenile Justice and Delinquency Prevention Act of 1974 brought both the prevention and control functions within the jurisdiction of U.S. Department of Justice, Law Enforcement Assistance Administration. To administer a unified national program, the Act also created the Office of Juvenile Justice and Delinquency Prevention.[20]

Going Away from Institutions

As the philosophy behind juvenile institutions kept changing, these institutions kept changing their names. When the destitute children of new immigrants were running about idle in the streets in the early nineteenth century, they were sent to a *house of refuge*. In the last quarter of the century, when the idea of reformation was raging, these institutions came to be called *reform schools*. When the emphasis shifted to industrial production, these schools were called *industrial schools*. When the children were considered deficient in character, the juvenile institutions were named *training schools*. With the current emphasis on group therapy and the therapeutic community, these resocializing communities are known as *boys' villages, boys' ranches,* and *girls' towns.* The names kept changing, but the institutions remained places of custody with few changes in the program content.

Most of these training schools have a very high rate of recidivism; it ran as high as 70 percent in Massachusetts. The Commonwealth of Massachusetts took a bold step in closing outright most of that state's training schools in the early 1970s. Their residents were moved into several alternative environments. These included foster homes, group homes (often a local YMCA), and nonresidential programs in which they lived with their own families while attending day or evening sessions at a nearby center.[21] So Massachusetts, which was one of the first states to start a training school, was the first to put an end to the training school. There are growing trends to divert more and more children from institutions to community services.

Thus, the history of juvenile delinquency has brought us back to eighteenth-century methods in some ways. Again, juvenile offenders are being treated in the community, rather than in training schools. It is to be hoped that the lessons learned in 150 years are worthwhile, and that we are better able to use our community resources to serve our children.

INCIDENCE

Juvenile delinquency is a problem of great enormity in the United States. The President's Commission on Crime has expressed great concern regarding the volume of delinquency:

> Rough estimates by the Children's Bureau, supported by independent studies, indicate that one in every nine youths—one in every six male youths—will be referred to juvenile court in connection with a delinquent act (excluding traffic offenses) before his 18th birthday.[22]

> A commission survey shows that in 1965 more than two million Americans were received in prisons or juvenile training schools, or placed on probation. Another commission study suggests that about 40 percent of all male children now living in the United States will be arrested for a nontraffic offense during their lives.[23]

In 1973, there were 1,717,366 arrests of persons under age 18. This represents 26.4 percent of all arrests, 22.7 percent of all arrests for violent crime, and 50.8 percent of all arrests for property crime. Note that the major juvenile problem is property crime, and not violent crime. Arrests for violent crime start appearing in crime statistics with offenders of 11 to 12 years of age, and the number of such arrests increases with each additional year of age. However, most people who are arrested for violent crime are over 18. For example, eight times as many people over 18 as under 18 are arrested for murder. It appears that situations possibly leading to murder are encountered most by people between ages 18 and 29 (Table 1–1).

Some offenses show a higher arrest rate for juveniles than for adults; two examples are arson (6491 versus 4605) and vandalism (83,428 versus 37,583). Some offenses are exclusively juvenile, as defined by law. These include curfew and loitering law violations and runaways. Runaway arrests peak at offender age 13 to 14 and taper off at age 17. Parents are quick to report to the police if a child of 13 runs away; and a child of 13 is more easily arrested than an older adolescent. Curfew violations understandably concentrate at offender age 16. Arrests under narcotic drug laws and for disorderly conduct and vagrancy peak at offender age 18.

Race and Delinquency

The most obvious findings from Table 1–2 are that Chinese Americans and Japanese Americans show minimum arrests, and American Indians come next with a slightly higher rate. American Negroes show the highest rate of arrests of all groups for violent crime (58 percent). This is disproportionate by more than five times, since blacks make up about 11 percent of the United States population. Among all arrests under offender age 18 for murder, rape, and robbery, Negro arrests account for an alarmingly high 54.4 to 68.5 percent. Similarly, Negroes have the proportionately highest arrest rate for prostitution and commercialized vice (58.9 percent) and gambling (73.3 percent). In the cities, the Negro arrest rate is still higher. As concerns prostitution and gambling, for example, Negroes are more exposed to the police, as they commit these offenses primarily on streets.

Whites, on the other hand, tend more to property crimes, for example, burglary, larceny, auto theft, and stolen-property crimes, and allied offenses such as forgery, counterfeiting, fraud, and embezzlement. They have more opportunity for the latter offenses, as they handle more property. The destructiveness of white youth is evident from their arrest rates for arson (79.8 percent), vandalism (85.0 percent), liquor law violations (94.8 percent), narcotic drug law violations (89.1 percent), and drunkenness (87.7 percent). White youth also show greater arrest rates for offenses against family and children (88.9 percent) and as runaways (88.2 percent).

To sum up, Negroes show a higher arrest rate for violent crimes. White youth tend toward property crimes and offenses of deceit and destruction.

Geographic Distribution of Delinquency

Delinquency is largely a big-city phenomenon. Delinquency rates are highest in the cities, lower in the suburbs, and lowest in rural areas. The total crime index rate per 100,000 inhabitants in standard metropolitan statistical areas is 4823; in other cities, 3349; and in rural areas, 1472.[24] We should, however, bear in mind that the crime index total is increasing at the rate of 4.1 percent in all cities, but it is increasing at a rate of 8.9 percent in suburban areas and 9.6 percent in rural areas.[25] Studies by Shaw and McKay and others have repeatedly borne out the following findings:

> **1.** Juvenile delinquents are not distributed uniformly over the city of Chicago and some other cities but tend to be concentrated in areas adjacent to the central business district and to heavy industrial areas.
> **2.** The rates of delinquency vary inversely with distance from the center of the city.[26]

Numerous studies indicate that what matters is where in the city one is growing up, and not religion, nationality, or race. For all immigrant groups, delinquency rates were highest in the center of the city, and lowest on the outskirts.

> There is no reason to expect a different story for Negroes. Indeed, McKay found Negro delinquency rates decreasing from the center of the city outward, just as they did for earlier migrant groups. And when delinquency rates of whites and Negroes are compared in areas of similar economic status, the differences between them are markedly reduced. But for Negroes, movement out of the inner city and absorption into America's middle class have been much slower and more

TABLE 1-1   Total Arrests by Age, 1973 (6,004 agencies; 1973 estimated population 154,995,000)

Offense charged	Grand total all ages	Ages under 15	Ages under 18	Ages 18 and over	10 and under	11-12	13-14	15	16	17	18	19	20
TOTAL	6,499,864	614,716	1,717,366	4,782,498	72,229	136,345	406,142	336,986	401,737	363,927	350,649	308,829	277,672
Percent distribution[1]	100.0	9.5	26.4	73.6									
Criminal homicide:													
(a) Murder and nonnegligent manslaughter	14,399	216	1,497	12,902	12	31	173	274	439	568	717	684	709
(b) Manslaughter by negligence	2,996	83	363	2,633	12	16	55	57	87	136	167	186	160
Forcible rape	19,198	813	3,772	15,426	43	130	640	687	1,061	1,211	1,309	1,226	1,193
Robbery	101,894	11,015	34,374	67,520	687	2,405	7,923	6,800	8,085	8,474	8,610	7,330	6,364
Aggravated assault	54,891	8,200	26,270	128,621	824	1,851	5,525	4,724	6,554	6,792	7,325	6,902	6,796
Burglary—breaking or entering	316,272	73,139	170,228	146,044	9,424	17,529	46,186	33,532	34,575	28,982	24,545	18,186	14,321
Larceny—theft	644,190	146,910	310,452	333,738	19,147	39,543	88,220	54,905	58,916	49,721	44,009	33,651	26,842
Auto theft	118,380	17,736	66,868	51,512	455	2,086	15,195	17,464	18,393	13,275	9,458	6,661	4,938
Violent crime[2]	290,382	20,244	65,913	224,469	1,566	4,417	14,261	12,485	16,139	17,045	17,961	16,142	15,062
Percent distribution[1]	100.0	7.0	22.7	77.3	.5	1.5	4.9	4.3	5.6	5.9	6.2	5.6	5.2
Property crime[1]	1,078,842	237,785	547,548	531,294	29,026	59,158	149,601	105,901	111,884	91,978	78,012	58,498	46,101
Percent distribution[1]	100.0	22.0	50.8	49.2	2.7	5.5	13.9	9.8	10.4	8.5	7.2	5.4	4.3
Subtotal for above offenses	1,372,220	258,112	613,824	758,396	30,604	63,591	163,917	118,443	128,110	109,159	96,140	74,826	61,323
Percent distribution[1]	100.0	18.8	44.7	55.3	2.2	4.6	11.9	8.6	9.3	8.0	7.0	5.5	4.5
Other assaults	275,105	21,013	53,044	222,061	2,690	5,342	12,981	9,380	11,174	11,477	12,173	11,976	12,052
Arson	11,096	4,420	6,491	4,605	1,452	1,097	1,871	896	659	516	479	358	297
Forgery and counterfeiting	41,975	729	4,657	37,318	41	133	555	791	1,353	1,784	2,437	2,636	2,599
Fraud	85,467	686	3,159	82,308	62	154	470	450	796	1,227	2,548	3,190	3,678
Embezzlement	5,612	87	429	5,183	7	18	62	46	117	179	240	240	303
Stolen property: buying, receiving, possessing	70,238	7,121	23,738	46,500	453	1,433	5,235	4,594	5,972	6,051	5,882	4,879	3,924
Vandalism	121,011	51,377	83,428	37,583	11,808	15,076	24,493	12,661	11,213	8,177	5,316	3,906	3,093
Weapons; carrying, possessing, etc.	115,918	4,756	18,635	97,283	315	921	3,520	3,418	4,988	5,473	6,316	5,727	5,407
Prostitution and commercialized vice	45,308	150	1,769	43,539	6	11	133	190	431	998	2,730	3,690	3,877
Sex offenses (except forcible rape and prostitution)	48,673	3,698	9,784	38,889	422	802	2,474	1,900	2,131	2,055	2,041	1,899	1,842
Narcotic drug laws	484,242	16,222	127,316	356,926	236	1,291	14,695	23,106	39,090	48,892	55,327	49,972	42,938
Gambling	54,938	270	1,544	53,394	30	38	202	257	435	582	876	814	934
Offenses against family and children	42,784	222	994	41,790	70	31	121	104	213	455	2,278	2,019	1,807
Driving under the influence	653,914	242	9,026	644,888	74	23	145	381	2,288	6,115	15,348	17,869	19,537

TABLE 1-1 (cont.)

Offense charged	Grand total all ages	Ages under 15	Ages under 18	Ages 18 and over	Age								
					10 and under	11–12	13–14	15	16	17	18	19	20
TOTAL	6,499,864	614,716	1,717,366	4,782,498	72,229	136,345	406,142	336,986	401,737	363,927	350,649	308,829	277,672
Percent distribution[1]	100.0	9.5	26.4	73.6									
Liquor laws	183,813	7,178	74,690	109,123	84	565	6,529	11,903	23,879	31,730	25,248	18,809	14,042
Drunkenness	1,189,489	4,207	34,722	1,154,767	180	444	3,583	5,338	9,925	15,252	28,470	27,278	26,671
Disorderly conduct	461,553	36,114	103,556	357,997	4,616	8,562	22,936	18,533	23,454	25,455	29,571	26,530	24,431
Vagrancy	50,310	1,272	6,016	44,294	65	220	987	1,090	1,648	2,006	2,900	2,834	2,635
All other offenses (except traffic)	848,835	87,475	231,018	617,817	12,569	18,547	56,359	46,111	49,766	47,666	50,283	46,403	43,813
Suspicion	40,927	4,383	13,090	27,837	623	942	2,818	2,569	3,025	3,113	4,046	2,974	2,469
Curfew and loitering law violations	118,003	33,651	118,003		1,932	6,112	25,607	26,785	39,438	18,129			
Runaways	178,433	71,331	178,433		3,890	10,992	56,449	48,040	41,626	17,436			

[1] Because of rounding, the percentages may not add to the total.
[2] Violent crime is offenses of murder, forcible rape, robbery, and aggravated assault.
[3] Property crime is offenses of burglary, larceny, and auto theft.

SOURCE: Federal Bureau of Investigation, *Uniform Crime Reports for the United States—1973*, U.S. Government Printing Office, Washington, D.C., p. 128.

TABLE 1-2 Total Arrests by Race, 1973

Offense charged	Arrests under 18							Percent distribution[1]						
	Total	White	Negro	Indian	Chinese	Japanese	All others	Total	White	Negro	Indian	Chinese	Japanese	All others
TOTAL	1,665,792	1,253,489	388,566	14,692	917	696	7,432	100.0	75.2	23.3	0.9	0.1	0.1	0.4
Criminal homicide:														
(a) Murder and nonnegligent manslaughter	1,247	437	779	15	10		6	100.0	35.0	62.5	1.2	0.8		0.5
(b) Manslaughter by negligence	285	226	48	2	1	1	9	100.0	79.3	16.8	0.7			3.2
Forcible rape	3,263	1,425	1,776	31		8	29	100.0	43.7	54.4	1.0			0.9
Robbery	27,068	8,221	18,539	159	25	3	116	100.0	30.4	68.5	0.6	0.1		0.4
Aggravated assault	23,335	12,263	10,746	147	60	43	77	100.0	52.6	46.1	0.6	0.3		0.5
Burglary – breaking or entering	161,860	113,371	46,354	1,204	77	43	811	100.0	70.0	28.6	0.7			0.5
Larceny – theft	304,786	214,926	85,929	2,099	295	210	1,327	100.0	70.5	28.2	0.7	0.1	0.1	0.4
Auto theft	62,232	42,836	18,132	776	40	26	422	100.0	68.8	29.1	1.2	0.1		0.7
Violent crime	54,913	22,346	31,840	352	96	12	267	100.0	40.7	58.0	0.6	0.2		0.5
Property crime	528,878	371,133	150,415	4,079	412	279	2,560	100.0	70.2	28.4	0.8	0.1	0.1	0.5
Subtotal for above offenses	584,076	393,705	182,303	4,433	508	291	2,836	100.0	67.4	31.2	0.8	0.1		0.5
Other assaults	50,897	30,051	20,207	348	44	21	226	100.0	59.0	39.7	0.7	0.1		0.4
Arson	6,231	4,970	1,208	21	3	2	27	100.0	79.8	19.4	0.3			0.4
Forgery and counterfeiting	4,461	3,424	984	32	2	1	18	100.0	76.8	22.1	0.7			0.4
Fraud	3,083	2,308	755	11	3	1	5	100.0	74.9	24.5	0.4	0.1		0.2
Embezzlement	405	325	77	3				100.0	80.2	19.0	0.7			
Stolen property: buying, receiving, possessing	22,410	14,848	7,334	80	8	8	132	100.0	66.3	32.7	0.4			0.6
Vandalism	81,168	68,971	11,453	383	26	27	308	100.0	85.0	14.1	0.5			0.4
Weapons: carrying, possessing, etc.	16,843	10,338	6,287	75	23	5	115	100.0	61.4	37.3	0.4	0.1		0.7
Prostitution and commercialized vice	1,711	684	1,008	13		1	5	100.0	40.0	58.9	0.8			0.3
Sex offenses (except forcible rape and prostitution)	9,249	6,191	2,932	43	37	7	39	100.0	66.9	31.7	0.5	0.4		0.4
Narcotic drug laws	123,934	110,402	12,393	598	40	81	420	100.0	89.1	10.0	0.5		0.1	0.3
Gambling	1,493	374	1,094	1		5	19	100.0	25.1	73.3	0.1		0.3	1.3
Offenses against family and children	997	886	91	13			7	100.0	88.9	9.1	1.3			0.7
Driving under the influence	8,859	8,220	421	141	1	2	74	100.0	92.8	4.8	1.6			0.8

TABLE 1-2 (cont.)

Offense charged	Arrests under 18							Percent distribution[1]						
	Total	White	Negro	Indian	Chinese	Japanese	All others	Total	White	Negro	Indian	Chinese	Japanese	All others
TOTAL	1,665,792	1,253,489	388,566	14,692	917	696	7,432	100.0	75.2	23.3	0.9	0.1	0.1	0.4
Liquor laws	73,895	70,089	2,128	1,358	16	18	286	100.0	94.8	2.9	1.8			0.4
Drunkenness	34,252	30,022	2,520	1,573	6	11	120	100.0	87.7	7.4	4.6			0.4
Disorderly conduct	101,760	73,760	26,918	690	24	11	357	100.0	72.5	26.5	0.7			0.4
Vagrancy	5,434	3,818	1,409	34	1		172	100.0	70.3	25.9	0.6			3.2
All other offenses (except traffic)	226,838	173,049	51,018	1,627	79	61	1,004	100.0	76.3	22.5	0.7			0.4
Suspicion	12,835	9,910	2,864	15		4	42	100.0	77.2	22.3	0.1			0.3
Curfew and loitering law violations	117,640	80,794	35,239	1,118	34	47	408	100.0	68.7	30.0	1.0			0.3
Runaways	177,321	156,350	17,923	2,082	62	92	812	100.0	88.2	10.1	1.2		0.1	0.5

[1] Because of rounding, the percentages may not add to the total.
SOURCE Federal Bureau of Investigation. *Uniform Crime Reports for the United States—1973.* U.S. Government Printing Office. Washington, D.C., p. 134

difficult than for any other ethnic or racial group. Their attempts to move spatially, socially, economically have met much stiffer resistance.[27]

In areas of high crime and delinquency rates, other related problems coexist, with similar high rates. (Such related problems include family disorganization, unemployment, alcoholism, and drug addiction.) Two current explanations of high-delinquency areas are high rates of transiency and lack of stable institutions and relationships which the inhabitants can trust. There is also a tendency for illegal practices and institutions (fences, houses of prostitution, gambling dens) to cluster in these areas of disorganization. It is also possible that criminals are attracted to such areas.[28]

TRENDS

The number of arrests, for almost all offenses, has been increasing for the past several years. The rate of increase for juveniles is much greater than that for adults. Table 1-3 shows this trend for a 13-year period (1960 to 1973). In the case of persons below 18 years of age, violent crime has gone up 246.5 percent, and property crime has increased by 104.6 percent. Among persons over 18 years of age, the rate of increase of violent crime was 109.4 percent. Thus, the rate of increase for juveniles was twice that for persons over 18 years of age.

Manslaughter by negligence, which decreased by 11.6 percent in the case of adults, went up by 63.6 percent in the case of juveniles. Other offenses which have shown an exceedingly high rate of increase among juveniles are fraud and embezzlement (205 percent); prostitution and commercialized vice (286.2 percent); robbery (299.0 percent); buying, receiving, or possessing stolen property (529.2 percent); and narcotic drug law violations (4673.3 percent). Drug arrests have shown an alarming increase (Table 1-3).

While there has been an overall increase in arrests, vagrancy laws are not as rigidly enforced as before. Fewer arrests are now made for vagrancy, and there are continuing trends in this direction. Perhaps the police are changing their attitude toward vagrancy, and are more likely nowadays to dismiss a vagrant child with a verbal warning.

TABLE 1–3 Total Arrest Trends, 1960–73 (2,378 agencies; 1973 population 94,251,000[1])

Offense charged	Total all ages			Number of persons arrested					
				Under 18 years of age			18 years of age and over		
	1960	1973	Percent change	1960	1973	Percent change	1960	1973	Percent change
TOTAL	3,242,574	4,381,968	+35.1	466,174	1,138,046	+144.1	2,776,400	3,243,922	+16.8
Criminal homicide:									
(a) Murder and nonnegligent manslaughter	4,541	10,629	+134.1	337	1,197	+255.2	4,204	9,432	+124.4
(b) Manslaughter by negligence	1,766	1,660	−6.0	132	216	+63.6	1,634	1,444	−11.6
Forcible rape	6,857	13,823	+101.6	1,185	2,753	+132.3	5,672	11,070	+95.2
Robbery	31,197	83,012	+166.1	7,352	29,336	+299.0	23,845	53,676	+125.1
Aggravated assault	50,402	108,076	+114.4	6,306	19,306	+206.2	44,096	88,770	+101.3
Burglary—breaking or entering	117,084	211,029	+80.2	55,149	112,606	+104.2	61,935	98,423	+58.9
Larceny—theft	190,443	431,506	+126.6	91,375	204,913	+124.3	99,068	226,593	+128.7
Auto theft	54,202	87,975	+62.3	32,939	49,747	+51.0	21,263	38,228	+79.8
Violent crime[2]	92,997	215,540	+131.8	15,180	52,592	+246.5	77,817	162,948	+109.4
Property crime[3]	361,729	730,510	+101.9	179,463	367,266	+104.6	182,266	363,244	+99.3
Subtotal for above offenses	456,492	947,710	+107.6	194,775	420,074	+115.7	261,717	527,636	+101.6
Other assaults	115,156	182,985	+58.9	11,938	36,287	+204.0	103,218	146,698	+42.1
Forgery and counterfeiting	21,329	28,175	+32.1	1,502	3,081	+105.1	19,827	25,094	+26.6
Fraud and embezzlement	30,551	56,208	+84.0	779	2,376	+205.0	29,772	53,832	+80.8
Stolen property: buying, receiving, possessing	9,147	48,141	+426.3	2,531	15,925	+529.2	6,616	32,216	+386.9
Weapons: carrying, possessing, etc.	30,865	85,749	+177.8	6,353	13,950	+119.6	24,512	71,799	+192.9
Prostitution and commercialized vice	24,331	40,354	+65.9	413	1,595	+286.2	23,918	38,759	+62.0
Sex offenses (except forcible rape and prostitution)	39,582	35,693	−9.8	8,738	7,078	−19.0	30,844	28,615	−7.2
Narcotic drug laws	29,889	328,670	+999.6	1,725	82,340	+4673.3	28,164	246,330	+774.6
Gambling	105,607	43,983	−58.4	1,230	1,239	+.7	104,377	42,744	−59.0
Offenses against family and children	35,906	24,063	−33.0	697	523	−25.0	35,209	23,540	−33.1
Driving under the influence	142,698	413,837	+190.0	1,125	5,640	+401.3	141,573	408,197	+188.3
Liquor laws	81,735	109,392	+33.8	17,207	43,329	+151.8	64,528	66,063	+2.4
Drunkenness	1,215,555	837,551	−31.1	12,209	22,959	+88.0	1,203,346	814,592	−32.8
Disorderly conduct	364,289	317,531	−12.8	46,271	69,864	+51.0	318,018	247,667	−22.1
Vagrancy	127,643	40,508	−68.3	7,151	4,089	−42.8	120,492	36,419	−69.8
All other offenses (except traffic)	411,799	841,418	+104.3	151,530	407,697	+169.1	260,269	433,721	+66.6
Suspicion (not included in totals)	123,196	30,876	−74.9	22,651	9,430	−58.4	100,545	21,446	−78.7

[1] Based on comparable reports from 1,854 cities representing 79,540,000 population and 524 counties representing 14,711,000 population.
[2] Violent crime is offenses of murder, forcible rape, robbery, and aggravated assault.
[3] Property crime is offenses of burglary, larceny, and auto theft.

SOURCE: Federal Bureau of Investigation, *Uniform Crime Reports for the United States—1973*, U.S. Government Printing Office, Washington, D.C., p 124

Female Arrests

If any group has shown a "spectacular" increase in delinquency, it is young females. Table 1–4 shows this trend. During the period 1960 to 1973, arrests of females under 18 increased overall by 264.1 percent. There was a 123.5 percent increase in arrests of males in the same age group during the same period. For females, there was an increase of 393.2 percent in arrests for violent crime, and an increase of 333.8 percent in arrests for property crime. There were also increases in arrests for prostitution (303.4 percent), driving under the influence (588.1 percent), and narcotic drug law violations (6045.1 percent). In all these arrest categories, girls have shown greater increases than boys.

Police Disposition of Juvenile Offenders

Table 1–5 shows the disposition of juvenile cases by type of area. It is gratifying to note that only about half the juvenile offenders taken into custody are referred to the juvenile courts. Most other cases are handled within the police department, and the offenders are released. A small minority (1.4 percent of the cases) are referred to welfare agencies. About the same percentage are referred to criminal or adult courts.

In suburban areas, about half the cases are handled within the police department, with the offender being released. In rural areas, fewer than one-third of the cases are handled within the department. It is reasonable to assume that rural police departments are not well equipped to handle juvenile offenders. Lacking a juvenile bureau, the police department is more likely to take the traditional approach of referral to the juvenile court. Thus, rural police refer about 60 percent of their juvenile offenders to juvenile courts, whereas suburban police refer only about 41 percent. The fact that many suburban areas have more delinquents from the middle class may also account for the fewer referrals to the juvenile court.

Also note that rural police refer a larger proportion (almost three times as many) of offenders to welfare agencies than do city police.

TABLE 1-4 Total Arrest Trends by Sex, 1960-73 (2,378 agencies; 1973 estimated population 94,251,000[1])

	Males						Females					
	Total			Under 18			Total			Under 18		
Offense charged	1960	1973	Percent change	1960	1973	Percent change	1960	1973	Percent change	1960	1973	Percent change
TOTAL	2,891,354	3,695,870	+27.8	397,862	889,333	+123.5	351,220	686,068	+95.3	68,312	248,713	+264.1
Criminal homicide:												
(a) Murder and nonnegligent manslaughter	3,761	9,048	+140.6	312	1,098	+251.9	780	1,581	+102.7	25	99	+296.0
(b) Manslaughter by negligence	1,580	1,469	-7.0	123	201	+63.4	186	191	+2.7	9	15	+66.7
Forcible rape	6,857	13,823	+101.6	1,185	2,753	+132.3						
Robbery	29,710	77,264	+160.1	6,993	27,265	+289.9	1,487	5,748	+286.6	359	2,071	+476.9
Aggravated assault	43,141	93,097	+115.8	5,668	16,435	+190.0	7,261	14,979	+106.3	638	2,871	+350.0
Burglary-breaking or entering	113,227	199,718	+76.4	53,497	107,009	+100.0	3,857	11,311	+193.3	1,652	5,597	+238.8
Larceny-theft	158,733	291,645	+83.7	78,222	143,789	+83.8	31,710	139,861	+341.1	13,153	61,124	+364.7
Auto theft	52,128	82,679	+58.6	31,640	46,614	+47.3	2,074	5,296	+155.4	1,299	3,133	+141.2
Violent crime[2]	83,469	193,232	+131.5	14,158	47,551	+235.9	9,528	22,308	+134.1	1,022	5,041	+393.2
Property crime[3]	324,088	574,042	+77.1	163,359	297,412	+82.1	37,641	156,468	+315.7	16,104	69,854	+333.8
Subtotal for above offenses	409,137	768,743	+87.9	177,640	345,164	+94.3	47,355	178,967	+277.9	17,135	74,910	+337.2
Other assaults	103,892	157,831	+51.9	10,173	28,844	+183.5	11,264	25,154	+123.3	1,765	7,443	+321.7
Forgery and counterfeiting	17,807	20,538	+15.3	1,153	2,173	+88.5	3,522	7,637	+116.8	349	908	+160.2
Fraud and embezzlement	26,015	38,911	+49.6	643	1,786	+177.8	4,536	17,297	+281.3	136	590	+333.8
Stolen property; buying, receiving, possessing	8,348	43,139	+416.8	2,355	14,580	+519.1	799	5,002	+526.0	176	1,345	+664.2
Weapons; carrying, possessing, etc.	29,114	78,675	+170.2	6,166	13,161	+113.4	1,751	7,074	+304.0	187	789	+321.9
Prostitution and commercialized vice	6,796	10,188	+49.9	119	409	+243.7	17,535	30,166	+72.0	294	1,186	+303.4
Sex offenses (except forcible rape and prostitution)	33,635	33,030	-1.8	6,311	6,203	-1.7	5,947	2,663	-55.2	2,427	875	-63.9
Narcotic drug laws	25,605	280,407	+995.1	1,488	67,776	+4,454.8	4,284	48,263	+1,026.6	237	14,564	+6,045.1
Gambling	96,244	40,175	-58.3	1,190	1,145	-3.8	9,363	3,808	-59.3	40	94	+135.0
Offenses against family and children	33,006	21,709	-34.2	483	368	-23.8	2,900	2,354	-18.8	214	155	-27.6
Driving under the influence	134,000	383,019	+185.8	1,066	5,234	+391.0	8,698	30,818	+254.3	59	406	+588.1
Liquor laws	70,180	92,604	+32.0	14,863	34,669	+133.3	11,555	16,788	+45.3	2,344	8,660	+269.5
Drunkenness	1,117,121	778,421	-30.3	10,963	19,731	+80.0	98,434	59,130	-39.9	1,246	3,228	+159.1
Disorderly conduct	314,416	256,316	-18.5	39,326	57,394	+45.9	49,873	61,215	+22.7	6,945	12,470	+79.6
Vagrancy	117,138	25,409	-78.3	6,327	3,366	-46.8	10,505	15,099	+43.7	824	723	-12.3
All other offenses (except traffic)	348,900	666,755	+91.1	117,596	287,330	+144.3	62,899	174,633	+177.6	33,934	120,367	+254.7
Suspicion (not included in totals)	108,785	26,431	-75.7	19,651	7,998	-59.3	14,411	4,445	-69.2	3,000	1,432	-52.3

[1] Based on comparable reports from 1,854 cities representing 79,540,000 population and 524 counties representing 14,711,000 population.
[2] Violent crime is offenses of murder, forcible rape, robbery, and aggravated assault.
[3] Property crime is offenses of burglary, larceny, and auto theft.

SOURCE: Federal Bureau of Investigation, *Uniform Crime Reports for the United States—1973*, U.S. Government Printing Office, Washington, D.C., p. 126.

TABLE 1-5 Police Disposition of Juvenile Offenders Taken into Custody, 1973 (1973 estimated population)

Population group	Total[1]	Handled within department and released	Referred to juvenile court jurisdiction	Referred to welfare agency	Referred to other police agency	Referred to criminal or adult court
TOTAL, ALL AGENCIES						
4,144 agencies; total population 100,816,000:						
Number	1,235,389	558,574	611,511	17,745	28,792	18,767
Percent[3]	100.0	45.2	49.5	1.4	2.3	1.5
TOTAL CITIES						
3,316 agencies; total population 77,708,000:						
Number	1,066,668	488,546	525,617	13,279	22,012	17,214
Percent	100.0	45.8	49.3	1.2	2.1	1.6
SUBURBAN AREA[3]						
2,076 agencies; population 38,114,000:						
Number	454,204	238,363	186,686	6,085	14,500	8,570
Percent	100.0	52.5	41.1	1.3	3.2	1.9
RURAL AREA						
631 agencies; population 9,619,000:						
Number	42,403	13,579	25,272	1,308	1,592	652
Percent	100.0	32.0	59.6	3.1	3.6	1.5

[1] Includes all offenses except traffic and neglect cases.
[2] Because of rounding, the percentages may not add to total.
[3] Includes suburban city and county police agencies within metropolitan areas. Excludes core cities. Suburban cities are also included in other city groups.

SOURCE: Adapted from Federal Bureau of Investigation, *Uniform Crime Reports for the United States—1973*, U.S. Government Printing Office, Washington, D.C., p. 119.

Nonreported Delinquency

Only a small portion of delinquency is reported. A much larger part goes unreported, and so remains hidden. Trivial delinquent acts are often ignored; less harmful acts are tolerated by the community. Some acts are condoned, and others are compromised. Parents tend to report only when they are unable to contain their children. Teachers may put up with a lot of mischief before reporting a delinquent act, so as not to get involved.

Several studies have shown that many high school students committed both minor and serious delinquency without having been reported.[29] The questionnaires in these studies sought information from the respondents anonymously, through self reports. When high school boys were compared with boys of a correctional school on self-confessed offenses, both groups were found to have committed offenses. The main difference is that the correctional school boys had committed offenses more persistently.[30]

There are several reasons why even the victims do not report offenses. The main reason is a belief that "nothing could be accomplished by reporting the incident." This belief not only reflects on the attitude of the victim, but also on the criminal justice system. People seem to have no trust in the system. The Census Bureau conducted a crime survey in five large cities in the United States in 1973. The survey included 10,000 households (some 22,000 persons) and approximately 2000 commercial establishments in each city. In all five cities, the level of criminal activity as determined by the surveys was appreciably higher than had previously been measured (or officially reported). Some of the highlights on victimization follow.

> For most types of victimization, males had higher rates than females. Also, persons under age 35 were more likely to have been victimized than those age 35 or older. Minority races, including blacks, had significantly higher victimization rates than whites for such offenses as robbery and aggravated assault; the rates for aggravated and simple assault were higher among persons never married than among persons married, widowed, divorced or separated. Persons from families with incomes of less than $10,000 had a higher rate of victimization for robbery, as well as for personal larceny with contact, than their more affluent counterparts. . . .
> Households headed by members of minority races were

more likely than white households to have been burglarized and except in New York, they were also more apt to have had their car stolen.³¹

It appears that the offender (whether juvenile or adult) most often

- Is a young male
- Is a member of a minority group
- Is somewhat estranged from his (or her) family
- Is from a lower socioeconomic stratum of society
- Tends to rob or hurt someone like himself (or herself)

The lower levels of society are thus hurt in two ways: They generate more offenders and produce more victims than the middle and upper classes.

INTERNATIONAL PERSPECTIVE

International delinquency statistics are not easily available. When they are available, they are in a form that defies comparison. To a great extent, this is because the definition of delinquency and the handling of delinquents vary from society to society. However, some generalizations may be made, on the basis of personal observation and a careful survey of the literature. Because delinquency is largely a product of societal conditions, every society has its style of delinquency. There is the delinquency of affluence at one end of the economic scale and the delinquency of poverty on the other, with intermediate categories between these two extremes. The author is of the opinion that, as a less developed society begins to modernize, the rate and the nature of its delinquency are influenced by its rate of development.

Delinquency and Affluence

Since World War II, delinquency has been on the increase globally. However, the rate of increase has been greater in the affluent societies. Some experts have suggested that affluence itself contributes to delinquency. Toby thinks that not only the level of affluence is important, but also the rate at which affluence is increasing. One way to measure affluence is in terms of automobile ownership. Then, by that measure, countries such as Japan, Italy, Greece, and Spain showed the fastest rate of increase in affluence. Although these countries have far more consumer goods than before, their expectations have risen faster than the supply of goods.

> When expectations are rising faster than the standard of living, the greater availability of consumer goods makes for greater rather than less dissatisfaction. . . . As car registration grows, so do the desires of adolescents to drive (as well as to own cameras, transistor radios, and new clothes). Few adolescents can get legitimate access to a car.[32]

Incidentally, the increasing number of cars has greatly increased the number of car accidents and traffic fatalities, along with the number of traffic offenders. Not only youth, but all segments of society are tempted and ensnared by the revolution of rising expectations. According to a Japanese government report in 1968, 12,685 government officials came to the attention of the public prosecutor for bribery and corruption. The report attributed this rate of corruption to a lack of self-restraint, slack discipline, and increasing craving for material possessions.[33] Material craving knows no end.

A noteworthy finding is that material prosperity has brought an increase in property offenses but no corresponding increase in offenses against the person. Urban affluence seems to invade the surrounding rural areas in several ways. Consequently, in Japan, the rural areas are fast approaching the city crime rate. Younger adolescents mostly commit larceny. Older adolescents and young adults have greater involvement in car theft, sex offenses, and violent crimes.

Affluent societies also offer *more opportunities* for delinquent acts—more cars, stores, night clubs, pubs, and more places to rob. According to a special survey in Japan, 17.5 percent of urban juvenile crimes were in some way connected with automobiles. "Rape was most closely connected with the use of motor vehicles: 40 percent of the total in urban areas and 37 percent in rural areas."[34] In Sweden, Toby found "the temptation to steal cars was proportional to the number of cars in use and the number of adolescents who felt dissatisfied with their share of them."[35]

In affluent societies, middle-class youth show a greater participation in delinquency, though not officially. Examples are to be found in Canada, Israel, Japan, the Scandinavian countries, Taiwan, the United Kingdom, the United States, and the Soviet Union. A large part of middle-class delinquency in these countries is oriented to seeking excitement through drugs, sex, vandalism, auto thefts, drinking, and mob activities. A portion of the delinquency in Japan and the Soviet Union is political in nature. Japanese students lately have been active on political issues.

Delinquency and Poverty

Delinquency in underdeveloped countries is a product of the culture of poverty. A youth in New York steals a car, joyrides in it, and then wrecks it. A youngster in New Delhi steals the loincloth of a bather in the river Jamna to clothe an ailing mother. Though so different, both youths are delinquents. The two youths indeed come from very different cultures. The delinquent youth in India make a pathetic profile—generally very poor, one-third of them orphans, with little or no schooling, unskilled, unemployed or earning pitifully low wages, living on the generosity of a relative, often runaways from home, occasionally having no place to live, sleeping on the pavement, subject to homosexual attacks by fellow pavement sleepers, and with no hope either in the present or the future. This description of delinquents in India is also true of delinquents in Iran, Afghanistan, Pakistan, Bangladesh, Burma, Thailand, Malaysia, and Indonesia.

Pickpockets There are no organized juvenile gangs in South Asia. However, there are loosely knit associations of pickpockets, each under the leadership of a master pickpocket. These associations occasionally recruit apprentices, usually boys. (There are a few female pickpockets, but they tend to operate individually.) The master may seek out a bright candidate, or the apprentice may approach the master and request his tutelage. The apprentice learns the art of pickpocketing and promises to pay the *guru* (master) a part of his daily or weekly gross earnings from pickpocketing. The guru buys him protection from the police, prosecution, and imprisonment. If the pickpocket boy is arrested, the guru arranges a lawyer for his defense and posts a bail bond. One guru may have eight or ten boys working for him.

These boys do not hang around a candy store or a corner drug store, because there are not many American style stores in Asian countries. The pickpockets mingle with the crowds at very busy places, such as railroad stations, bus stops, cinemas, fairs, markets, temples, mosques, and bazaars. Pickpocketing is easy in rushing crowds. At the railway stations, they pick out likely victims to rob, and follow the victims until they are off guard. Many times, a pickpocket will travel with his "mark" in the train. The pickpockets work late at night for better opportunities. They are either lone wolves or move about in pairs. They sleep in the parks or on the tops of buses. When they make good money, they drink, visit prostitutes, and consequently get venereal disease in the bargain.

The railroads are special victims for many delinquents. They steal batteries from underneath the railway carriages, remove water taps, electric bulbs, fans—anything that they can sell to a fence. There are many cases of extreme hardship. Many younger boys and girls steal discarded coal from the railway tracks to cook their morning meals. This kind of delinquency is very different from the senseless vandalism, needless theft, and meaningless violence of delinquents in the rich countries.

Offenders or Victims? Many of the youth are exploited by older criminals. The latter employ them for smuggling illicit liquor, drugs, and other contraband. In those countries where consumer goods are scarce and commodities run short, smuggling has good prospects. Younger girls are lured to prostitution by retired prostitutes and pimps. The latter make much money out of these exploited girls. Many cities maintain red-light areas where young girls, all attractively made up, sit at the doorsteps to attract customers. Illicit trafficking in women still goes on in some parts of Asia. Many poor single men with no prospects of marriage are left with no recourse but to buy a young woman. These girls are often runaways from their parents, and they do not stay with the husbands who buy them.

Until recently, house servants, both male and female, were quite common in upper- and middle-class households. They are not easily available these days, as they can make better money elsewhere. Yet, younger boys and girls driven by extreme poverty do work as domestic servants. Many times they "live in" with the family they work for. They are generally honest persons, but they are often tempted to steal, as they see money, jewelry, and watches handled carelessly in the house. They are paid poorly, which can also motivate them to steal.

Large-City Phenomenon In many Asian countries, juvenile delinquency is a large-city phenomenon. In India, there is very little delinquency in rural areas. The rural boys become vulnerable to delinquency when they move to the impersonality and anonymity of large cities. Their home community loses control of its members, and the family is not able to give prompt guidance when needed. One finds some female delinquency in very large cities, but there is hardly any female delinquency in rural areas or small towns. The state of Punjab in the northwestern part of India has a population of about 30 million. Yet it did not have a single training school for girls until the late 1960s. Punjab is mainly an agricultural state; agricultural families, being cohesive, either do not generate delinquency or are very tolerant of their children's mischiefs. The children of farming families are brought up in extended families of parents, grandparents, uncles, and aunts. They thus have much emotional security.

SUMMARY

Human groups have always been fearful of unknown phenomena and unknown persons. The delinquent is more of an unknown person in industrial societies than in agricultural societies. On account of their fear of the delinquent, industrial societies have tried to safeguard themselves by enacting a comprehensive body of juvenile laws. Juvenile delinquency is defined to include the violation of both adult penal code laws and the additional laws intended to restrain juveniles' movements and activities.

Until what age should a youth be treated as a delinquent? Each society has set its own age limits for juvenile delinquents. Societies move this limit up or down to accommodate social and political pressures.

Historically, Americans have taken a dim view of juvenile mischief. The colonists had a moralistic attitude toward delinquents. Delinquents were whipped and even executed during the eighteenth century. Then, in the nineteenth century, came the development of the penitentiary and the house of refuge. These were followed by the reformatory and the training school. The founders of these institutions had a strong belief in their effectiveness. They thought of these institutions as instruments of reform, not only of the offenders but of the entire society. The myth of the institutions has, however, exploded. Today, correctional services are moving to the community.

Even though only a small part of delinquency is reported, the number of youthful offenses reported to the police is enormous. According to one estimate, one in every nine youths will be referred to juvenile court in connection with delinquent acts (excluding traffic offenses). About 1¾ million children under 18 years of age were arrested in 1973. About half of all property offenses are committed by juveniles. Statistically, Negro youth commit a larger proportion of violent offenses, and white youth commit more property crimes. Females have shown an unparalleled increase in delinquency. In the 13 years from 1960 to 1973, their delinquency rate has grown threefold in violent crime, property offenses, and prostitution. Female drug offenses have increased by a factor of sixty in the same period.

Juvenile delinquency is a property of affluent societies. Before World War II, juvenile delinquency was relatively unknown in agricultural and preindustrial societies. The social controls of the family and other social institutions were intact. With rapid industrialization, urbanization, and modernization, people in the developing countries experienced rising expectations. When these rising expectations were not met, they gave way to discontent. Toby contends that, more than affluence, the rate of increase in affluence is associated with an increase in delinquency. Juvenile delinquents in poor societies either pick pockets or steal shoes, clothes, or food to survive. They do not form violent gangs, they use no guns, and they do not indulge in vandalism.

Discussion Questions

1. How does the public react to the fear of delinquency?
2. Are you in favor of limiting juvenile laws only to the extent of adult laws? If so, how would you deal with incorrigible and ungovernable behavior?
3. Are you in favor of lowering or raising the age limit for juvenile delinquency? What are the implications in both cases?
4. What kinds of delinquents do you feel should be sent to institutions?
5. Violent crime abounds after offender age 18. Do you believe that violent offenders develop their violent tendencies during their juvenile years?

6. Why do Negroes commit more violent offenses, and whites more property offenses?
7. How do you account for the very large increase in female delinquency?
8. How has rapid social change affected family controls? Discuss this with reference to developing countries.

Glossary

Adjudication Act of a court in making an order, decree, disposition, or judgment.

Aggravated Assault A violent attack on a person with intent to kill or for the purpose of inflicting severe bodily injury by shooting, cutting, stabbing, maiming, poisoning, scalding, or by the use of acids, explosives, or other means. Excludes simple assault.

Arson Willful or malicious burning of property with or without intent to defraud. Includes attempts.

Auto Theft Unlawful taking or stealing of a motor vehicle.

Burglary Breaking or entering. Burglary, housebreaking, safecracking, or any breaking or unlawful entry of a structure with the intent to commit a felony or a theft. Includes attempted forcible entry.

Criminal Homicide (1) Murder and nonnegligent manslaughter, includes all willful felonious homicides, as distinguished from deaths caused by negligence. Excludes attempts to kill, assaults to kill, suicides, accidental deaths, or justifiable homicides. Justifiable homicides are limited to (a) the killing of a person by a peace officer in the line of duty, and (b) the killing by a private citizen of a person who is in the act of committing a felony. (2) Manslaughter by negligence includes any death which police investigation establishes to be primarily attributable to the gross negligence of some individual other than the victim.

Deviant One who does not conform to a social norm.

Embezzlement Misappropriation or misapplication of money or property entrusted to one's care, custody, or control.

Forcible Rape Rape by force, assault to rape, and attempted rape. Excludes statutory offenses (in which no force is used but the victim is under the age of consent).

Fraud Fraudulent conversion and obtaining money or property by false pretenses. Includes bad-check offenses, except forgeries and counterfeiting. Also includes larceny by bailee.

Gemeinschaft Generalized or ideal type of society in which social bonds are based on close personal ties of friendship and kinship, emphasizing tradition and informality.

Gesellschaft Type of society in which secondary relations predominate. Social relationships are formal, contractual, expedient, impersonal, and specialized.

Incorrigible A legal term used in delinquency literature to mean uncontrollable behavior.

Jurisdiction The power and authority of a court to pronounce the sentence of law or to award the remedies provided by law after proper procedures.

Larceny Theft (except auto theft). The unlawful taking and removing of another person's property. Thefts of bicycles, automobile accessories, property, or other articles which are not taken by force and violence or by fraud. Excludes embezzlement, con games, forgery, worthless checks, etc.

Narcotic Drug Laws Laws controlling the possession, sale, use, growing, and manufacturing of narcotic drugs.

Offenses Against the Family and Children Nonsupport, neglect, desertion, or abuse of family and children.

Penal Institutions Penitentiaries, prisons, and reformatories where offenders are held for punishment, deterrence, and only incidentally for reformation.

Penology The branch of criminology which studies the effects of punishment and treatment given to offenders.

President's Commission on Crime The commission established by President Johnson in 1965 to evaluate the nation's crime problem. Its formal name, President's Commission on Law Enforcement and Administration of Justice, was shortened by many writers to U.S. President's Commission on Crime or even President's Crime Commission. In 1967, the Commission gave its general report, *The Challenge of Crime in a Free Society*, which was supplemented by several task force reports. One of these reports was entitled *Juvenile Delinquency and Youth Crime*.

Prostitution and Commercialized Vice Sex offenses of a commercialized nature and attempts, such as prostitution, keeping a bawdy house, procuring, and transporting women for immoral purposes.

Recidivism The repeated return to criminal or delinquent behavior, especially in the case of an individual (recidivist) who has been imprisoned.

Rehabilitation Restoration of ex-offenders to a social, vocational, and mental status which is satisfactory to the former offenders and also acceptable to the society.

Robbery Stealing or taking anything of value from the care, custody, or control of a person by force or violence or by the fear of violence. Includes strong-arm robbery, stickups, armed robbery, assaults to rob, and attempts to rob.

Sex Offenses (except forcible rape, prostitution, and commercialized vice) Statutory rape offenses against chastity, common decency, morals, and the like. Includes attempts.

Stolen Property: Buying, Receiving, and Possessing Buying, receiving, and possessing stolen property. Includes attempts.

Vagrancy The act of wandering about by a person without visible means of support.

Vandalism Willful or malicious destruction, injury, disfigurement, or defacement of property without the consent of the owner or the person having custody or control.

Footnotes

[1] Paul W. Tappan, *Juvenile Delinquency*, McGraw-Hill, New York, 1949, p. 30.

[2] *Juvenile Court Statistics 1971*, U.S. Department of Health, Education, and Welfare Publication 73–03452, Washington, D.C., 1972, p. 7.

[3] President's Commission on Law Enforcement and Administration of Justice (also known as President's Crime Commission), *Task Force Report: Juvenile Delinquency and Youth Crime*, U.S. Government Printing Office, Washington, D.C., 1967, p. 27.

[4] President's Commission on Law Enforcement and Administration of Justice, p. 28.

[5] U.S. Department of Justice, *Children in Custody*, U.S. Government Printing Office, Washington, D.C., 1974, pp. 1–2.

[6] "The Crime Wave," *Time*, June 30, 1975, p. 24.

[7] President's Commission on Law Enforcement and Administration of Justice, *The Challenge of Crime in a Free Society*, U.S. Government Printing Office, Washington, D.C., 1967, p. 56.

[8] Ronald C. Federico, *The Social Welfare Institution*, Heath, Lexington, Mass., 1973, p. 9.

[9] David J. Rothman, *The Discovery of the Asylum: Social Order and Disorder in the New Republic*, Little, Brown, Boston, 1971, p. 17.

[10] David J. Rothman, p. 14.

[11] David J. Rothman, p. 55.

[12] David J. Rothman, p. 212.

[13] David J. Rothman, p. 213.

[14] David J. Rothman, p. 215.

[15] David J. Rothman, p. 217.

[16] David J. Rothman, p. 218.

[17] Arthur E. Fink, *The Field of Social Work*, 6th ed., Holt, New York, 1974, p. 83.

[18] Hazel Frederickson, *The Child and His Welfare*, Freeman, San Francisco, 1948, p. 23.

[19] U.S. Department of Health, Education, and Welfare, *Delinquency Today*, U.S. Government Printing Office, Washington, D.C., 1969, p. 22.

[20] U.S. Department of Justice, *Indexed Legislative History of the Juvenile Justice and Delinquency Prevention Act of 1974*, Office of the General Counsel, Law Enforcement Assistance Administration, Washington, D.C., 1974, p. 2.

[21] Law Enforcement Assistance Administration, U.S. Department of Justice, *First Annual Report of the National Institute of Law Enforcement and Criminal Justice*, U.S. Government Printing Office, Washington, D.C., 1974, p. 19.

[22] President's Commission on Law Enforcement and Administration of Justice, *The Challenge of Crime in a Free Society*, p. 55.

[23] President's Commission on Law Enforcement and Administration of Justice, p. v.

[24] Federal Bureau of Investigation, *Uniform Crime Reports for the United States—1973*, U.S. Government Printing Office, Washington, D.C., p. 58.

[25] Federal Bureau of Investigation, pp. 98–99.

[26] President's Commission on Crime, *Task Force Report: Crime and Its Impact—An Assessment*, U.S. Government Printing Office, Washington, D.C., 1967, pp. 60–61.

[27] President's Commission on Law Enforcement and Administration of Justice, p. 57.

[28] President's Commission on Crime, p. 75–76.

[29] F. Ivan Nye, *Family Relationship and Delinquent Behavior*, Wiley, New York, 1958.

[30] James F. Short, Jr., and F. Ivan Nye, "Extent of Unrecorded Juvenile Delinquency," *Journal of Criminal Law, Criminology and Police Science*, Vol. 49, p. 297, Northwestern University School of Law, 1958.

[31] U.S. Department of Justice, *Crime in the Nation's Five Largest Cities: Annual Report*, Law Enforcement Assistance Administration, Washington, D.C., 1974, pp. 2–3.

[32] Jackson Toby, "Affluence and Adolescent Crime," a consultant paper appended to *Task Force Report: Juvenile Delinquency and Youth Crime* published by the U.S. President's Commission on Law Enforcement and Administration of Justice, U.S. Government Printing Office, Washington, D.C., 1967, pp. 133–134.

[33] Research and Training Institute, Ministry of Justice, *Summary of the White Paper on Crime, 1969*, Ministry of Finance Printing Bureau, Tokyo, Japan, p. 21.

[34] Research and Training Institute, p. 52.

[35] Jackson Toby, p. 137.

The Making of a Delinquent

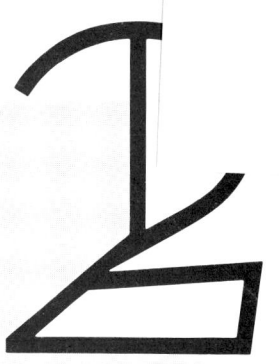

The search for the causes of delinquency has led to much theorizing and scientific enquiry. Scientists from various disciplines—medical doctors, anthropologists, psychologists, psychoanalysts, sociologists, and social workers—have attempted to determine what causes delinquent behavior. In their search, these theorists and researchers were, of course, influenced by their respective disciplines (medical, psychoanalytical, sociological). They were, to an extent, also influenced by the prevailing philosophy of their time (Darwinian, Freudian, Durkheimian), by historical events (war, depression, immigration), and by social changes (urbanization, migration, norm erosion).

Scholars have attributed delinquency to sociological factors, to the individual, and to social psychological factors. For better understanding, the causation theories can be classified in terms of three loci:

1. Delinquency-generating sources in the society (sociological perspective)
2. Delinquency-generating sources in the individual (psychogenic perspective)
3. Delinquency-provoking sources in the interaction of the individual and the society (social psychological or interactionist perspective)

The theories presented in this chapter overlap and may fall into more than one of these classifications. The difference between the three sets of theories is one of emphasis—whether on the individual, the group, or the interaction between the two. As the reader will note shortly, these theories explain delinquent behavior in general, but do not explain specific acts of delinquency. The latter will be dealt with in Chapters 3 and 4.

DELINQUENCY-GENERATING SOURCES IN THE SOCIETY

To most sociologists, delinquency is a property of the society. They believe the sources of delinquency are embedded in the social process. The society, as it is structured, exerts pressure on some individuals to be delinquent (the structural or cultural approach). A society may drive certain individuals away from the mainstream of life. These individuals are then forced to seek belongingness in a delinquent gang (the subcultural approach). A few other sociologists think the dominant groups design and execute the laws so that they are able to label opposing groups as criminal (the conflict approach). In fact, conflict is a common ingredient in all sociological theories. Let us examine some of the sociological explanations.

Anomie

Anomie is usually defined as a state of deregulation. The sociologists have used this concept, with slight variations in interpretation, to suit their theories. According to Durkheim, persons may go on extending their needs without placing any limit on those needs. The unsatiated pursuit of human needs can be very tormenting if there is no end to the needs. One who knows no goal or aspires for unattainable goals is condemning oneself to a state of perpetual unhappiness. So, society alone can put a limit on one's demands and regulate one's needs. If society fails in this regulatory function, it creates for the individual a state of deregulation. Durkheim contends that "society alone can play this moderating role; for it is the only moral power superior to the individual, the authority of which he accepts."[1] Although Durkheim uses the concept of anomie in the explanation of suicide, its application to delinquency is understandable.

Merton seems to equate anomie to a disregard of the institutionally prescribed means to reach a greatly coveted goal. He raises the question of "why it is that the frequency of deviant behavior varies within different social structures and how it happens that the deviations have different shapes and patterns in different social structures."[2] He answers this question by saying that a society may hold up exalted goals but may not define, regulate, and control "the acceptable modes of reaching out for these goals."[3]

People will use both fair and foul means to reach that goal.

With a strong emphasis on the culturally sponsored goal, some individuals try expedient but illegitimate routes to the goal. "Social structures exert a definite pressure upon certain persons in the society to engage in a non-conforming rather than a conforming conduct."[4] The persons adopting the deviant routes may be "responding normally to the social situation in which they find themselves."[5] Merton goes on to add that this "dissociation between culturally prescribed aspirations and socially structured avenues for realizing these aspirations"[6] leads to instability of the society. He thinks "there develops what Durkheim called 'anomie' or normlessness."[7]

The relation of anomie to delinquency was highlighted by Lander in an ecological analysis of Baltimore. He sought a relationship between the delinquency rates of several census tracts and variables such as education, monthly rent, substandard housing, and home ownership. Many of these variables were found to be associated with the delinquency rate. However, the associations turned out to be only surface relationships.

One variable which was a strong predictor of delinquency rate was *home ownership*. Lander argues that lack of home ownership in itself cannot be a cause of delinquency. Instead, it is the social instability associated with homelessness that could cause delinquency.

> The delinquency rate is fundamentally related only to the *anomie* and not specifically to the socio-economic conditions of an area. The delinquency rate in a *stable* community will be low in spite of its being characterized by bad housing, poverty and propinquity to the city center. On the other hand, one would expect a high delinquency rate in an area characterized by normlessness and social instability. In such sections there is a deficiency in the traditional social controls.[8]

Opportunity

In his theory of anomie, Merton says that the separation between success goals and legitimate opportunities to reach those goals forces individuals to use illegitimate opportunities. Cloward and Ohlin contend that illegitimate opportunity is not easily and equally open to all. It is not easy to become a successful thief. The aspiring thief has to learn the art of theft, develop associations with the criminal world, and make contact with a bonding agent, a fence, and with the police and lawyers. These opportunities, though illegitimate, are not easy to find. The underworld of career criminals does not open its opportunity structure to novices without testing them. The criminal opportunity structure is also very competitive and monopolized. Cloward and Ohlin assert that "access to illegitimate roles, no less than access to legitimate roles, is limited by both social and psychological factors."[9]

Legitimate and illegitimate opportunities are interwoven with each other. The community provides the opportunity, the means, the setting, and the milieu for the criminal to commit a crime. Different communities offer varying opportunities to commit a particular criminal act. The actors have to adapt to the situation in which they find themselves:

> [Their adaptation] may depend upon the kind of support for one or another type of illegitimate activity that is given at different points in the social structure. If, in a given location, illegal or criminal means are not readily available, then we should not expect a criminal subculture to develop among adolescents. By the same logic, we should expect the manipulation of violence to become a primary avenue to higher status only in areas where the means of violence are not denied to the young. To give a third example, drug addiction and participation in subcultures organized around the consumption of drugs presuppose that persons can secure access to drugs and knowledge about how to use them.[10]

Illegal opportunities, as described above, generate different kinds of subcultures which Cloward and Ohlin call criminal, conflict, or retreatist (drug) subcultures.

Lower-Class Culture

Miller found that lower-class cultures tend to generate gang delinquency. He asserts that the street-corner groups in a lower-class community violate laws in order to behave as they are expected to within that community. Miller collected extensive data on twenty-one street-corner groups in a slum district of a large eastern city over a period of 30 months. The data that were collected included observational data on behavior patterns of group members and other community residents, workers' contact reports, and direct tape recordings of group activities and discussions.

According to Miller, gang delinquency is not motivated by the delinquency subculture. Instead, it is guided by the long-established traditions of the lower-class community itself. Also, lower-class gang members are not trying to negate the values of the middle class. They are trying to live up to the values of their own class. By the act of affirming the values of their own lower class, they are violating the values of the middle-class or dominant culture. The focal concerns (values) of the lower class are trouble, toughness, smartness, excitement, fate, and autonomy. These focal concerns are the basis of the lower-class cultural system. Miller points out a certain amount of duality in their behavior: While the members of the lower class have an outward commitment to law violation, inwardly they are committed to abide by the law.

The concept of *trouble* generally concerns getting into trouble with the law. "Getting into trouble" and "staying out of trouble" are matters of daily concern to the lower class. One's experience in crime or delinquency and involvement with law enforcement agencies may result in a certain amount of prestige and status. Such experience may qualify a person for membership in a gang or leadership in the criminal underworld.

Toughness—physical prowess and bravery—is generally admired in the lower class. In order to acquire material goods and personal status, the lower class has to use *smartness* to outwit, to dupe and con, others. Bored by routine or repetitive activity, lower-class individuals seek much needed excitement through alcohol, gambling, and fighting.

> For many lower class individuals the venture into the high risk world of alcohol, sex and fighting occurs regularly once a week, with interim periods devoted to accommodating to possible consequences of these periods, along with recurrent resolves not to become so involved again.[11]

Many lower-class individuals attribute their woes and worries to *fate*. Personal efforts do not seem to take one very far without a good deal of luck. There is also a great emphasis on *autonomy* —personal independence and resentment of authority. Miller contends that this, in some cases, may be a front put up by some individuals. That is, behind this attitude, there may be an inward dependence on authority.

Individuals may have varying commitments to these focal concerns, or values. Miller thinks that a substantial segment of present-day American society subscribes to these focal concerns of the lower class. He adds that most of the adolescents in the street-corner groups came from "female-based" households, and they find a sense of belonging and status in a peer group.

Criminal Ways, Criminal Society

Bell says: "From the start America was at one and the same time a frontier community where 'everything goes' and the fair country of Blue Laws." In this country prostitution, liquor, and gambling grew into big business. When prostitution declined into small business and big liquor profits dried up, organized crime filtered into legitimate business. Bell continues:

> Moreover, for the young criminal, hunting in the asphalt jungle of the crowded city, it was not the businessman with his wily manipulation of numbers but the "man with the gun" who was the American hero. [He was] acquiring by personal merit what was denied to him by complex orderings of a stratified society.[12]

In the same vein, Reckless talks about the strong tradition of lawlessness in America:

> People in America do not have the respect for law that people in England, Holland, Germany, Sweden, and other countries have. The law-abiding tradition is not as strong. On the contrary, America has a sort of lawless tradition—at least a fairly strong subculture of lawlessness, which came with the settlement of a new country and the pushing out to new frontiers.[13]

Schur asserts that criminal behavior represents a part of our social system and is a fact of social life. In his book, *Our Criminal Society,* he advances several major grounds for legitimately describing American society as criminal. According to him, America is a criminal society because:

1. It is an unequal society.
2. It places emphasis on cultural values that help generate crime.
3. It has created much unnecessary crime.
4. It has adopted an unseeing and unworkable orientation to crime problems.[14]

Delinquent Subculture: Status Seeking

According to Cohen, "The process of becoming a delinquent is the same as the process of becoming, let us say, a Boy Scout. The difference lies only in the culture pattern with which the child associates."[15]

The children of the working class find themselves stifled in a world dominated by middle-class standards. One place where they find it particularly difficult to compete with middle-class children is in the school. The school is managed by a board and teachers, all of whom foster middle-class values. Judged by standards which are alien to the children of the working class, they feel defeated and degraded in status. Hemmed in by the status problem, these boys try to find something to compensate for the loss of status. They find it in boys' gangs that flourish most conspicuously in the "delinquent neighborhoods" of our large cities. These gangs revel in the delinquent subculture.

According to Cohen, the delinquent subculture is nonutilitarian, malicious, and negativistic.[16] These boys don't steal things because they want them; they steal for the fun of it. There is malice in their actions. They like to terrorize other children. They take delight in the discomfort of others. They misbehave in school, play hookey, disturb other children, and irritate the teachers.

Cohen contends that the delinquent subculture takes its norms from the larger culture but turns them upside down.[17] They negate the norms of the middle class to such an extent that they would not like to do anything that the middle class does. According to Cohen, the middle class places a great premium on ambition, individual responsibility, resourcefulness, cultivation of skills, postponement of immediate satisfactions in the interest of long-term goals, industry, thrift, rationality, cultivation of manners, control of physical aggression and violence, wholesome recreation, and respect for property.[18] The boys from the delinquent subculture flout and oppose the norms. By the mechanism of reaction formation, their activities may run counter to these norms.

These boys are *versatile* in the sense that they get into all kinds of mischief—mostly theft, but also vandalism, malicious mischief, trespassing, truancy, and drugs. They are *impulsive hedonists*. They seek excitement, and instant fun. Short-run hedonism is characteristic of the social class from which they come.[19] Also characteristic is the *group autonomy* or intolerance of restraint. The delinquent subculture has a special allergy to restraint and regulation. "Gang members are unusually resistant to efforts of home, school and other agencies to regulate, not only their delinquent activities, but any activities carried on within the group."[20]

Cohen thinks that a breakdown in family controls may lead to recruitment in gangs. He is also not oblivious to the role of psychogenic factors. Psychogenic factors may be causing delinquency independently; or, in the majority of cases, these factors may be interacting with subcultural factors.[21] Subcultural factors act as a pollen for a susceptible person who being allergic to pollen could easily get hay fever. To illustrate, a child who was brutally treated by his stepfather developed a tendency to set small fires around his home. When he was punished for setting fires, he switched to stealing. When he was 17, his city was struck by race riots. This triggered the arsonist in him and he set a dozen buildings ablaze.

Next, we examine some theories which look at crime as a by-product of conflict.

Culture Conflict

Sellin associated delinquency and crime with intensive culture conflict. He contended that "culture conflict can arise because of the interpenetration of conduct norms. Conflicts of culture are inevitable when the norms of one cultural or subcultural area migrate to or come in contact with those of another."[22] One noteworthy example is that of the immigrants who travel with their native norms to the host country. It has been observed that the first generation of immigrants does not show a high crime rate. They mostly seem to use their own native norms and consequently do not experience much cultural conflict. The cultural conflict seems to occur in their children. These children of foreign-born parents are faced with a conflict between the culture under the roof and that in the street. They commit crime in the American style. The conflict is particularly acute if the immigrant family moves from rural Europe to urban America.

It is noteworthy that Asian immigrant groups have not shown

very many of the adverse effects of culture conflict. Consequently, their delinquency rate has remained low. Since the Orient is so different from the Occident, one would expect Orientals to be more heavily damaged by the culture conflict. But it appears that Orientals have insulated themselves against the invasion of their heritage. They have maintained family discipline and loyalty and have actively pursued the study of Oriental religion, language, and culture.

Conflict of Group Interests

Whereas Sellin discussed conflict of group norms, Vold explained crime on the basis of opposing group conflicts. Groups with different religious, political, cultural, and economic orientations have often come into conflict with each other. History is replete with wars, battles, religious strifes, and labor-business rivalries. Vold says: "A group must always be in a position to defend itself in order to maintain its place and position in the world of constantly changing adjustments. The principal goal, therefore, of one group in contact with another, is to keep from being replaced."[23]

Some of the most powerful groups have very strong lobbies working with the legislatures. They influence legislators to enact laws relating to health, food, drugs, manufacturing, trade, and recreation, thus safeguarding and promoting their interests. When one group promotes its interests at the cost of another group, it quite often comes into conflict with a group with opposing interests. Some of the laws restricting the use of alcohol, drugs, and abortion are resented by youth. Similarly, laws concerning obscenity, nudity, and morality are sponsored by some and resisted by others, including those whose living might be at stake. The Supreme Court found that some juvenile laws were infringing upon the constitutional rights of children. There are still many practices, carried out in the name of juvenile justice, which conflict with the interests and legitimate freedom of children. Reckless remarks:

> The prevalence of the companionship factor in crime and delinquency means to Vold that delinquency and crime are collective defensive behaviors. The delinquent boys' gang is a

minority group at odds with the rest of the community. . . . Many of these young gang members in American cities become members of adult gangs, of organized crime, of political machines, who are doing battle against the majority group.[24]

There are ideological conflicts between the conscientious objectors to military service and the majority group which demands military service. There are political differences, and the party in power may send its opponents to prison. Elections generate conflict, violence, dishonesty, bribery, perjury, corruption, and sometimes political burglary—all for the sake of winning or keeping control of political power.[25] Vold says:

> The whole political process of law making, law breaking, and law enforcement becomes a direct reflection of deep seated and fundamental conflicts between interest groups and their more general struggles for the control of the police power of the state. Those who produce legislative majorities win control over the police power and dominate the policies that decide who is likely to be involved in violation of the law.[26]

Vold asserts that in many conflict situations, criminal reaction is the natural and normal reaction for the maintenance of the way of life to which the individuals stand committed.[27]

Quinney also explains crime in terms of class conflict and power. The definitions of crime and the criminal are written by the people in power to suit their interests. They change and rewrite these definitions (or laws) to match their changing interests. The dominant class not only defines crime, but it also lays down the procedures for applying penal sanctions to those who are defined as criminals. The powerful groups formulate legal policies and appoint their agents to enforce these policies against the "criminal." When the interests of the powerful are threatened, those in power extend the "protective" laws and enforce them more repressively. This has unfortunate consequences for the persons or groups who are defined and treated as criminal. They start looking upon themselves as criminals, and they act as criminals. The dominant class thus constructs an ideology of crime: who the criminals are, what the dangers from them are, and how they should be controlled. The dominant class spreads these ideas through mass communication.[28]

DELINQUENCY-GENERATING SOURCES IN THE INDIVIDUAL

In this section, we discuss theories that tend to place more emphasis on the individual than on the group. The physical anthropologists attribute delinquency to a particular body type. The neo-Freudians blame the inborn asocial instincts which were never socialized during childhood. The psychoanalysts also try to diagnose the quality of the typical adjustment made by an individual offender. The sociologists relate the factor of self with delinquency. Organic psychosis can contribute to delinquency indirectly.

Mesomorphy

Sheldon indentified three body types: endomorph (fat), mesomorph (muscular), and ectomorph (lean). He found that mesomorphy predominated in delinquent boys.[29] While Sheldon's research method is not free from criticism, his findings received support initially from the Gluecks and lately from Cortes and Gatti. The Gluecks found that 60.1 percent of delinquents were mesomorphic, as compared with only 30.7 percent of non-delinquents.[30] Cortes and Gatti found *three times* as many mesomorphs in their group of delinquents as compared with non-delinquents.[31] They interpret the mesomorphy-delinquency association in the following words:

> We do not mean to imply that there is a *direct* relationship between mesomorphy and delinquent behavior. Body build will intervene, through interaction with the environment, in the sense that a person born with an athletic body is more likely to engage in certain adventurous and aggressive types of activity than a person born with a very ectomorphic body.[32]

Sociologists also agree that we expect mesomorphs to play the role of a tough person. They merely try to live up to the expectations demanded of their role. They would, perhaps, be ridiculed if they played the role of a weakling.

Asocial Instincts

Before presenting psychoanalytical explanations of delinquency, it is necessary that we discuss some basic Freudian concepts. According to Freud, the two great drives which dominate personality are the *life instinct* and the *death instinct*. The life instinct strives for self preservation and love; the death instinct stands for destruction and hate. These instincts, which are sexual and aggressive in nature, seek satisfaction. The instincts are invested with a strong psychic energy. Using the force of this psychic energy, the instincts give rise to a tension in the personality. The personality system reacts to eliminate tension and restore the steady state.

The mind has two states: *conscious* and *unconscious;* they overlap, interact, and influence each other. The unconscious is the more important state of the mind. It contains our ideas, instinctive urges, and repressed memories originating in traumatic experiences in early childhood. We may not always be able to easily recall these ideas to our conscious mind.

The total personality, as conceived by Freud, consists of three major subsystems—id, ego, and superego. The *id* is a reservoir of instincts (love and hate) which demand immediate gratification. "The id cannot tolerate tension. It is demanding, impulsive, irrational, asocial, selfish and pleasure-loving."[33] *Id* wishes are mostly sexual and aggressive in character. The *ego* is the executive of the personality and tends to contain id wishes in accordance with the demands of reality. Unlike the id, the ego is reality-oriented. The *superego* is a conscience, a moral part of the personality. All three subsystems are both conscious and unconscious. Acting as a moderator between the wishes of the id and the prohibitions of the superego, the ego relieves tension and restores the steady state.

Freud believed that the child passes through a series of dynamically differentiated psychosexual stages in developing into an adult. The early stages of psychosexual development are the oral, anal, and phallic stages during which the mouth, elimination, and sexual identification are successive areas of concern for the personality. This is followed by a period of quiescent latency and, finally, the emergence of the genital stage of adolescence.

The way in which each stage is met and resolved is significant in determining personality. For example, during the anal stage the crucial issue in the child's development is not the control of toilet functions per se. Rather, it is how the child's mother and others interact with the child concerning toilet training. A mother who is repressive and anxious about toilet training could produce undue aggression in the child. From then on, the child might generalize this in other expulsive traits, such as cruelty, destructiveness, and temper tantrums.

According to "instinct" theories, we are all born with asocial instincts which are sexual and aggressive in nature. If these asocial instincts are properly tamed and trained, we become social beings; otherwise we remain asocial individuals. Proper socialization requires the proper parent-child love relationship. August Aichhorn, a close friend of Freud, asserts that behind every act of manifest delinquency, there is latent delinquency. In fact, we all have the seeds of latent delinquency in us, but these seeds do not sprout into actual delinquency unless the contributory conditions are present. A faulty parent-child relationship contributes to manifest delinquency.

In *Wayward Youth*, a classic in the field, Aichhorn presents the case histories of several youths whose manifest delinquency was triggered by a particular event. An analysis of these cases invariably reveals, in childhood, the existence of psychic trauma, guilt, hostility, and fear. The youths were either overprotected or not loved at all. Faulty family relationships nursed their latent delinquency.

> The predisposition to delinquency is not a finished product at birth but is determined by the emotional relationship, that is, by the first experiences which the environment forces upon the child. This does not mean that every child so predisposed will become delinquent. Bad company, street influences, and the like, factors which are not the underlying causes of delinquency but the direct or indirect provocation, also may play a part.[34]

According to Aichhorn, emotional illness in a child often gives the appearance of delinquency. Aichhorn was the pioneer of the child guidance movement, and he himself directed a youth guidance center for a number of years.

Children Who Hate

Fritz Redl, a neo-Freudian, together with Wineman, a social worker, closely watched and treated a group of children in a home named the Pioneer House, in Detroit. The house admitted only a small group of preadolescents between the ages of 8 and 11. These children had received little or no love from their parents or any other person in the family. These were the children whom nobody wanted, and they had passed through events of an extraordinarily traumatic nature. Nothing good had ever happened to them. They displayed a pathological backlog of hostility and aggression, and they impulsively attacked anything that came their way. They had no control of their impulsivity and hate. Their egos and superegos had failed in the job of behavioral control.

Redl lists twenty-two functions which the ego is supposed to perform in handling life situations. They include frustration tolerance; coping with insecurity, anxiety, and fear; resistance to temptation; assessing social reality; learning from experience; and drawing inferences from what happens to others. The delinquent ego fails in such functions and substitutes evasive excuses.[35] Similarly, the delinquent superego is deficient, sick, and spotty. The superego fails to forewarn hyperaggressive children when they are going to commit an offense; and it fails to punish them after the offense is committed. The children who hate constitute a special problem because their deficient and sick consciences happen to coincide with a deficient or delinquent ego.[36]

The Delinquent Act: A Solution

When faced with a problem, we seek a solution. Many of our solutions are unconscious. Depending on the state of health of our personality and the interaction of id, ego, and superego, a solution may be normal, neurotic, psychotic, or delinquent. The nature of the solution one finds depends both on the situation one is facing and the dynamics of one's personality. Aichhorn contends, "The manner in which the psychic energy is utilized determines the direction in which the individual develops; whether he will be subjected to nervous illness, or whether he will become dissocial."[37]

A person with a problem must use the usual mechanisms of adjustment: projection, rationalization, substitution, sublimation, and reaction formation. One may *fight* out the problem or resort to a *flight* mechanism. An individual may solve a problem in a way which is typical of that individual, or choose a different solution every time: a neurotic or psychotic solution one time, and a delinquent solution another time. Generally, an individual seeks a solution which involves the least amount of psychic energy. Such a solution is relatively comfortable, or least uncomfortable, to the individual. In many cases, compulsive stealing, shoplifting, compulsive fire setting, or compulsive peeping signifies an effort to solve an unconscious problem.

Neurotic Solution

Neurosis is not generally considered an important causal factor in delinquency. Generally, one may be either a neurotic or a delinquent but not both. After a good survey of related literature, Mannheim says:

> If the individual has, unconsciously, to choose between neurosis and delinquency, his choice may depend on the source of the conflict responsible for his difficulties. If they are rooted in himself, he is likely to develop a neurosis; if, however, they are caused by other people, he is more likely to commit delinquent acts, but he may also take refuge in a neurosis as a defense against his aggressive impulses. The delinquent who is somehow deprived of his delinquent outlets may occasionally develop neurotic symptoms, especially if his victory over his delinquent tendencies was achieved through over-great self control.[38]

How does one choose either a neurotic solution or a delinquent solution to a problem? According to the Freudian school of thought, when id wishes seek instinctual gratification they come into conflict with the ego and superego. Because of the incompatibility of these wishes with the demands of the outside world, they cannot be allowed expression. To repress these wishes, the ego has to put in a lot of effort and has to remain on constant alert against id wishes. This kind of perpetual threat from id wishes can lead to neurotic anxiety. The struggle between the id on the one hand, and the ego and superego on the other, can lead to unconscious inner conflicts, anxiety, and guilt. If these conflicts are acted out inside oneself, they may lead to neurosis; if they are acted out on others, these conflicts may contribute to delinquency. Also, a superego that is too punitive may inflict neurosis, and if it is deficient it may generate a delinquent solution. Neurotics are highly moral people, and a delinquent act greatly torments them. However, someone who is suffering an anxiety neurosis due to irrational fears may blackmail other people, steal money to keep face with friends, or be driven to sexual behavior such as peeping, exhibitionism, or setting fires. Because of an extreme sense of guilt in some cases, neurotics may seek self punishment to allay their guilt feelings.

Psychotic Solution

Some of the better known forms of psychoses are schizophrenia, manic-depressive, and paranoia. A schizophrenic patient generally suffers from hallucinations, delusions, and incoherent thinking. There is a partial or complete loss of contact with reality, resulting in bizarre flights into fantasy. In the case of some juveniles, these symptoms may not at times be very apparent. The diagnosis may become obvious only after the patient has committed a serious delinquent act.

The manic-depressive has alternate moods of elation and depression, with some periods of apparent normality. During elation, the manic-depressive may swindle, steal, vandalize, drink, and misbehave sexually. During the depressive phase, the patient may attempt suicide or homicide.

The paranoid generally has grandiose feelings alternating with a sense of being persecuted. A paranoid who imagines that he or she is being harmed by someone may hurt or kill the imagined enemy.

Organic Psychoses

Organic psychoses are generally caused by brain injuries, syphilitic infection (traumatic psychosis), or acute infectious fever producing an inflammation of the brain (encephalitis lethargica). Persons affected by organic psychoses may commit almost any kind of crime without realizing what they are doing. They are not capable of hiding their crimes, and they commit crimes with an astonishing openness and silliness.

Brain injuries caused by accidents may also produce profound personality changes leading to criminality and/or vagabondage. Patients may become easily excited and prone to crimes of violence. A person suffering from brain infection is likely to show lasting aftereffects and changes in physique, intelligence, and character. Highly antisocial acts, often of an explosive or sexual nature, may easily be a part of the postencephalitic period. Similarly, epileptics are prone to sudden outbreaks of apparently motiveless violence and other antisocial acts.[39]

Self Factor

Why does one person react normally in a given situation, while another reacts in a delinquent fashion? Many sociological theories are not able to answer this question satisfactorily. Naturally, the answer to this difference in reactions lies in the *actor* and the *self*. Reckless has identified several factors of self which veer an individual away from or toward delinquency: self-concept, images, and perceptions; awareness of limited opportunity; rejection of middle-class values; norm retention or norm erosion; techniques of neutralization of offenses; types of alienation; and acceptance or rejection of blame.[40] The operation of only some of them can be discussed here.

Reckless and Dinitz attempted to find a self factor that might provide some insight into the reasons why most boys in areas of high delinquency rates do not get involved in official delinquency. They asked the teachers of 12-year-old white boys to nominate good and bad boys. The nominees were interviewed, and it was found that they corroborated the estimation of their teachers. The good boys saw themselves as good boys, planned to finish high school, and looked upon their friends and families in a favorable light. They scored high on Gough's Socialization Scale and Responsibility Scale and made favorable responses on Reckless's Self-concept Questionnaire. In contrast, the bad boys had already developed an unfavorable self-image. They believed that they and their friends would get into trouble. They did not like their families. They did not hope to finish school. They scored low on socialization and responsibility and showed an unfavorable self-concept.

In a longitudinal comparison 4 years later, practically all the good boys were still in school, and they had had little or no trouble with the law. On the other hand, 39 percent of the bad boys had been in the juvenile court an average of three times. This proved that a good self-concept insulates the individual against delinquency.

> We believe we have some tangible evidence that a good self-concept, undoubtedly a product of favorable socialization, veers slum boys away from delinquency, while a poor self-concept, a product of unfavorable socialization, gives the slum boy no resistance to deviancy, delinquent companions, or delinquent sub-culture.[41]

Delinquents' Subterranean Values

The common belief that a delinquent's values, norms, and attitudes are totally opposed to the norms of the larger society is erroneous. According to Matza:

> Many delinquents are essentially in agreement with the larger society, at least with regard to the evaluation of delinquent behavior as "wrong." Rather than standing in opposition to conventional ideas of good conduct, the delinquent is likely to adhere to the dominant norms in belief but render them ineffective in practice.[42]

Matza goes on to argue that the values behind much juvenile delinquency are far less deviant than commonly portrayed. He has observed three major themes in the values of delinquents.

First, delinquents show a restless search for excitement, thrills, or kicks. They like to undertake daring adventures, even at the cost of risk. They court physical danger, experiment with the forbidden, and provoke the authorities.[43] Second, juvenile delinquents commonly exhibit a disdain for "getting on" in the realm of work. They don't believe in occupational goals, hard work, a steady job or slow but steady advancement. If they have aspirations, they are very unrealistic about their goals and ambiguous about the means to reach those goals. They look for easy ways to make money, and tend toward chicanery and manipulation. In matters of money the delinquent knows no frugality and thrift.

> Money is frequently desired as something to be squandered in gestures of largesse, in patterns of conspicuous consumption. The sudden acquisition of large sums of money is his goal—the "big score"—and he will employ legal means if possible, and illegal means if necessary.[44]

A third theme running through accounts of juvenile delinquency centers on aggression. Delinquent boys lay great stress on toughness, masculinity, and machismo.

Matza and Sykes liken delinquents to Veblen's "gentlemen of leisure" and call them "leisured elite." However, they do not think that the values of delinquents are very different from those of the dominant classes. The subterranean values of the dominant classes are the same as those of the delinquents. The middle classes "seek their 'kicks' in gambling, nightclubbing and the big night on the town."[45] While the middle and upper classes revel in these luxuries behind the protection of the nightclubs in a sophisticated manner, the delinquents are left to gamble and steal on the streets. They also show a poor sense of timing. Matza and Sykes say:

> The delinquent may not stand as an alien in the body of society but may represent instead a disturbing reflection or a caricature. . . . These subterranean values, similar in many ways to the values Veblen ascribed to a leisure class, bind the delinquent to the society whose laws he violates. And we suspect that this sharing of values, this bond with the larger social order, facilitates the frequently observed reformation of delinquents with the coming of adult status.[46]

DELINQUENCY-PROVOKING SOURCES IN THE INTERACTION OF THE INDIVIDUAL AND THE SOCIETY

The previous two sets of theories do not exclude interaction between the group and the individual. However, the third set of theories seems to be based on such interaction. For example, the family and school generate conditions that give rise to delinquency; vulnerable children are more likely to react to these conditions in a delinquent fashion. Similarly, according to learning theories, society provides conditions suitable to the learning of delinquent ways; vulnerable children readily yield to these ways.

In the containment theory, the group puts pressures of poverty, minority status, discrimination, and deprivation on the individual. The group pulls the individual to the lures of a criminal life. The individual reacts to the pressures and pulls of the group on the strength of his or her inner and outer containments. If the impact of the pressures and pulls is too severe for these containments, then the individual succumbs.

Nye's theory is based on the interaction between the family group which controls and the youngster who is the object of control. According to the interactionist perspective, delinquency is generated by the reactions of other people. Society, by reacting severely to even a minor deviation, gives the individual a deviant identity. This can drive the individual to more serious delinquent behavior.

Family Life

Undoubtedly, the family has a lot to do with raising children as delinquents as well as nondelinquents. The family is the first and the chief socializing agent for the child. As such, it sets the foundation for behavior patterns. Several aspects of family life have been greatly researched in relation to delinquency: family structure (family intactness or brokenness), family functioning, parent-child relationships, and family size. Let us look at some of the results of this research.

The *broken home* has been the subject of many investigations.[47] Many of the studies show a larger percentage of broken homes among delinquent children than among nondelinquent children. Apparently, a break in the family structure through separation, divorce, desertion, or death does place some strain on the family. But a case has been made that a broken home may be more peaceful for a child who is saved the traumatic experience of parents constantly fighting with each other. The McCords have shown that quarrelsome and negligent homes lead to more delinquency than broken homes.[48] In other words, the structure of the family is not at fault as much as *family functioning*.

Many researchers have indicated that a broken home does not have the same effect on all children. The delinquency-producing effects of a broken home are greater for preadolescents than for adolescents. Similarly, a broken home has a greater effect on girls than on boys. It is understandable that younger children and girls are more dependent on the family unit than older children. More delinquent girls than delinquent boys come from broken homes. Girls seem to react more rebelliously to the broken home.[49] Also, families generally exercise more control on girls than on boys. The impact of the broken home also depends on the attitude of the affected members. Cavan and Ferdinand contend that the most common type of reduced family that remains after a break is that of the mother and children.

> The way in which the mother speaks of the father affects the attitude that children have for the father. . . . When the mother always spoke of the absent father in derogatory terms, the child's fantasies pictured the father as fearful and aggressive. The opposite was true when the mother always spoke favorably of the father.[50]

Analyzing the *family soil* in which the children are raised, the Gluecks found a larger incidence of criminalism (including both serious offenses and drunkenness) in the families of delinquent children. The parents and close relatives of delinquents were more heavily burdened with physical and mental illnesses than those of nondelinquents.[51] The Gluecks are cautious not to infer any direct causal link between family criminalism and delinquency. The McCords also found that when the father and mother were both deviant, the association with adult criminality was very high. If one parent was nondeviant, the association was not high.[52] The mother's absence for a prolonged period of time during early childhood, which is generally regarded as a cause of mental illness, has not been found as a foremost causal factor in delinquency. However, studies have shown an association between maternal deprivation and inability to enter an affectionate relationship.[53]

In the parent-child relationship, *parental discipline* is a significant factor in delinquency. The consistency and fairness of discipline have been found to be significantly associated with conforming behavior. The Gluecks found that in disproportionately large numbers of families of delinquents, disciplinary practices were erratic and unsound. That is, the mother or the father was either extremely lax or unreasonably rigid in control.[54] Firm and kind techniques were practiced much more frequently by the parents of nondelinquents. More of the delinquents' families resorted to physical punishment, whereas more of the nondelinquents' parents used reasoning as a disciplinary method. Since most of these studies are based upon the perceptions and recollections of delinquents and controls, the Task Force Report makes a cautionary comment:

> It is possible that delinquents and non-delinquents perceive their parental discipline differently despite similarities in disciplinary techniques; it is also possible that the actual differences in disciplinary techniques are due to the parents' differential responses to delinquent and non-delinquent behavior, such behavior having been triggered by other variables.[55]

Affectional relations between parents and children are of vital importance to the development of personality and character. According to the Gluecks, the delinquents were much more the victims of indifference or actual hostility of their fathers and mothers and were, in turn, less attached to their parents.[56] The most important, however, seemed to be the father's affection for the boy. That is, 40.2 percent of the delinquents had affectionate fathers, but 80.7 percent of the controls had affectionate fathers. The McCords found that the presence of at least one loving parent, coupled with consistent parental discipline, was enough to reduce the delinquency-producing effect of a criminal father. With two loving parents, the type of discipline used has no effect upon the delinquency of sons. But with one loving parent, erratic or lax discipline produces significantly more delinquency than consistent discipline.[57] So, the differential relationship between the family and delinquency varies with the child's "self" and the situation.

> The problem of ferreting out the influences of the family in the causation of delinquent behavior is complicated by the fact that any given family situation is not the same situation for the sibling living in it. . . . It may be that the delinquent child is reared on storm clouds, seeks them, and even helps to generate them.[58]

School Failure

School conditions can generate a high rate of educational failure and alienation. This sense of failure and exclusion, in turn, leads to delinquency. The consultants' paper written by Schafer and Polk for the task force report on delinquency and youth crime can be interpreted to imply these two stages:

1. The public school system generates alienative conditions for disadvantaged youth.
2. These conditions contribute to the delinquency of the youth who perceive these school conditions as most alienative.

American school programs, curricula, and instructional techniques are geared to middle-class standards. These do not meet the needs of low-status and low-income youth. The school adds to the cumulative failure of disadvantaged youth and their deep sense of frustration. The teachers are from the middle class and speak the middle-class language. Culturally handicapped children are not accommodated in any special way in the school. The teachers believe that these students have limited potential so that there is no use in working with them. The program content is irrelevant to the students, as it is not useful in their daily life. They learn from the street. The teaching style is not conducive to their proper learning. With low grades, these disadvantaged students are placed in slow-learning groups and lower tracks. In this way, they are deprived of what other students are getting. The gap continues to widen, and no remedial action is taken to bridge this gap. The lower-income schools have inferior teachers, poor facilities, and outdated equipment. There is also a woeful lack of communication between the school and the community.[59] All this heightens failure and subsequent delinquency.

The frustration of school failure seems to affect the youth of all classes, but it affects lower-class youth in particular.

> Polk found that boys [who failed and were] from white collar homes have five times greater chance of becoming delinquent than those who did not fail, while boys from blue collar backgrounds who failed were delinquent almost seven times more often than those who did not fail.
>
> The evidence suggests, then, that educational failure is one experience, especially when combined with a desire for success, that contributes to delinquency.[60]

The underprivileged youth do not see how they can use this education for their work. They do not believe that the education will bring them any rewards, or payoff. Short found that poor articulation between school experience and future orientation was associated with higher rates of delinquency. Similarly, Polk found that delinquency was greater among noncollege-bound than college-bound students, even when their grades were the same.[61]

Criminal Behavior Is Learned

A few theorists emphasize that criminal behavior (as well as noncriminal behavior) is learned. It is learned through differential association, imitation, or identification.

Sutherland explains crime through his famous theory of *differential association*. According to Sutherland, a criminal act occurs when a situation appropriate for it, as defined by the person, is present. He makes the following statements which refer to the process by which a particular person comes to engage in criminal behavior.

1. Criminal behavior is learned.
2. Criminal behavior is learned in interaction with other persons in a process of communication.
3. The principal part of the learning of criminal behavior occurs within intimate personal groups.
4. When criminal behavior is learned, the learning includes (a) techniques of committing the crime, which are sometimes very complicated, sometimes very simple; and (b) the specific direction of motives, drives, rationalizations, and attitudes.
5. The specific direction of motives is learned from definitions of the legal codes as favorable or unfavorable.
6. A person becomes delinquent because of an excess of definitions favorable to violation of the law over definitions unfavorable to violation of the law. (This is the principle of differential association.)
7. Differential associations may vary in frequency, duration, priority, and intensity.
8. The process of learning criminal behavior by association with criminal and anti-criminal patterns involves all of the mechanisms that are involved in any other learning.
9. While criminal behavior is an expression of general needs and values, it is not explained by those general needs and values since non-criminal behavior is an expression of the same needs and values.[62]

Sutherland and Cressey go on to say that:

> The person's associations are determined in a general context of social organization. . . . Crime is rooted in the social organization and is an expression of that social organization. A group may be organized for criminal behavior or organized against criminal behavior. Most communities are organized both for criminal and anti-criminal behavior and in that sense the crime rate is an expression of the differential group organization.[63]

Gabriel Tarde, a French magistrate and social psychologist, explained behavior on the basis of imitation. The laws of imitation which apply in crime as well as in all other aspects of social life are basic to Tarde's theories. In his studies of criminal behavior, Tarde noted three types of repetitive patterns. This led him to formulate three laws of imitation.

> The first and most obvious law is that men imitate one another in proportion as they are in close contact. In crowds or cities where contact is close and life is active and exciting,

imitation is most frequent and changes often. [Tarde defined this phenomenon as fashion.]

The second law concerns the direction in which imitations are spread. Usually the superior is imitated by the inferior. . . . The last law of imitation Tarde called the law of insertion. When two mutually exclusive fashions come together, one can be substituted for the other. When this happens, there is a decline in the older method and an increase in the newer method. An example of this would be murder by knifing and murder by the gun. Tarde found that the former method had decreased while the latter had increased.[64]

Tarde recognized that both the element of individual choice and the factor of chance operate in a criminal career. He also reckoned the importance of social environment in producing criminals. He thus brought about the happy marriage of psychology and sociology in his theories.

Earlier, we examined Sutherland's theory of differential association, which assumes that criminal behavior is learned in interaction with other persons, especially in *intimate personal groups*. We know of several criminal patterns being copied from a distance without the actors coming into personal contact with each other. Skyjacking, with all its changing techniques, including that of parachuting with a bag of money, is one of many appropriate examples. These practices spread from continent to continent through mass media. Glaser explains this in terms of *differential identification*. He describes identification as "the choice of another, from whose perspective we view our own behavior."

> During any period, prior identification and present circumstances dictate the selection of the persons with whom we identify ourselves. Prior identifications which have been pleasing tend to persist.[65]

According to Glaser, the essence of rehabilitation lies in the offender's identification with the noncriminal models. Commenting on Glaser's theory, Reckless says,

> Hidden individual factors are what push the offenders to embrace or succumb to confronting models. Why an individual gravitates toward a certain model, why the model has importance, meaning, drawing power for him, why it is retained, modified, or rejected during a long or short period, are questions which Glaser's theory cannot answer.[66]

The Failure of Containments

A most useful theory, the one that explains the largest amount of criminal and delinquent behavior, is the containment theory of Reckless. It not only combines both the sociological and psychological theories, but also fills in the gap between the two. It satisfactorily answers the persistent question: Who succumbs and who remains immune to crime when exposed to a crime-provoking situation? It takes into account both the group and the individual, and both the macro and micro levels of explanation.

Briefly, when one is pressured (by unemployment), lured or pulled (by bad companions), and pushed (by compulsions), one protects oneself by the use of outer and inner containments. If the containments are strong enough, the individual is immune; if they break down, the individual succumbs. The *outer containment* "is the holding power of the group. Society, and particularly nuclear groups, contain, steer, shield, divert, support, reinforce, and limit its members."[67] Folk communities and religious sects are very strong containing groups. They provide to the individual clearcut, meaningful roles and a sense of belonging and identity. The components of *inner containment* are self-image, self-concept, goal orientation, aspiration level, frustration tolerance, and commitment to norms.[68]

The following discussion refers to the diagram in Figure 1.

> While external containment and internal containment, in combination or singly, can be stated in terms of the degree of risk for becoming involved in reportable violations of norms, rules, and laws, they can also be described as operating as buffers against deviance. A buffer paradigm can be constructed for the democratic world of flux following a pattern of concentric circles. In the outer circle (1) is the social stratosphere of pressures and pulls. In the next circle (2), coming from outside to inside, lies the buffer of external containments— the person's groups and organizations. Then there is the circle (3) of inner containment—the self. Finally, there is the innermost circle (4) of organic and psychological pushes. Circle (2) is the external containing buffer, if and when it is strong enough. Circle (3) is the internal containing buffer (the self), if and when it is strong enough.
>
> The pressures and pulls are exerted for the most part in a sphere outside the nuclear containing groups, such as the family or organizations. Pressures consist of adverse living

conditions (relative to region and culture), such as poverty, unemployment, economic insecurity, group conflicts, minority group status, lack of opportunities, inequalities. Some break through the weakness in the buffer of circle (2). Some of the pressures are diluted or diverted by circle (2). Those that break through the buffer of group containment confront the person head on. If he has the strength to fend them off, the buffer in circle (3) holds. If not, he succumbs to deviance and violation of law. The same can be said for the pulls which also are located in circle (1). The pulls draw the person away from his original way of life and accepted forms of living. Pulls consist of prestige individuals, bad companions, delinquency of criminal subculture, deviant groups, mass media, propaganda. They must break through the buffer of circle (2) (outer containment) and break through also the buffer of circle (3) (the self).

In addition to the pressures and pulls which batter at outer and inner containment, there are the organic and psychological pushes which batter the self. These are located in circle (4), the innermost circle. Some of the pushes which are rather uncontainable are extreme restlessness and discontent, marked

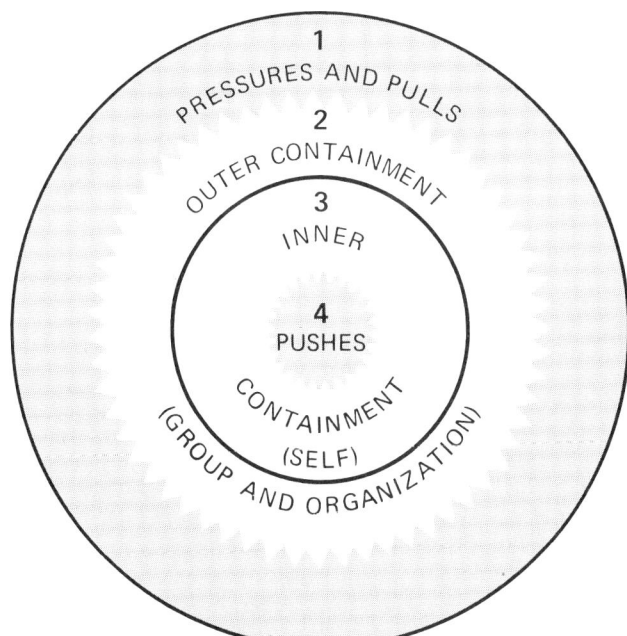

FIGURE 1   Diagram of the Theory of Containment.

inner tensions, extreme hostility and aggressiveness, aggrandizement and need for immediate gratification, extreme suggestibility, strong rebellion against authority, strong feeling of inadequacy and inferiority, guilt reactions, mental conflicts, anxieties, compulsions, phobias, organic impairments (brain damage, epilepsy), psychoses. Many of these pushes are too strong for the self to handle or for nuclear groups such as the family to contain. The buffers of circle (2) and circle (3) can carry ordinary disappointments, frustrations, restlessness, but they are no match for the big thrusts."[69]

Social Control

Nye takes the position that "when controls internal and external are weak and alternative routes to goal achievement are restricted, delinquent behavior can be anticipated."[70] He identifies four types of control:

1. Direct control imposed from without
2. Internalized control exercised from within through conscience
3. Indirect control related to affectional identification with parents and other noncriminal persons
4. Availability of alternative means to goals and values[71]

In order to relate the family attitudes to delinquent behavior, he departed from the usual practice of using the institutionalized population as his respondents. Instead, he administered his questionnaire to high school students. His use of a self-reported delinquency scale and other family attitude scales was both extensive and impressive. Nye found that all social control indicators, both in the family structure and in the parent-adolescent relationship, supported his theory. Delinquency was associated with low church attendance, high mobility, urban family, unhappy broken home, employment of mother, mutual rejection by parents and children, lack of appropriate discipline, nonsharing of responsibility, too much or too little freedom, father's low status and low acceptance in the community, antisocial or unethical parental behavior, lack of close value agreements between parents and children, dissatisfaction with parents' allocation of funds to children, and lack of advice on appropriate matters."[72] "The analysis of freedom and delinquent behavior suggests that direct control techniques have greater significance for girls than for boys. More measures of direct control were significantly related to delinquent behavior of girls than of boys."[73]

In general, delinquent behavior is minimal where a moderate amount of direct control is exercised. For example, in the case of girls, delinquent behavior is greatest where complete freedom is allowed, lowest where considerable freedom is allowed, and higher where no freedom is the practice. Again, a middle way, giving major responsibility but not discontinuing supervision and guidance entirely, appears to be associated with least delinquent behavior.[74]

> The more efficient the provision that is made for meeting adolescent needs in institutionalized behavior patterns, the less need there is for control of any other type; the more effective are the mechanisms of indirect control the less need for direct control. The more effective are internalized controls, the less need there is of any other type.[75]

Interactionist Perspective

A group of sociologists and social psychologists have greatly added to our understanding of the process of becoming a delinquent. Becker contends:

> Social groups create deviance by making the rules whose infractions constitute deviance, and by applying those rules to particular people and labeling them as outsiders. From this point of view, deviance is not a quality of the act the person commits, but rather a consequence of the application by others of rules and sanctions to an "offender." The deviant is the one to whom that label has successfully been applied; deviant behavior is behavior that people so label.[76]

The degree to which other people will respond to a given act as deviant varies greatly from time to time and from person to person. Homosexuality, which was viewed seriously in the 1940s, is viewed leniently in the 1970s. Slum children are more likely to be processed through the juvenile justice system than are middle-class children. Becker claims that "deviance is not a quality that lies in behavior itself, but in the interaction between the person who commits an act and those who respond to it."[77]

To be involved in a delinquent career, one may have to go through a series of steps. To be a burglar, a youth drops out of school, mingles with a gang of burglars, learns the "ropes" of burglary, makes appropriate contact with the fence, and, to escape arrest and punishment, gets to know some police officers and lawyers. In the progression of such a delinquent career, other persons' reactions in terms of their labeling, degrading, and rejection, are of great consequence to the delinquent.

At first, delinquents may commit a deviant act casually, unconsciously, or with only a weak intention. They may rationalize their act and may think of themselves as being only slightly deviant. They may suffer only minor psychic or social damage. Lemert calls this *primary deviance*. But the situation changes if such delinquents are arrested and presented before the juvenile court, labeled as delinquents, and placed under probation supervision. This branding in the open may bring about a drastic change in their public identity. Having been typed as delinquents, all the attributes of a delinquent will be applied to them, rightly or wrongly. The children so typed will suffer the usual social, psychological, or moral consequences of having been classified as delinquents. With the reputation of having been a delinquent, they may find it difficult to get good jobs. Worse, they too may start thinking of themselves as delinquents and join a delinquent group. This is the onset of *secondary deviance*. Lemert states:

> *Secondary deviation* is deviant behavior, or social roles based upon it, which becomes means of defense, attack, or adaptation to the overt and covert problems created by the societal reaction to primary deviation. In effect, the original "causes" of the deviation recede and give way to the central importance of the disapproving, degradational and isolating reactions of the society.[78]

These persons who are labeled, typed, punished, and rejected are propelled to a deviant or delinquent subculture. They are pulled toward the subculture to solve problems of adjustment, and to seek belongingness and company. The members of an organized delinquent group tend to develop "a set of perspectives and understandings about what the world is like and how to deal with it, and a set of routine activities based on these perspectives."[79]

Rubington and Weinberg say, "Identity results from operations that people go through when they wish to answer the question 'Who am I?' "[80] There is a private identity and a social identity. Youths may think of themselves as delinquents, drug users, or auto thieves (personal identity), or others may think of them in the same way (social identity). At times, there is a conflict between the two identities. Ex-delinquents may consider themselves reformed, but society may still consider them as cons and refuse to reintegrate them into the community.

The central point in the interactionist perspective is that a delinquent could be produced in the first instance by the response of others. The child may then be confirmed in this role by the reaction of other persons, particularly those in the juvenile justice system.

SUMMARY

The main theme in sociological theories is that of norm erosion. These theories seem to fall into two broad categories: theories of anomie and theories of conflict. Norm erosion is evident in both anomie and conflict. Durkheim uses anomie to indicate the failure of the society to regulate the limitless needs of some individuals. Merton uses anomie to point out the pressure generated by the society to use unfair means. And Lander refers to the same concept to maintain social controls.

A common ingredient in all these thoughts is that norms have lost their regulatory hold. The theories of conflict signify disrespect for the norms and protest against the laws. Sellin talks about the clash of norms based on cultural differences; Vold attributes crime to conflict of interests; and Quinney explains crime in terms of conflict between the dominant and powerless sections of society. All these theories express disenchantment with the present norms.

> Much of the ordinary criminal and delinquent behavior, perhaps the largest sector of it, represents erosion of conventional norms and also, to a much more limited extent, an alienation from the norms and the people who reinforce them. . . . "Bad companions" help the norm erosion process. Conflict engenders abrogation of norms.[81]

The individual theories which explain delinquency in terms of mesomorphic body type do not enjoy much of a following. The amount of crime resulting from organic psychoses, brain lesion, and epilepsy is negligible. The psychoanalysts attribute delinquency to asocial instincts which have not been tamed. When they mention faulty socialization, they are also implying the failure of internalization of norms. Redl blames it on the failure of ego functioning. The problem-solving theories suggest that the adjustment sought by some of the delinquents is antisocial in character.

Reckless lists several self factors as possible determinants of the direction a youth will take—toward or away from delinquent behavior. They include self-concepts, images, and perceptions; awareness of limited opportunity; rejection of middle-class values; norm retention or norm erosion; techniques of neutralization; types of alienation; and acceptance or rejection of blame.[82]

According to the sociopsychological explanations, when the most important social institution—the family—offers a poor quality of life, a vulnerable child succumbs. Similarly, when a school generates conditions conducive to delinquency, the disadvantaged child drops out to become a delinquent. When situations appropriate to the learning of delinquency exist, a suggestible youth learns delinquent behavior. According to the containment theory, youths subjected to many pressures, pulls, and pushes give in when their inner and outer containments break down. The interactionist perspectives imply that a minor deviant can develop into a delinquent if the persons and the agencies dealing with the deviant overreact or react improperly.

It is hoped that this discussion will be helpful to caseworkers and probation officers in their diagnoses. Some factors affect the individual closely, others remotely; similarly, some factors predispose the individual to delinquency, whereas others precipitate and trigger delinquent behavior.

Discussion Questions

1. What societal conditions generate anomie?
2. Do Durkheim, Merton, and Lander interpret anomie differently? If so, what are the differences in their interpretations?
3. How does Schur describe American society as a criminal society? Do you agree with him?
4. Both Cohen and Miller attribute delinquency to the lower class and its values. What is the difference in their positions?
5. Can conflict theories explain all delinquent behavior? If not, what kind of offenses are not easily explainable from the conflict perspective?

6. Do you recall any case of a psychotic youth who committed serious delinquent acts? What disposition was made in the case?
7. In a family living in a slum, one sibling becomes a delinquent, and the other becomes a police officer. Both siblings are males, born less than 2 years apart. How do you explain this phenomenon?
8. What are the advantages of the containment theory?

Glossary

Anomie A state (of a society or an individual) in which there is a lack of regulations or behavioral norms. It may be a personal disorganization, in which the individual has little reference to or concern for the social structure and its norms; a situation in which a society's laws and norms are themselves in conflict, so that an individual cannot easily conform to the contradictory requirements; or a society or group that has no norms and therefore no guidance for conduct—such a society sees no conformity.

Asocial Indifferent to social values, customs, and norms.

Child Guidance Movement A movement directed to the identification, diagnosis, and treatment of behavioral problems of children.

Impulsive Hedonist One who seeks excitement on an impulse without any thought of consequences.

Instinct An enduring tendency or disposition to act in an organized and biologically adaptive way.

Interactionist Perspective In the context of explaining delinquent behavior, an interpretation of the delinquency label as a product of the reaction of other persons to a certain act, not as a property of the act itself.

Learning Theories The theories which emphasize that delinquent behavior is learned through imitation, suggestion, association, and identification.

Longitudinal Comparison A study of the similarities and differences among a group of people over a period of time.

Lower Class That section of society which has low income and low education. This low status is perceived as such by people in the lower class as well as by people in other classes.

Middle Class Those members of society who perceive their social status as neither very low nor exceptionally high.

Neurosis A psychological disorder which generally arises as a defense against anxiety-ridden conflicts suffered by an individual. A neurotic may have inhibitions and obsessions which must be released through compulsive acts. The neurotic anxiety is mostly irrational and free-floating in nature.

Norm A standard of conduct shared by the members of a society or other group. Adherence to norms is often enforced by positive and negative sanctions.

Self The way an individual regards himself or herself. Mainly the result of experiences with others, and their reactions toward and expressed views of that individual.

Subculture An identifiable portion of a society that differs from the larger society in one or more cultural respects. The difference may be one of language, customs, or norms, for example.

Subterranean Values Hidden or secret, but coveted, values.

Trauma A stressful event in early life that inflicts permanent psychic injury.

Upper Class Upper stratum of a society which is able to dominate the lower strata by virtue of its greater authority, wealth, and prestige.

Working Class Usually used to denote manual workers, either skilled or unskilled. Sometimes includes low-paid clerical workers.

Footnotes

[1] Talcot Parsons et al., *Theories of Society*, Free Press, New York, 1961, vol. II, p. 91, quoting Emile Durkheim, *Suicide*, translated by John A. Spaulding and George Simpson, Free Press, Glencoe, Ill., 1951.

[2] Robert K. Merton, *Social Theory and Social Structure*, rev. ed., Free Press, New York, 1957, p. 131.

[3] Robert K. Merton, p. 133.

[4] Robert K. Merton, p. 132.

[5] Robert K. Merton, p. 132.

[6] Robert K. Merton, p. 134.

[7] Robert K. Merton, p. 135.

[8] Barnard Lander, *Towards An Understanding of Juvenile Delinquency*, Columbia, New York, 1954, p. 89.

[9] Richard A. Cloward and Lloyd E. Ohlin, *Delinquency and Opportunity*, Free Press, New York, 1960, p. 148.

[10] Richard A. Cloward and Lloyd E. Ohlin, pp. 151–152.

[11] Walter B. Miller, "Lower Class Culture as a Generating Milieu of Gang Delinquency," *Journal of Social Issues*, vol. 14, no. 3, p. 11.

[12] Daniel Bell, "Crime as an American Way of Life," *The Antioch Review*, vol. 13, pp. 131–154, June 1953, in Marvin Wolfgang et al., *Sociology of Crime and Delinquency*, 2d ed., Wiley, New York, 1970, pp. 165–166.

[13] Walter C. Reckless, *The Crime Problem*, 3d ed., Appleton Century Crofts, New York, 1961, p. 2.

[14] Edwin M. Schur, *Our Criminal Society: The Social and Legal Sources of Crime in America*, Prentice-Hall, Englewood Cliffs, N.J., 1969, pp. 16–20.

[15] Albert C. Cohen, *Delinquent Boys: The Culture of the Gang*, Free Press, Glencoe, Ill., 1955, p. 4.

[16] Albert C. Cohen, p. 23.

[17] Albert C. Cohen, p. 28.

[18] Albert C. Cohen, pp. 88–91.

[19] Albert C. Cohen, pp. 29–30.

[20] Albert C. Cohen, p. 31.

[21] Albert C. Cohen, p. 17.

[22] Thorsten Sellin, *Culture Conflict and Crime*, Social Sciences Research Council Bulletin 41, New York, 1938, p. 63.

[23] George B. Vold, *Theoretical Criminology*, Oxford University Press, Fair Lawn, N.J., p. 205.

[24] Walter C. Reckless, *The Crime Problem*, 3d ed., Appleton Century Crofts, New York, 1961, p. 319.

[25] George B. Vold, p. 215.

[26] George B. Vold, p. 208–209.

[27] George B. Vold, p. 218.

[28] Richard Quinney, *Criminology, Analysis and Critique of Crime in America*, Little, Brown, Boston, 1975, pp. 39–40.

[29] William H. Sheldon, *Varieties of Delinquent Youth*, Harper & Row, New York, 1949, referred to in Juan B. Cortes with Florence M. Gatti, *Delinquency and Crime*, Seminar Press, New York, 1972, p. 16.

[30] Sheldon Glueck and Eleanor Glueck, *Physique and Delinquency*, Harper & Row, New York, 1956, p. 9.

[31] Juan B. Cortes with Florence M. Gatti, *Delinquency and Crime*, Seminar Press, New York, 1972, p. 28.

[32] Juan B. Cortes with Florence M. Gatti, p. 42.

[33] Calvin S. Hall, *A Primer of Freudian Psychology*, New American Library, New York, 1954, p. 27.

[34] August Aichhorn, *Wayward Youth*, Viking Press, New York, 1963, p. 40.

[35] Fritz Redl and David Wineman, *The Aggressive Child*, Free Press, New York, 1957, passim pp. 76–128.

[36] Fritz Redl and David Wineman, p. 209.

[37] August Aichhorn, p. 63.

[38] Hermann Mannheim, *Comparative Criminology*, Houghton Mifflin, Boston, 1965, p. 258.

[39] Hermann Mannheim, passim pp. 243–245.

[40] Walter C. Reckless, *The Crime Problem*, 4th ed., Appleton Century Crofts, New York, 1967, p. 467.

[41] Simon Dinitz et al., "Delinquency Vulnerability: A Cross Group and Longitudinal Analysis," *American Sociological Review*, vol. 27, no. 4, p. 517, 1962.

[42] David Matza and Gresham M. Sykes, "Juvenile Delinquency and Subterranean Values," *American Sociological Review*, vol. 26, no. 5, p. 712, 1961.

[43] David Matza and Gresham M. Sykes, p. 713.

[44] David Matza and Gresham M. Sykes, p. 714.

[45] David Matza and Gresham M. Sykes, p. 716.

[46] David Matza, and Gresham M. Sykes, pp. 717–718.

[47] President's Commission on Law Enforcement and Administration of Justice, *Task Force Report: Juvenile Delinquency and Youth Crime*, U.S. Government Printing Office, Washington, D.C., 1967, pp. 188–200.

[48] William McCord and Joan McCord with Irving K. Zola, *Origins of Crime*, Columbia, New York, 1959, quoted in *President's Commission on Law Enforcement and Administration of Justice*, p. 198.

[49] President's Commission on Law Enforcement and Administration of Justice, p. 196.

[50] Ruth S. Cavan and Theodore N. Ferdinand, *Juvenile Delinquency*, 3d ed., Lippincott, Philadelphia, 1975, p. 206.

[51] Sheldon Glueck and Eleanor Glueck, *Of Delinquency and Crime*, Charles C Thomas, Springfield, Ill., 1974, pp. 57–58.

[52] William McCord and Joan McCord with Irving K. Zola, pp. 93–116.

[53] President's Commission on Law Enforcement and Administration of Justice, p. 197.

[54] Sheldon Glueck and Eleanor Glueck, p. 65.

[55] President's Commission on Law Enforcement and Administration of Justice, p. 199.

[56] Sheldon Glueck and Eleanor Glueck, p. 67.

[57] Joan McCord and William McCord, "The Effects of Parental Role Model on Criminality," in President's Commission on Law Enforcement and Administration of Justice, p. 199.

[58] Walter C. Reckless, *The Etiology of Delinquency and Criminal Behavior*, Social Sciences Research Council, New York, p. 27.

[59] President's Commission on Law Enforcement and Administration of Justice, passim pp. 234–244.

[60] President's Commission on Law Enforcement and Administration of Justice, p. 231.

[61] President's Commission on Law Enforcement and Administration of Justice, p. 232.

[62] Edwin H. Sutherland and Donald R. Cressey, *Criminology*, 9th ed., J. B. Lippincott, Philadelphia, 1974, pp. 75–76.

[63] Edwin H. Sutherland and Donald R. Cressey, p. 77.

[64] Margaret S. Wilson, "Pioneers in Criminology, I—Gabriel Tarde," *Journal of Criminal Law, Criminology and Police Science*, vol. 45, no. 1, pp. 5–6, May–June, 1954.

[65] Daniel Glaser, "Criminality Theories and Behavior Images," *American Journal of Sociology*, vol. 61, p. 441, 1956.

[66] Walter C. Reckless, *The Crime Problem*, 4th ed., Appleton Century Crofts, New York, 1967, p. 441.

[67] Walter C. Reckless, p. 470.

[68] Walter C. Reckless, pp. 470–471, 476.

[69] Walter C. Reckless, *The Crime Problem*, pp. 479–480.

[70] F. Ivan Nye, *Family Relationships and Delinquent Behavior*, Wiley, New York, 1958, p. 4.

[71] F. Ivan Nye, p. 5.

[72] F. Ivan Nye, pp. 34, 154.

[73] F. Ivan Nye, p. 156.

[74] F. Ivan Nye, pp. 94, 100.

[75] F. Ivan Nye, pp. 156–157.

[76] Howard S. Becker, *Outsiders,* Free Press, New York, 1963, p. 9.

[77] Howard S. Becker, p. 14.

[78] Edwin M. Lemert, *Human Deviance, Social Problems and Social Control,* 2d ed., Prentice-Hall, Englewood Cliffs, N.J., 1972, p. 48.

[79] Howard S. Becker, p. 38.

[80] Earl Rubington and Martin S. Weinberg, *Deviance: The Interactionist Perspective,* 2d ed., Macmillan, New York, 1973, p. 359.

[81] Walter C. Reckless, pp. 37–38.

[82] Walter C. Reckless, p. 467.

The Diversity of Delinquent Expression

Delinquency has many modes of expression—that is, there are many forms of youth behavior that are viewed and treated as delinquent by society. Adolescence is a very active, dynamic, romantic, and adventurous period of life, when youth is full of energy. Yet, it is during this stage of life that youngsters must put up with many restraints. Below a certain age, they cannot drink when everyone else around is drinking. They cannot work, although they are tempted to buy things in this materialistic world. They cannot get a marriage license, even though the circumstances may be pressing. They cannot sign a contract, even though they are vulnerable to be drafted. They must stay in school until age 16, and be home before curfew.

Adolescence is called a stormy period of life. It is admittedly full of tensions and pressures in the industrial societies. These tensions can be released and expressed in a variety of ways, a few of which are dealt with in this chapter.

Excitement is a common theme in many youth activities. What may start out as some frolic and fun, as an innocent, harmless activity, may end up in serious acts of willful destruction and malicious vandalism. Most delinquency is peer-oriented group activity, as is much of normal youth activity. In large groups, mob behavior is generated; a beach rally may end in an unintended riot. Intoxicated by the power of the group, the members may become violent—often to no purpose.

Just as each society produces its own brand of delinquency, each social class expresses its delinquency in its own way. Middle-class delinquency, for example, is largely nonviolent; it expresses itself through group drinking, drugs, and sex. The form of delinquency also differs with different age groups, mainly between early and late adolescents. The most feared form of delinquency comes from gangs, though not all gangs are violent. Gang delinquency has something to do with the community setting in which the gang is located. Most gang violence is directed against its own members or against other gangs. Gangs have a long history in America.

The use of drugs by delinquents is quite common, although drugs may not be a direct cause of delinquency. The legal and social consequences of drug use depend on the user's status in society. The lower-class user is sent to a prison, whereas the middle- or upper-class user is diverted to a psychiatrist. The alienated youth have found drugs a medium of communication in groups. But perhaps the most harmful and perplexing form of delinquency is psychopathy.

REBELLIOUS AND FUN-ORIENTED DELINQUENCY: VANDALISM

Vandalism is defined as the willful or malicious destruction, injury, disfigurement, or defacement of property without consent of the owner or the person having custody or control.[1] Even though acts of vandalism frequently go unreported, in 1973 as many as 121,011 persons were arrested for vandalism. The typical vandal is a young white male. About 69 percent of those arrested for vandalism in 1973 were below age 18, and 79 percent were below age 21; 82 percent were white, and 92 percent were male. Although persons from 10 to over 65 years of age have been arrested for vandalism, it is predominant among young teen-agers. The maximum number of arrests was of offenders between the ages of 13 and 15 years; the modal age for a vandal at present is about 14 years.

From 1968 to 1973, vandalism generally has increased by 6.3 percent. For persons under 18 years of age, it has decreased by 4 percent; but it has gone up by 38 percent for persons over 18 years of age. Although the reasons for this foray of older adolescents and adults into vandalism are not known, the growing trend for adult Americans to be arrested as vandals is disturbing.

While 85 percent of all those under 18 who are arrested for vandalism are white, it should be noted that white youth also have a high rate of arrest for allied offenses: liquor law violations, 95 percent; driving under the influence, 93 percent; and drunkenness, 88 percent. It is interesting to note that black boys have a lower rate of arrest for these types of offense. Vandalism, then, remains mainly a male behavior, as females contribute only about 8 percent to total arrests for vandalism.[2]

Martin studied the characteristics of juvenile vandals in New York City in 1955. According to him, vandals were drawn from a variety of class levels. One significant finding was that 62 percent of the vandals came from families in which there was parent-child conflict and tension.[3] Martin classified vandals into three types: disturbed vandals (16 percent), essentially law-abiding vandals (17 percent), and subculture vandals (67 percent). The disturbed vandals were truants and were poorly adjusted in school; most of them suffered from psychotic disorders. The essentially law-abiding vandals did not have a prior record of delinquency, and their involvement in vandalism was temporary. The subcultural vandals were gang members who vandalized in the company of others.[4]

Martin also classified vandalism into three types, depending on the objective and subjective situations in which the behavior took place. The three categories are overlapping: predatory vandalism, vindictive vandalism, and wanton vandalism. Predatory vandalism is fun, or a "sport." Vindictive vandalism is an expression of the antagonism and hatred the vandals feel toward special individuals and groups. Wanton vandalism appears to be spontaneous and wild destruction by individuals who are in open conflict with the community.[5] Predatory vandalism can at times be motivated by a desire to steal some scarce goods.

Railways are among the worst victims of vandals. According to a federal report, there appear to be four major acts of vandalism common to railroads: stoning and shooting at trains, tampering with switches and causing derailments, damaging signals and crossing gates, and placing obstructions on tracks. Railroad vandalism is reported more in urban than in suburban or rural areas.[6] Obviously, vandalism against railroads can be extremely hazardous to the passengers and the railroad crew.

Wade thinks of vandalism as spontaneous and unplanned behavior. Vandalism is generally a group activity. Wade views it as a product of the social process growing out of the group interaction. Some of the social preconditions to the act of vandalism are (1) the participant's self-image, (2) the situational and cultural variables, and (3) the functional variables involved in the episode.

The vandal's self-image partially affects the act of vandalism. A vandal who views the act as a prank or a good joke is more likely to vandalize with impunity. The situational and cultural support come from the vandal's group. The group may start something, with the members having to join in the act to show their loyalty. They are activated by the subculture of the group. A functional variable would be an opportunity to vandalize. "Obvious opportunity structures would be such situations as abandoned houses with broken windows, buildings under construction where doors are left unlocked and water pipes and electrical wires exposed, or a closed school building in a secluded area."[7]

According to Wade, there are usually five stages in an act of vandalism:

1. *Waiting* for something to turn up
2. *Exploring* the possibilities of indulging in vandalism
3. *Mutual conversion* of the group members and daring each other
4. *Joint elaboration of the act,* when all members of the group jump in to join in the wholesale destruction
5. *Aftermath and retrospect,* when the members rationalize their vandalism and gloat over the misfortunes of the victim[8]

Wade contends that acts of vandalism result from a sequence of events and individual and group attitudes. Generally there is a waiting period, followed by exploration for excitement. This leads to group activity in which every member wants to make a contribution. The contagion of destruction spreads to all members. After the deed is done, there is a cooling-off period until the group finds another escapade.

Some vandalism is rebellious in nature, as is seen in the destruction often accompanying student protests or political demonstrations. On at least one Midwest college campus, an evening of "streaking" culminated in some of the participants causing frivolous property damage. The whole affair seemed to be fueled by a mixture of rebelliousness, the need for fun, and the exhilaration of being part of a large group of several thousand people. Rebellious vandalism is also evident in the vengeful destruction that youngsters may cause their parents or other authority figures—although pent-up vengeance and anger often express themselves through behaviors other than vandalism. Finally, rebellious vandalism may occur between members of opposing social groups. Recently, for example, a Ku Klux Klan member in a white residential area of Oklahoma City destroyed a black homeowner's yard. At almost the same time, some black youths in Boston went so far as to burn a white woman whose car happened to run out of gasoline.

MIDDLE-CLASS DELINQUENCY

According to the literature accumulated until the middle of the 1960s, delinquency patterns keep changing. However, children from high-income areas are more likely to be involved in violations of liquor laws and traffic regulations. They also have a relatively higher involvement in car theft and vandalism. Children from low-income areas, on the other hand, are involved in gainful property offenses and offenses of personal injury to others.

> Children from high income areas are more likely to come into court for property offenses that do not lead to personal gain, or for violation of rules intended to control the driving, drinking, and late hours of teen-agers. Approximately 52 percent of all offenses involving children from high income areas fall into this last category. Only 30 percent of the offenses of children from low income areas fit this description.[9]

Middle-class youth do not seem to be as involved in the conventional property offenses of burglary and robbery or in violent offenses. They do steal more cars, but they use the cars for joyriding and then wreck them. They steal cars in the company of their peers to establish themselves with the group and to seek excitement. In fact, much of middle-class delinquency revolves around the car. The car is used both as an instrument of delinquency (to get away from the scene of the crime) and as a setting for delinquency (for drinking, stealing, assault, and rape).

The Myerhoffs are of the opinion that "the primary middle-class problem to which delinquency is a response is the establishment of masculine identity."[10] Middle-class male delinquents use the car as a means of proving their masculinity—for example, by drag racing, making noise, and driving around in circles on busy streets. These activities, though annoying, stop short of being delinquent acts requiring official attention. Although they are looking for "kicks," the middle-class gangs do use some discretion, judgment, caution, and restraint.[11] However, to prove their masculinity, they have to demonstrate their sophisticated skills.

Great pride was evidenced in the cleverness with which the thefts were executed and a good performance seemed more important than the acquisition of goods. . . . The stolen goods were by no means small, inexpensive, or easily portable, but included such items as tires, car radios, phonographs, tape recorders, and television sets.[12]

The Myerhoffs conclude that "middle class deviants may differ from lower class delinquents not in the frequency of their antisocial activities, but only in the form which they take and the sophistication, social intelligence, judgment and skill with which they are executed."[13]

This emphasis on technique is the product of the self-concept of middle-class teen-agers. Fannin and Clinard found that middle-class white delinquents have a self-concept of being clever, smart, smooth, loyal, and daring comrades. In matters pertaining to sexuality, they believe in sophistication, dexterity, and verbal manipulation. Lower-class white delinquents, on the other hand, conceive of themselves as more powerful, fierce, fearless, dangerous, and tough. In their attitudes to sex they believe in toughness, callousness, and physical prowess.[14] Vaz suggests that "certain kinds of delinquency in the middle class are related to the social roles of boys and to their differential participation in legitimate teen-age activities."[15] (Edmund W. Vaz is an ardent scholar of middle-class delinquency. His compilation of articles, cited in footnote 15, is a very useful reference.)

Teen-age culture, being a creature of the larger middle-class society, derives many of its values from the parent culture. The middle class implants in its youngsters the values of social success, social mixing, and social status. Vaz thinks that "the pursuit of status is intense among middle class adolescents, and often it is to his peers that the adolescent looks for respect."[16] In the legitimate activities of dating and dancing, there is a veiled competition among the adolescents to do something new and extraordinary to establish themselves. In their explorations for something funny and exciting, they may transgress beyond acceptable behavior.

Based on the self-reported delinquency of middle-class boys on a checklist of twenty-one items of behavior, Vaz found the following differences between the roles of younger boys (13 to 14 years) and older boys (15 to 19 years).

> Ironically, the world of younger boys is a masculine world, girls occupy little of their time. . . . The values of adventure, bravado, manliness, and muscular prowess circumscribe their role, and usually they make every effort to prove that they are "all boy."
>
> The older adolescent role requires increased participation in dominant youth culture activities. Parties, dances, sport events, cars, and girls occupy a large part of a boy's time. "Sophistication" replaces masculinity, and a premium is put on the cultivation of social skills and a "social personality."[17]

Vaz asserts that the delinquency of middle-class adolescents is different in content from conventional delinquency. Many of their activities have the blessing of the middle class.

Wise contends that the delinquency of middle-class girls resembles that of middle-class boys. Responding to a checklist of thirty-seven delinquency items, boys and girls admitted having participated about equally in sex and alcohol offenses. In all other offenses, boys participated to a greater extent than girls.[18] However, middle-class boys and girls both engage in essentially noncoercive and nonviolent forms of delinquent behavior.[19] Furthermore, girls tend to experiment with delinquency but are less likely to persist in their offenses.[20]

Theories of Middle-Class Delinquency

According to Scott and Vaz, "the bulk of middle-class delinquency occurs in the course of customary, non-delinquent activities and falls within the limits of adolescent group norms."[21] Ever since World War I, there has been an emergence of a mass youth culture. Several patterns of youth behavior, both delinquent and nondelinquent, have developed as part of this mass culture.

There has been a great change in the family, which used to be a character-building institution. This institution has lost some of its regulatory controls, and the peer group has come to hold sway. The old norms of industry, diligence, and self-discipline have gradually eroded, giving greater prominence to hedonistic pursuits. These new forms of behavior are approved by the families as part of the growing-up process. "Delinquent sex behavior among middle-class adolescents emerges from culturally approved activity, and can be explained as a variation on the encouraged patterns of dating."[22] England thinks that when youngsters were gradually removed from the labor force through protective labor legislation and the compulsory education movement, they faced status ambiguity. It was

> ... the first time a major society deactivated a large and energetic segment of its population without clearly redefining the status and function of that segment. ... The middle class teenager, with his typically lengthened period of ambiguous status compared with working class youngsters, is faced with contradictory expectations.[23]

According to England, teen-agers since World War II have developed strong in-group feelings and hedonistic pursuits. They either resist the nonhedonistic pressures from the adult world or alter adults' norms to suit their own needs.

Kvaraceus and Miller opine that middle-class behavior patterns have been influenced by lower-class behavior through a process of "upward diffusion." Some examples are the infiltration into the middle class of jazz music and rock and roll, which were the products of lower-class culture. Middle-class youth have also started imitating lower-class behavior by playing hookey, failing in school, threatening to quit school, and belittling the worth of college.[24]

Bohlke also thinks that working-class values have diffused up to middle-class youth, but in a different way. With the income revolution of the postwar period, many working-class families have moved up to the status of new middle-class families without adopting middle-class values.

> The middle class youth who appear to have taken on working class values and behavior patterns are in reality boys from families who were in the lower income group until fifteen to twenty years ago. ... They have not taken on middle class values and behavior patterns because their families, despite a dramatic rise in income, have not had to renounce working class values in the cultural context of economic abundance.[25]

GANG DELINQUENCY

The most intimate account of the gang has come from Thrasher, who studied 1313 gangs in the gangland of Chicago over a period of 7 years in the early 1920s. To Thrasher, gangland represents an interstitial area in the city. That is, gangs seem to flourish in the geographic and social "spaces" between other groups.

Probably the most significant concept of the study is the term *interstitial*—that is, pertaining to spaces that intervene between one thing and another. In nature foreign matter tends to collect and cake in every crack, crevice, and cranny—interstices. There are also fissures and breaks in the structure of social organization. The gang may be regarded as an interstitial element in the framework of society, and gangland as an interstitial region in the layout of the city. The gang is almost invariably characteristic of regions that are interstitial to the more settled, more stable, and better organized portions of the city.[26]

The gang begins in the crowded slums of the city. Play groups —gangs in embryo—form in the crowds of children. These play groups develop "we" feelings and come into conflict with other play groups on the matter of play spaces, territorial privileges, and so on. Each group is faced with a real struggle for existence.[27] The group members may develop similar interests which keep them together. But a play group does not develop into a gang unless it comes into opposition or conflict with adult authorities or other gangs. With opposition, suspicion, and hostility directed against them, the members develop group consciousness and some group organization. Natural leaders emerge,[28] and a gang begins to develop. However, there is little permanence in most of the gangs—the ganging process is one of continuous flux and flow. The gang is constantly forming and re-forming itself.

Both conflict and competition threaten the embryonic gangs with disintegration. The attention of the individual is often diverted to some new pal or to some other gang that holds more attractions. When delinquency is detected the police break up the group and at least temporarily interrupt its career.[29]

Among the psychological rewards of belonging to a gang, one must include social identity, social support, and social reality.[30] Social identity is the sense of belonging or attachment a gang member may feel toward the gang or individuals in it. Social support is the favorable response that individuals receive for their actions from other gang members. Social reality is the shared outlook or frame for viewing the world provided by the gang. Individual gang members may give these rewards to others as well as receive them from others. Thus, a gang meets the unmet needs of its members. In Thrasher's words, "It offers a substitute for what society fails to give; and it provides a relief from suppression. . . . It fills a gap and affords an escape."[31]

Each gang is different. Each gang meets the different needs of its members, or meets similar needs in different ways. Girls make relatively few gangs, and the female gangs generally do not fight with other gangs. For a slum boy who is denied other leisure activities, a gang has great appeal. The group gives him an escape from monotony and offers opportunities for new experiences, excitement, and thrills.[32] The gang boy "likes to be in the thick of the play, the bigger the melee, the better he enjoys it."[33] To seek relief from dullness and routine, the gang members seek games involving action, rivalry, and chance. Gambling is a popular sport. Among the predatory activities, stealing, burglarizing, and robbing drunks are common types of gang enterprises.[34] Alcohol and drugs make a favorite pastime. "In its struggle for existence a gang has to fight hostile groups to maintain its play privileges, its property rights and the physical safety of its members."[35]

The older adolescents and young adults have a definite though half-concealed interest in girls. Dances are exceedingly popular. The dance halls are reserved for certain gangs for special nights. In return, the gang protects the management from other gangs and individuals who try to create trouble by forcing their way into the dance halls for free. Although sex represents a secondary activity in the gang, Thrasher found much evidence of illicit sex relations, stag parties, nude dances, and sex orgies. "While wives of successful gangsters are well protected, sweethearts and paramours often take part in criminal enterprises, sometimes acting as lures, sometimes actually holding a gun and participating as any other gangster in a holdup."[36]

Group Control in the Gang

Loyalty is a universal requirement in the gang, and squealing is probably the worst infraction of the gang code.[37] In a fight between members to settle some difference, the combatants must follow rules set up by the group. At times, the leader acts as an arbiter. The members also show brotherly kindliness to each other at the appropriate times. The group greatly influences the behavior of the members. According to Thrasher, the group "will also make a boy one person under group influence and quite another when apart from it."[38] The leader has considerable power over his subordinates, as long as he does not abuse it.

Leadership According to Thrasher, the chief trait of a leader is his gameness.

> He leads. He goes where others fear to go. He goes first—ahead of the gang—and the rest feel secure in his presence.[39] . . . He "sells himself to the gang." . . . Other things being equal, the imaginative boy has an excellent chance to become the leader of the gang. He has the power to make things interesting for them. He "thinks up things for us to do."[40]

There is some democracy in the gang, and the leader emerges as a result of the members' interaction.

The Delinquent Gang as a Near-Group

Yablonsky gives a slightly different account of gangs in the city of New York. It could be that each large city has its own gang traditions. It could also be that history makes the difference: Thrasher's gangs in Chicago came about 25 years before Yablonsky's gangs in New York. Yablonsky does not think that the gang is as organized and cohesive a group as is claimed by Thrasher. He also observes that the gang members do not have clearly defined roles; that there is no consensus on goals; and that the leader is generally self-appointed, usually a dictatorial type.

Yablonsky calls the delinquent gang a near-group. The gang is neither organized like a group nor disorganized like a mob, but stands somewhere midway on the group-mob continuum. Gangs possess characteristics of both the group and the mob, and yet are characterized by factors not found fully in either. Yablonsky worked directly with some thirty delinquent gangs in New York City. He found press and police reports concerning gang fights greatly distorted. When Yablonsky talked to the boys in the jail, he found that many of them did not have any stable and permanent membership in gangs; in fact, they had only flimsy affiliations with a gang, if any. Some were not fully aware of the impending fight, and their involvement in the fight was only incidental and accidental.

Analyzing the structure of the thirty gangs, Yablonsky found that each gang had three levels of membership. In the center of the gang were the most psychologically disturbed members—the leaders.

It is these youths who require and need the gang most of all. This core of disturbed youths provides the gang's most cohesive force. In a gang of some 30 boys there may be five or six who are central or core members because they desperately need the gang in order to deal with their personal problems of inadequacy.[41]

Around the inner circle, there is a second level of organization where members "claim affiliation to the gang, but only participate in it according to their emotional needs at given times."[42] When they are rejected by their primary group, they turn to the gang for acceptance. The outer (third) circle has peripheral members who are only occasional visitors to the gang.

With this kind of organization, the gang is actually much smaller in size than what the members claim. The leaders tend to make exaggerated claims in regard to the size and territory of the gang. This is just to satisfy their phantasy of prestige and power. Also, the roles and functions of the members are not clearly defined. All this leads Yablonsky to conclude that the gang is not a group, but at best a near-group. The gang serves as a vehicle for the acting out of varied individual needs and problems.[43]

Types of Gangs

Gangs are the products of communities. Therefore, as communities differ in their social structures and their circumstances, so do gangs differ in their orientation and activities. In Chapter 2, we discussed Cloward and Ohlin's three types of delinquent subcultures—criminal subculture, conflict (violent) subculture, and retreatist (drug) subculture. Gang members make these adaptations to different subcultures subject to the availability or nonavailability of illegitimate opportunities.

Spergel modified Cloward and Ohlin's formulation by dividing the criminal subculture into a racket subculture and a theft subculture. He accepted Cloward and Ohlin's conflict (violent) subculture, but he considered the drug-addiction pattern to be a subtype common to all three subcultures instead of being a separate subculture. Spergel selected three kinds of neighborhoods with individual reputations for racket activity, violence, or car thefts. Analyses pointed out the subcultural differences among the three neighborhoods.

In the racket subculture, the numbers game and loan-sharking were common. There was cooperation between the older criminals and young boys. These criminal groups cooperated with local businesspersons, political leaders, and the police.

> The racketeer played a variety of significant economic and social roles in the neighborhood. He was the sponsor and subsidizer of legitimate and illegitimate business enterprise. He was helpful when others were in trouble by raising bail money and making appropriate "payoffs." He was a parent surrogate for recalcitrant youth.[44]

The conflict or violent subculture developed in one of the worst slums of the city, where social breakdown was the highest. The older criminals and the youth gangs were in open conflict. There were threats of violence and actual violence. There was no intermeshing between conventional and criminal opportunities. Delinquents in the conflict subculture generally had weak and negative relationships with adults, but positive associations with peers.

In the theft subcultural area there was a higher incidence of car thefts and burglary of apartments and stores. Some workers in radio and television stores, automobile shops, and restaurants served as fences for stolen goods.[45]

These descriptions of different subcultures suggest that different areas of the city produce different kinds of gangs. Similarly, different societies produce gangs of different characteristics. Vaz made a study of gangs in Paris in 1961. He found Parisian gangs different from their American counterparts in some respects. He attributed these variations to "certain structural and normative differences between the two societies, and the differential development of major, adult criminal institutions."[46] Parisian gangs were smaller and much less violent. Beyond France, many Asian societies did not have delinquent gangs until recently. These family-centered societies do not seem to impel teen-agers to street gangs. In those societies that did have gangs, the gang members did not possess firearms. In a country such as India, the delinquents were always too poor to buy guns, guns were not easily available, and they did not have the technology to improvise guns.

The Violence of the Gang

The most frightening aspect of the gang is its violence. It is appropriate, therefore, to look into the accounts given by Yablonsky, who worked closely with violent gangs. Reviewing the history of gangs in American society, Yablonsky opines that at the turn of this century gangs were not senselessly violent. They did not kill just for "kicks" or ego gratification. A new era of violence was ushered in by the bootleg gangs of the twenties, but they too used violence for their business. But the gangs of the midcentury used violence unprovoked, senselessly, and pathologically.

The gangs with whom Yablonsky worked were "a moblike collectivity that forms around violence in a spontaneous fashion, moving into action—often on the spur of an evening's boredom—in search of kicks."[47] The members of the violent gangs use the gang to cope with a variety of personality problems and to channel their pent-up aggression. The leaders have both grandiose and persecutory thoughts and seek power to neutralize their unhappy and insecure past. Gangs start a fight over trivia: territory, an argument over a girl, or a nasty remark.[48] They are very arrogant and at times brutal in their relationships with women. Yablonsky concludes:

> The demise of a community into a modern disorganized slum produces bewildered youths with defective personality systems. They are exposed to confusing adult role models and value systems. . . . The anonymity and conflict of the disorganized slum produces an asocialized individual. . . . For this type of sociopathic youth the violent gang functions as an adequate adjustment pattern in the sea of social confusion he confronts in the disorganized slum.[49]

Gangs in the Soviet Union

Looking at youth gangs in other countries, Geis points out two traits which occur with some regularity in all settings: the gang members' distinctive dress and their hostility to authority. The dress gives them status, and their hostility is directed against the power system of the society. The presence of gangs in the Soviet Union "throws into striking perspective many of the fundamental problems of rebellion and nonconformity among young people."[50]

The Russian gangs came into being following the Soviet Revolution of 1917. Large groups of youth formed themselves into marauding bands when they were left without any adult supervision. The Soviets did all they could do in accordance with their philosophy. They put them in boarding schools, indoctrinated them, trained them for factory work, and tried to tame them into conformity. Geis reports that it has not worked. There are many youth movements in the Soviet Union that strongly resemble gang behavior in the United States. Geis contends that Russian teen-agers are so attracted to American ways that they even try to imitate American deviant behavior. He says that neither the demands for rigid conformity of the Soviet Union nor the laissez faire and permissive attitude of the United States seems to succeed. We should try a middle-of-the-road approach.

DRUGS AND DELINQUENCY

Drug abuse in America is far more extensive than what is shown by the statistics. For purposes of uniform crime reports, the Federal Bureau of Investigation (FBI) includes among narcotic drug law violations "offenses relating to narcotic drugs, such as unlawful possession, sale, use, growing, manufacturing, and making of narcotic drugs." Although only a small percentage of total drug offenses is reported, in 1973 there were 127,316 arrests under offender age 18 (see Table 1–1). There were three times as many drug arrests above offender age 18.

Drug arrests start very early for some children: There were 236 arrests at offender age 10 and under. The number of arrests increases with offender age, until it peaks at offender age 18. Thereafter, the number of arrests dwindles. There are two reasons for this peak in drug arrests at offender age 18: (1) younger offenders are easier to catch, and (2) older offenders are better at concealing their drugs and related offenses.

Most drug abusers are young people: 57 percent of all drug arrests were of individuals under the age of 21. According to 1962 statistics, the modal age group for narcotic addicts at that time was 21 to 30 years. However, from all accounts, narcotic addiction has been seeping down to lower age groups. The people being admitted to Lexington Hospital are, on the average, younger today than those admitted in 1962.

The increase in narcotic drug law violations has reached tremendous proportions. From 1960 to 1973, while violent crime increased by 132 percent and property crime by 77 percent, narcotic drug law violations increased by 995 percent for all ages. Arrests, under narcotic drug laws, of males below the age of 18 have increased by 4455 percent. The most staggering increase has been in arrests of female juveniles (Table 3–1).

Drugs that are liable to be abused are classified as either narcotics or dangerous drugs. Under federal laws, *narcotics* include

86 Juvenile Delinquency

TABLE 3-1 Total Arrest Trends by Sex, 1960-1973

Offense charged	Males under 18			Females under 18		
	1960	1973	Percent change	1960	1973	Percent change
Narcotic drug laws	1,488	67,776	+4455	237	14,564	+6045
Liquor laws	14,863	34,669	+133	2344	8,660	+270
Drunkenness	10,963	19,731	+80	1246	3,228	+159

SOURCE: Federal Bureau of Investigation, *Uniform Crime Reports for the United States—1973*, U.S. Government Printing Office, Washington, D.C., p. 126.

opiates and cocaine. Under most state statutes, marihuana is also a narcotic. The term *dangerous drugs* commonly refers to three classes of nonnarcotic drugs that are habit-forming or have a potential for drug abuse because of their stimulant effects (amphetamines, "speed"), depressant effects (barbiturates, "goof balls"), or hallucinogenic effects (LSD, "acid").[51]

The Opiate User's Social and Personal Characteristics

Opiates include opium, morphine, and heroin. Public concern is focused primarily on heroin, a morphine derivative. How the user responds to the drug depends more on the individual and his or her circumstances than on the drug itself. About the effects of heroin, the President's Commission on Crime reports:

> The effects of any drug depend on many variables, not the least of which are the mood and expectation of the taker. . . . [Heroin] relieves anxiety and tension and diminishes the sex hunger and other primary drives. . . . Among the symptoms of the withdrawal sickness, which reaches peak intensity in 24–48 hours, are muscle aches, cramps and nausea.[52]

All the heroin that reaches the American user is smuggled into the country from abroad. All heroin transactions and the possession of heroin are, therefore, criminal.

Opiate addicts come from the most deprived areas of large cities, where "a delinquent orientation to life exists comprised of pessimism, futility, mistrust, negativism, defiance, quick pleasures, exploitation of others, etc."[53] Perhaps a very cohesive, loving, and secure family can neutralize or counterbalance the devastating effects of such an environment. But in such a deteriorated neighborhood, the strength of the family itself is sapped. And it is precisely from such disrupted families that the bulk of our delinquents and drug users come.[54] Addicts are reared in the less cohesive families with high rates of disorder, criminality, neurosis, addiction, and the like. These family disabilities can be a great handicap to the proper development of the personality.

There are many descriptions of the *personality* of addicts. Most of them suggest that addicts lack initiative and self-reliance and are passive, inadequate, and immature. One personality trait that stands out in these drug users is their peer-oriented sociability, a quality that is necessary to bring together drug-using friends. "The Chein work also calls attention to the fact that heroin, like most other mind-altering drugs, is not only a social drug in the sense that one is initiated to it by and with others, but that use may continue to be a social rather than a private event."[55] Some other characteristics of addicts are constricted emotional responsivity, withdrawal under stress, lack of close relations with others, underutilization of abilities, and oversensitivity to rejection. Blum cautions his readers that some of these disorders may be the result of drug use and the resultant social stigmatization, and not the original characteristics of the user.[56]

Drug Abuse and Delinquency

How do narcotic use and delinquency come to coincide in the life experiences of many adolescents? In describing how young people begin using drugs in the slums, Finestone puts great emphasis on the influence and role of the peer group. This group assumes sole and complete control over the behavior of the individual adolescent. The youth is, meanwhile, actively seeking the drug and its accompanying "kicks." The peers are very hospitable to experimentation with narcotics. They graciously provide the first dose and the excitement. The use of narcotics has many of the characteristics of a fad. There is an aura of prestige about drugs, and their use spreads. The young emulate the adult models in the neighborhood who have achieved notoriety, glamour, and material success through crime. Both criminality and narcotics use come to be prestigeful forms of activity.[57]

> In this sense, it is irrelevant to ask whether the delinquency preceded the addiction or vice versa. Many of those who became addicted and were forced to engage in crime to support

the high cost of their addiction would probably have gone on to engage in crime as adolescents regardless of whether or not they had become addicted.[58]

Many addicts were delinquents before they were identified as opiate addicts, and they continued to be delinquents after their release from the hospital or prison. There is no evidence that the use of opiates inevitably and independently leads to crime.

Addiction itself is not a crime, but drug addicts are crime-prone persons. To maintain their addiction, addicts have a constant need for drugs, which obviously must be purchased and possessed before they can be consumed. Purchase and possession violate criminal laws. So does sale, to which many addicts turn to provide financial support for their habits. The drugs are very expensive. Addicts must raise a lot of money, so they are compelled to steal. Contrary to popular impressions, addicts do not commonly commit violent and assaultive acts.[59] How many of the delinquents charged with nondrug offenses use drugs is not reliably known.

> Insofar as the use of a drug is itself illicit then there can be no drug use without criminality; if however one attends to crimes against person or property as opposed simply to the violation of law occurring because a drug is used, then the best evidence to date suggests that the drug-crime relationship depends upon the kinds of persons who choose to use drugs, the kinds of persons one meets as a drug user, and on the life circumstances both before drug use and those developing afterward by virtue of the individual's own (e.g., dependent or addictive) response and society's response to him (prohibition of use, arrest, and incarceration, etc.).[60]

Marihuana

Although there is no reliable drug census, marihuana's extensive use among the juvenile and youth population is widely recognized. The effects of marihuana have been debated. Users advocate it; medical researchers have conflicting and inconclusive findings on its effects; and law enforcement officials wish to relate it to other crimes. One view is that marihuana is a major cause of crime and violence. Another is that marihuana has no association with delinquency or crime, and only a marginal relation to violence. The La Guardia study did not observe any increase in aggression in subjects to whom marihuana was given.[61]

Several studies have investigated the use of drugs (marihuana in particular) by students, professionals, and members of the middle class. In the late 1960s, Carey found that college-age youth in and around Berkeley who used drugs came from respectable middle-class families. They associated almost exclusively with people of similar backgrounds. "They appeared on the surface to be clinically no 'sicker,' 'needier,' or more inadequate than others of their age and social status."[62]

Some of these users' predominant attitudes involved rejection of parents, denigrating university education, subscribing to new-left politics, and questioning the legitimacy of society's norms. Legal and social pressures forced the users to organize into groups. They spoke approvingly of the sexual freedom "which would permit affectional-sexual liaisons between persons, without love being involved."[63] Boy-girl relationships were limited to physical love, thus allowing maximization of personal freedom for both persons. Many of them expressed a sense of disillusionment and dissatisfaction with society's hypocrisy, duality of standards and rigidity.

Another study, focused on the suburban youth of Pleasant Hill, California, talks about *Kids, Cops and Kilos* in the same vein. In the 1960s there was a phenomenal increase in drug abuse among middle-class youth. They felt alienated from contemporary society. In turn, they rejected middle-class values in favor of a "drop-out" or "hang-loose" ethic. The hang-loose ethic shows disenchantment with the traditional values of society.[64]

American youth are not alone in entertaining such thoughts. In Swedish institutions, a study of narcotic offenders found that one of the basic differences between Swedish addicts and nonaddicts was the addicts' dissatisfaction with their social relationships. At the Fourth United Nations Congress on the Prevention of Crime, an Egyptian representative said that the "angry younger generation was seeking ways to have different experiences, rather than deserting life."

> There was a drift into a pill culture so that even happiness was not something to be pursued and attained; it was only something to be swallowed. Hallucinations had replaced insight. Nobody could possibly fail to see that there was a kind of affinity between the drug revolution and the sexual revo-

lution, and both appeared to be associated with the current emancipatory movement of youth. The drug wave might not be altogether an evil thing. It might be a reminder that the current social system needed readjustment and reevaluation.[65]

FEMALE DELINQUENCY

The alarming increase in delinquency by female juveniles was mentioned earlier in this chapter and in Chapter 1. A glance through Table 1–4 shows that, from 1960 to 1973, female delinquency grew at two to three times the rate of male delinquency. Furthermore, the increase has been recorded in all kinds of delinquency: violent crime, property crime, forgery, fraud, embezzlement, prostitution, weapon carrying, violation of narcotic drug laws, gambling, and drunkenness. As is evident from this wide spectrum of delinquent behavior, the female juvenile is offending both against others and against herself. This is partly attributable to women's changing roles and changing perceptions of self, and to their desire for expanded horizons.

> As women become more liberated from hearth and home and become more involved in full-time jobs, they are more likely to engage in the types of crime for which their occupations provide them with the greatest opportunities. They are also likely to become partners and entrepreneurs in crime to a greater extent than they have in the past. Traditionally, women who have engaged in criminal activity have played subservient roles. They have worked under the direction and guidance of men who have been their lovers, husbands, or pimps.[66]

The Female Delinquent

Most of the factors which cause male delinquency also cause female delinquency. Most of the theories of causation explained in Chapter 2 apply to both sexes. The exception is the subcultural theories, which explain the gang delinquency of boys and, obviously, do not apply to female delinquency. Girls generally do not form gangs, and their role in gang delinquency is insignificant. The gang does not serve the same purpose for girls as it does for boys.

The pattern of girls' offenses differs somewhat from that of boys. More girls are apprehended for sex offenses (sexual vagrancy and sexual promiscuity), incorrigibility, and unmanageability. There are more runaways among girls than boys: In 1973, among every 100 runaways there were 56 girls and 44 boys.[67] (It could be that parents more readily report a girl runaway.)

The Sex Theme No matter for what offense the female juvenile is arrested, there is a *sexual theme* underlying her delinquency. This is strikingly evident from a survey of the literature, perusal of case histories, and professional interviews with delinquent girls. In their analysis of *Five Hundred Delinquent Women*, the Gluecks found these women heavily involved in illicit sexual activity. They found that 52 percent of the women were professional or occasional prostitutes; 13 percent were promiscuously adulterous; 22 percent were promiscuous; 11 percent were unconventional in their sex life; and only 2 percent did not engage in illicit sexual activity.[68] Most of the women began their illicit sex lives during their teens.

The Gluecks found a close association between the age at the first illicit sex experience and the onset of other delinquent conduct, such as truancy and stealing.

> It is impossible to determine, merely by correlation, which factor is cause and which effect. All that can be said is that the evidence clearly points to the practically simultaneous occurrence of the phenomena of sex delinquency and the onset of various other misbehavior manifestations; and of sex delinquency with unstabilizing environmental experiences.[69]

It is quite possible that whatever triggers delinquency also generates illicit sexual activity. The Gluecks, however, repeat: "Illicit sex practices were extremely common among these women, began surprisingly early, and carried in their train disease, illegitimacy, and unhappy matrimony."[70] The girls were heavily burdened with illegitimate pregnancies (54 percent) and venereal disease (67.8 percent) before 21 years of age.[71] They did not know how to protect themselves. A British study dealing with younger girls found only 14 percent of them infected with either gonorrhea or syphilis.[72]

Sexual activity is also very common among nondelinquent adolescents. Thus, one must be careful not to exaggerate the problem as it concerns delinquent girls. However, it is fair to say that these girls are generally not able to restrain their sexual impulses. Delinquent girls are somewhat unfortunate in their social situation and, therefore, more vulnerable to official action. A middle-class girl may also become sexually ungovernable, but she is more likely to be referred to a private psychiatrist than to a juvenile court. The girls' motives for sexual misconduct are the usual ones: curiosity, the need for self expression and assertiveness, defiance and rebellion, a wish to prove their adequacy, imitation of adults, and acceptance by their peers.[73]

Allied to these sexual difficulties is a recurring theme of *loneliness*, either expressed or implied. Konopka cites several excerpts from interviews that reflect the girls' loneliness as well as their overt and covert reactions against this loneliness.[74] The girls seem to seek company with whom to discuss their problems. Given an opportunity, girls in institutions like to talk to the staff or engage visitors in conversation. They develop emotional friendships with other residents. They phantasize highly romantic love relationships with complete disregard for reality. Tormented by years of neglect, some of these girls try to help other people in their suffering. They become quite altruistic and want to become welfare workers. Konopka noticed in these girls a very strong desire for travel and adventure,[75] which may well be another way out of their loneliness and boredom.

The author gained a similar impression from interviews with these girls. Many girls wanted to travel abroad, to see other lands. The most adventurous ones, though just a few, had already visited many parts of the country. The travel funds were raised by selling sexual favors. It appeared that some of the girls were too unconventional for society to contain. A few other girls suffered a sense of guilt and, as a result, developed a low self-concept.

Although marriage could stabilize them, many delinquent girls are likely to have marital difficulties. Sandhu and Allen desired to evaluate delinquent girls' perceptions of marriage. The responses to a questionnaire indicated that delinquent girls had significantly less commitment to marital goals than nondelinquent girls. Some of them may not consider marriage to be in their best interest. Instead, they may have found greater excitement in illicit sexual adventures.[76]

Konopka's findings are somewhat similar to these. According

to her, these girls have lived through the horrible realities of sexual abuse in broken homes. They are afraid of marriage, which, to them, has a fairy-tale quality about it.[77] They tend to replace marital goals with impulsive, hedonistic innovation.

Family Dynamics and Female Delinquency A part of the explanation of the sexual promiscuity of delinquent girls is to be sought in their home lives. The home is structurally broken or functionally pathological. According to a British study, 23 percent of these girls were illegitimate, 12 percent were raised in institutions, and 46 percent were brought up in broken homes.[78] The incidence of broken homes among delinquent girls differs from study to study: Sandhu and Allen found 50 percent in Florida;[79] Vedder and Somerville found 62 percent in California;[80] and Shaw and McKay found 66.8 percent in Chicago.[81]

Moreover, the incidence of broken homes is higher among delinquent girls than among delinquent boys. The effects of a broken home are much more devastating for girls. Since the family exercises more control over girls, they are affected to a greater extent by a broken home.[82]

Vedder and Somerville studied delinquent girls under the aegis of the California Youth Authority. They found that these girls' families had little or no self-respect, and below-average family cohesiveness. Their families also had a record of delinquency, particularly among the many siblings of the delinquent girl.[83] In another study of eighty delinquent girls, Felice and Offord found their economically disadvantaged families heavily burdened by inadequate parents. The fathers were either absent or abusive, and the mothers overworked and often alcoholics or prostitutes.[84]

Riege replicated a study to find that girl truants lacked paternal love and affection at home. The girls were likely to suffer from excessive loneliness, low self-esteem, estrangement from adults, and a lack of capacity for friendships with contemporaries. The delinquent girls perceived their fathers' roles as defective, and they wanted their fathers to be more strict.

The father's role as head of the family makes him the chief source of security for a daughter. If his love or affection is perceived as deficient, the girl is likely to feel a lack or loss of security as well. To compensate for this lack of security and affection at home, the girl seeks out a substitute relationship, often sexual, outside her home. Many of these relationships end in frustration. Although delinquent girls report strong ties with their mothers, they prefer that both parents deal with them in case of trouble.[85]

In summary, some of the family dynamics that are considered contributory to female sexual delinquency are: primary emotional deprivation and an unfulfilled need for closeness and tenderness in the girl; longing for a missing father; overpermissiveness and inconsistent parental controls; hostility, a flight from incest threat within the family; and combinations of the above factors.[86]

Sexuality for these girls is usually an empty gesture. Personal satisfaction is often totally lacking. Girls have a distinctive way of expressing their anger and hostility. Barker and Adams found significant differences as well as significant similarities between girl offenders and boy offenders in Colorado training schools.

Girls express their conflicts and anger in a direct manner, whereas boys who are seeking identification and acceptance as well as an expression of their masculinity seem to launch their protests through group misbehavior calculated to gain status through various devices. . . . The striking out of the girls in a direct line against authority, the home, and themselves would frequently make them more noticeable in their misbehavior.[87]

Delinquent girls cannot be treated as a single homogeneous or uniform group. For the purpose of treatment, these girls should be classified into typologies. Butler administered the Jesness Psychological Inventory to 139 delinquent girls on their admission to a training school in California. He derived three major types: Type 1, disturbed-neurotic; Type 2, immature-impulsive; and Type 3, covert manipulators.

The girls in Type 1 get into trouble because of some social situation with which they cannot cope. They suffer from a sense of guilt and anxiety and are willing to accept cultural norms. Type 2 girls, being impulsively hedonistic, seek immediate gratification. The girls in Type 3 are self-assertive and attempt to control their environment. Their overt behavior is that of a conformist, but in their latent attitudes they believe in manipulation. They tend to use their intelligence sociopathically.[88]

The rate of recidivism for female juvenile delinquents is lower than that for males. In Lexington, Kentucky, Ball found that, over a period of 9 years, 48 percent of the girls recidivated as against 60 percent of the boys. The mean number of court appearances for the boys was 4.2, and for the girls 3.2.[89]

In a study on recidivism at Girls Training School, Ocala, Florida, Offord et al. found a tendency on the part of the Negro girls to cling to the institution. The steps toward recidivism through which these girls proceed are as follows: unsettled and inadequate home situation, early contact with the juvenile court, admission to the institution at an early age, a pattern of clinging to the institution, and finally discharge to an unsettled and inadequate home. The vicious circle starts with an unsettled and inadequate home and finally returns these unfortunate girls to the situation which gave rise to their delinquency. It does not take very long to trigger delinquency once again. The researchers found more or less the same cycle for white girls, with the exception of the clinging behavior.[90]

PSYCHOPATHIC EXPRESSION

Psychopathic behavior has a quality of sickness, dangerousness, selfishness, destructiveness, and strange brutality about it. Most criminal acts are marked to some degree by these characteristics. However, we consider a behavior pattern to be psychopathic when there is a morbid persistency to the antisocial acts, but no remorse. The McCords define the psychopath as "an asocial, aggressive, highly impulsive person, who feels little or no guilt and is unable to form lasting bonds of affection with other human beings."[91] Mannheim adds the following attributes to the psychopathic syndrome:

1. Disregard of community or group standards, along with antisocial behavior on a verbal, acquisitive, personal, or sexual plane
2. Apparent absence of guilt feelings and failure to learn by punishment
3. Lack of foresight
4. Continued sexual experimentation, immaturity, or aberration[92]

The main problem is to diagnose psychopathy. How does the psychopath differ from other hardened delinquents? The McCords insist that only an individual who exhibits the two critical psychopathic traits—guiltlessness and lovelessness—should be categorized as psychopathic.[93] Unresponsiveness to treatment, or incurability, is another distinguishing trait. Some psychological inventories, such as the Minnesota Multiphasic Personality Inventory and the California Psychological Inventory, are supposedly capable of distinguishing the psychopathic personality. The projective tests, particularly the Rorschach and the Thematic Apperception Test, have also been used advantageously. On the Rorschach, the "normal" criminals and the psychopaths were differentiated by the intense explosiveness and excessive egocentricity of the psychopaths.[94]

Some psychopaths are generalists who commit a variety of crimes; others tend to be specialists. Most of the psychopathic delinquents with whom the author has dealt could be classified as "specializing" in three areas: (1) consistent cheating, conning, swindling, and impersonation; (2) brutal assaults and fighting; and (3) offenses against women. The offender against women takes particular pleasure in duping and cheating women. He lies to them; takes advantage of them; lures them into some kind of trap; robs, molests and threatens to blackmail them; and experiments with a series of loveless marriages. The female psychopathic offender also takes pleasure in duping and cheating men. She has the added incentive of knowing that, very often, her male victim will not report the crime because such an admission would damage his own reputation.

SUMMARY

This chapter describes the different paths delinquency takes, and the different ways in which youth express their delinquent urges. Although vandalism remains predominantly an activity of young teen-agers, vandalism arrests of persons above 18 years of age have recently (from 1968 to 1973) increased by 38 percent. The typical vandal in the United States is a white male below the age of 18. Whites below 18 years of age are also responsible for about 90 percent of the arrests for violations of liquor laws, driving under the influence, and drunkenness. With all this, the white male delinquent below 18 years of age emerges as a rowdy person. There is an element of antagonism and hatred in some forms of vandalism. Although most vandalism is fun-oriented, a small part is rebellious in nature, particularly in politically disturbed societies. Vandalism is a group phenomenon, and it arises out of group interaction.

Middle-class delinquency is not utilitarian in nature; it is not focused on personal gains. A good part of middle-class delinquency marks an attempt on the part of the young boy to establish his masculinity. The middle-class delinquent is a manipulator and wants to show off his skills. He has the self-concept of a clever, smart, smooth, and daring comrade. Younger adolescents want to do something new and extraordinary to establish themselves. Older adolescents like parties, dances, cars, girls, alcohol, and drugs. Their activities have the blessings of the middle class. Middle-class delinquency, however, is nonviolent. Scholars have presented different theories to explain middle-class delinquency: that the family has lost its regulatory controls; that young persons have been deactivated and made idle; that today's youth subscribe to an impulsive hedonistic ethic; and, that the values of the lower class have infiltrated into the middle class.

The gang is another vehicle of expression for the delinquent. A gang develops, according to Thrasher, in the interstitial spaces within the city and society. The gang grows out of a play group. The play group becomes a gang when it faces opposition and conflict. A gang meets the unmet needs of the youth. Yablonsky does not think of the gang as an organized and cohesive group. Only those members who constitute the central core of the gang have a long-term commitment. The members on the periphery are only occasional visitors. Different areas produce different kinds of gangs. With some variations, gangs exist in many societies.

The use of drugs has gone up tremendously at the teen-age level. Arrests for narcotic drug law violations reach their peak at offender age 18. Most drug addicts come from deprived areas of large cities, where there is pessimism, futility, and distrust. Drug users are peer-oriented people; this is their common characteristic. Their other characteristics are underutilization of abilities, oversensitivity to rejection, and withdrawal. There is no direct causal relationship between drugs and delinquency. Addiction itself is not a crime, but drug addicts are crime-vulnerable people. The effect of drugs on the user depends on the user's personality and circumstances.

Female juveniles have shown an alarming increase in all categories of crime: violent crime, property crime, forgery, fraud, embezzlement, prostitution, weapon carrying, and drunkenness. In one decade, there has been an increase of 6000 percent in the number of girls arrested on drug charges. Such increases are attributed to the female's changing role in society. Her pattern of offenses differs from that of boys: Most delinquent girls are apprehended for sex offenses (sexual vagrancy, sexual promiscuity, ungovernable behavior). Also, more girls than boys are runaways.

There are sexual undertones even to the nonsexual offenses of female delinquents. Sex delinquency seems to exist alongside the conventional delinquency. The grounds for sexual promiscuity are found in maladjusted homes. Such homes are characterized by crime, alcoholism, prostitution, and neglect. Tired of all this, the girls turn to sexual promiscuity as a way of striking out against authority figures. Close to the sexual theme is the recurring theme of loneliness. Girls react to loneliness either by actually running away or by entertaining a desire for extensive travel.

Discussion Questions

1. In which areas of a city would you expect the highest incidence of vandalism?
2. Which of the theories on the causes of middle-class delinquency makes the most sense to you? Discuss the merits of each theory.
3. How is a gang an interstitial element in the framework of society?
4. Why does Yablonsky call the delinquent gang a near-group?
5. What is the relationship between drug abuse and delinquency?
6. How do you account for the widespread use of marihuana among middle-class youth?
7. How do you account for the increase in weapon carrying by girls?
8. How do juveniles make contact with drug pushers?

Glossary

Adolescent A person who is passing through the transitional period between puberty and maturity. The period falls roughly between early teens and early twenties.

Cultural Variables Culture is made up of the values, folkways, customs, norms, beliefs, attitudes, and language of a society. Cultural variables are the different characteristics of culture which shape and affect human behavior.

Family Dynamics Different kinds of physical, social, and emotional forces in the family which affect the behavior of its members.

Functionally Pathological A condition where one component breaks down, causing the entire system to break down. An example is the situation where a drinking parent cannot provide adequately for the family, causing severe emotional and financial stress among family members.

Gang A group of persons, generally young, who associate closely with each other to pursue normal or deviant activities.

Hedonism A doctrine or behavior pattern that implies that the ultimate human goal is the avoidance of pain and the seeking of pleasure.

Primary Group A social group, with common standards of behavior, whose members are in continual contact. The group has a strong effect on many aspects of the individual member's personality and attitudes. The family is the most common example of a primary group.

Retreatism A behavior pattern in which an individual rejects or abandons both the success goals of a society and the recognized means of attaining them. Retreatism is one way of adapting to the frustration of not being able to attain these goals. Hoboism and alcoholism are, to an extent, this type of behavior.

Situational Variables A combination of physical and social circumstances that affect an individual.

Footnotes

[1] Federal Bureau of Investigation, *Uniform Crime Reports for the United States—1973*, U.S. Government Printing Office, Washington, D.C., p. 55.

[2] Federal Bureau of Investigation, p. 125–134 (see Tables 27, 30, 32, 34).

[3] John M. Martin, *Juvenile Vandalism*, Charles C Thomas, Springfield, Ill., 1961, p. 26.

[4] John M. Martin, pp. 31–48.

[5] John M. Martin, pp. 73, 77, 90.

[6] Mark Sanders et al., *Vandalism*, Federal Railroad Administration, Washington, D.C., 1972 (reproduced by National Technical Information Serv-

100 Juvenile Delinquency

ice, PB 214–36), in *Crime and Delinquency Literature*, vol. 6, no. 1, p. 92, 1974.

[7] Andrew L. Wade, "Social Processes in the Act of Juvenile Vandalism," in Marshall B. Clinard and Richard Quinney, *Criminal Behavior Systems: A Typology*, Holt, New York, 1967, pp. 97, 108.

[8] Andrew L. Wade, pp, 98–105.

[9] Roland J. Chilton, "Middle-Class Delinquency and Specific Offense Analysis," in Edmund W. Vaz, editor, *Middle-Class Juvenile Delinquency*, Harper, New York, 1967, pp. 96–97.

[10] Howard L. Myerhoff and Barbara G. Myerhoff, "Field Observations of Middle Class 'Gangs'," *Social Forces*, vol. 42, no. 3, p. 331, March 1964.

[11] Howard L. Myerhoff and Barbara G. Myerhoff, p. 332.

[12] Howard L. Myerhoff and Barbara G. Myerhoff, p. 332.

[13] Howard L. Myerhoff and Barbara G. Myerhoff, p. 335.

[14] Leon F. Fannin and Marshall B. Clinard, "Differences in the Conception of Self as a Male among Lower and Middle Class Delinquents," *Social Problems*, vol. 13, no. 2, pp. 213–217, Fall 1965.

[15] Edmund W. Vaz, editor, *Middle-Class Juvenile Delinquency*, Harper, New York, 1967, p. 116.

[16] Edmund W. Vaz, p. 133.

[17] Edmund W. Vaz, p. 139.

[18] Nancy Barton Wise, "Juvenile Delinquency among Middle-Class Girls," in Edmund W. Vaz, editor, pp. 180–181.

[19] Nancy Barton Wise, p. 187.

[20] Nancy Barton Wise, p. 186.

[21] Joseph W. Scott and Edmund W. Vaz, "A Perspective on Middle-Class Delinquency," *Canadian Journal of Economics and Political Science*, vol. 29, no. 3, pp. 324–355, August 1963, in Edmund W. Vaz, editor, p. 208.

[22] Joseph W. Scott and Edmund W. Vaz, p. 216.

[23] Ralph W. England, "A Theory of Middle Class Juvenile Delinquency," *Journal of Criminal Law, Criminology and Police Science*, vol. 50, p. 536, March–April 1960.

[24] William Kvaraceus and Walter B. Miller, "Norm Violating Behavior in Middle-Class Culture," *Delinquent Behavior: Culture and the Individual*, National Education Association of the United States, Washington, D.C., 1959, in Edmund W. Vaz, editor, pp. 236–237.

[25] Robert H. Bohlke, "Social Mobility, Stratification, Inconsistency and Middle Class Delinquency," *Social Problems*, vol. 8, no. 4, pp. 351–363, Spring 1961.

The Diversity of Delinquent Expression 101

[26] Frederic M. Thrasher, *The Gang*, University of Chicago Press, Chicago, 1927, p. 22.

[27] Frederic M. Thrasher, p. 26.

[28] Frederic M. Thrasher, p. 30.

[29] Frederic M. Thrasher, p. 35.

[30] Edwin P. Hollander, *Principles and Methods of Social Psychology*, Oxford University Press, New York, 1971, p. 21.

[31] Frederic M. Thrasher, p. 38.

[32] Frederic M. Thrasher, pp. 79–84.

[33] Frederic M. Thrasher, p. 84.

[34] Frederic M. Thrasher, pp. 88, 92, 93.

[35] Frederic M. Thrasher, p. 174.

[36] Frederic M. Thrasher, p. 239.

[37] Frederic M. Thrasher, p. 288.

[38] Frederic M. Thrasher, p. 291.

[39] Frederic M. Thrasher, p. 345.

[40] Frederic M. Thrasher, p. 349.

[41] Lewis Yablonsky, "The Delinquent Gang as a Near-Group," *Social Problems*, vol. 7, no. 2, p. 113, Fall 1959.

[42] Lewis Yablonsky, p. 113.

[43] Lewis Yablonsky, pp. 113–116.

[44] Irving Spergel, "An Exploratory Research in Delinquent Subcultures," *Social Service Review*, vol. 35, p. 38, March 1961.

[45] Irving Spergel, passim pp. 35–40.

[46] Edmund W. Vaz, "Juvenile Gang Delinquency in Paris," *Social Problems*, vol. 10, no. 1, p. 30, Summer 1962.

[47] Lewis Yablonsky, *The Violent Gang*, Penguin, Baltimore, 1966, p. 5.

[48] Lewis Yablonsky, passim pp. 147–151.

[49] Lewis Yablonsky, p. 188.

[50] Gilbert Geis, "Juvenile Gangs," *Report of the President's Committee on Juvenile Delinquency and Youth Crime*, 1965, p. 13.

[51] President's Commission on Law Enforcement and Administration of Justice, *The Challenge of Crime in a Free Society*, U.S. Government Printing Office, Washington, D.C., 1967, pp. 212, 214.

[52] President's Commission on Law Enforcement and Administration of Justice, p. 212.

102   Juvenile Delinquency

[53] Richard H. Blum, "Mind-Altering Drugs and Dangerous Behavior: Narcotics," a consultant's paper in U.S. President's Commission on Law Enforcement and Administration of Justice, *Task Force Report: Narcotics and Drug Abuse,* U.S. Government Printing Office, Washington, D.C., 1967, p. 50.

[54] Isidor Chein, "Narcotics Use Among Juveniles," *Social Work,* vol. 1, pp. 50–60, April 1956.

[55] Richard H. Blum, p. 52.

[56] Richard H. Blum, p. 51.

[57] Harold Finestone, "Narcotics and Criminality," *Law and Contemporary Problems,* vol. 22, p. 75, Winter 1957.

[58] Harold Finestone, p. 76.

[59] President's Commission on Law Enforcement and Administration of Justice, *Task Force Report: Narcotics and Drug Abuse,* U.S. Government Printing Office, Washington, D.C., 1967, p. 10.

[60] Richard H. Blum, p. 23.

[61] President's Commission on Law Enforcement and Administration of Justice, *The Challenge of Crime in a Free Society,* p. 224.

[62] James T. Carey, *The College Drug Scene,* Prentice-Hall, Englewood Cliffs, N.J., 1968, 210 pp.

[63] James T. Carey, p. 25.

[64] Thomas G. Gitchoff, *Kids, Cops, and Kilos,* Malter-Westerfield, San Diego, 1969, p. 178.

[65] United Nations, *Fourth United Nations Congress on the Prevention of Crime and the Treatment of Offenders,* New York, 1971, p. 41.

[66] Rita J. Simon, *The Contemporary Woman and Crime,* National Institute of Mental Health, Center for Studies of Crime and Delinquency, Rockville, Md., 1975, pp. 3–4.

[67] Federal Bureau of Investigation, p. 131.

[68] Sheldon Glueck and Eleanor T. Glueck, *Five Hundred Delinquent Women,* Knopf, New York, 1934, p. 89.

[69] Sheldon Glueck and Eleanor T. Glueck, p. 90.

[70] Sheldon Glueck and Eleanor T. Glueck, p. 97.

[71] Sheldon Glueck and Eleanor T. Glueck, p. 93.

[72] John Cowie et al., *Delinquency in Girls,* Heinemann, London, 1968, p. 11.

[73] Herbert H. Herskovitz, "A Psychodynamic View of Sexual Promiscuity," in Otto Pollak et al., *Family Dynamics and Female Sexual Delinquency,* Science and Behavior Books, Palo Alto, 1969, p. 90.

[74] Gisela Konopka, *The Adolescent Girl in Conflict*, Prentice-Hall, Englewood Cliffs, N.J., 1966, pp. 38–45.
[75] Gisela Konopka, p. 82.
[76] Harjit S. Sandhu and Donald E. Allen, "Female Delinquency: Goal Obstruction and Anomie," *Canadian Review in Sociology and Anthropology*, vol. 6, no. 2, pp. 109–110, 1969.
[77] Gisela Konopka, pp. 74–75.
[78] John Cowie et al., p. 96.
[79] Harjit S. Sandhu and Donald E. Allen, p. 108.
[80] Clyde B. Vedder and Dora B. Somerville, *The Delinquent Girl*, Charles C Thomas, Springfield, Ill., 1970, p. 17.
[81] Clifford R. Shaw and Henry D. McKay, "Are Broken Homes a Causative Factor in Juvenile Delinquency," *Social Forces*, vol. 10, pp. 514–524, 1932, in President's Commission on Law Enforcement and Administration of Justice, *Task Force Report: Juvenile Delinquency and Youth Crime*, U.S. Government Printing Office, Washington, D.C., 1967, p. 196.
[82] Clifford R. Shaw and Henry D. McKay, p. 196.
[83] Clyde B. Vedder and Dora B. Somerville, p. 19.
[84] Marianne Felice and D. R. Offord, "Three Developmental Pathways to Delinquency in Girls," *British Journal of Criminology*, vol. 12, no. 4, p. 376.
[85] M. G. Riege, "Parental Affection and Juvenile Delinquency," *British Journal of Criminology*, vol. 12, no. 1, pp. 55–73, 1972.
[86] Alfred S. Friedman, "The Family and the Female Delinquent: An Overview," in Otto Pollak et al., p. 120.
[87] Gordon H. Barker and William T. Adams, "Comparison of Delinquencies of Boys and Girls," *Journal of Criminal Law, Criminology and Police Science*, vol. 53, no. 4, pp. 474–475, 1962.
[88] Edgar W. Butler, "Typologies of Delinquent Girls: Some Alternate Approaches," *Social Forces*, vol. 44, pp. 404–405, 1966.
[89] J. C. Ball, "The Extent of Recidivism among Juvenile Delinquents in a Metropolitan Area," *Journal of Research in Crime and Delinquency*, vol. 2, p. 81, 1965.
[90] D. R. Offord et al., "A Study of Recidivism among Female Juvenile Delinquents," *Corrective Psychiatry and Journal of Social Therapy*, vol. 14, no. 3, p. 172, 1963.
[91] William McCord and Joan McCord, *The Psychopath*, Van Nostrand, Princeton, N.J., 1964, p. 3.
[92] Hermann Mannheim, *Comparative Criminology*, Houghton Mifflin, Boston, 1965, p. 264.
[93] William McCord and Joan McCord, p. 20.
[94] Robert Lindner, "The Rorschach Test and the Diagnosis of Psychopathic Personality," *Journal of Criminal Psychopathology*, vol. 5, pp. 69–93, 1943, in William McCord and Joan McCord, p. 41.

Delinquents: Types and Characteristics

The delinquents form a very diverse population. They range from truants to murderers, from exhibitionists to rapists, from kleptomaniacs to professional robbers. While there are some similarities among these types of delinquents, there are even more differences. Each individual in a delinquent typology is unique in personality and circumstances but shares some common characteristics and attitudes with other members of the typology.

There are several criteria by which delinquents are classified. Juvenile laws differentiate juvenile offenders as delinquents or nondelinquents. The latter include neglected youth, those in need of supervision, and those beyond control (see Chapter 1). Administrators separate female from male, young adolescents from older ones, serious delinquents from less serious delinquents, and those needing intensive supervision from those needing minimum supervision. The psychologists and sociologists tend to classify delinquents according to their own particular orientations. To construct a diagnostic classification, the psychologists and psychiatrists like to assess ego and superego strengths, or to analyze an individual's typical solution patterns (neurotic, psychotic, psychopathic). To construct a typology based on the social behavior system, sociologists have used, as criteria, social orientation to a particular subculture (conventional or delinquent); subscription to values (middle class or lower class); social control (presence or absence); and attitude to norms (obedience or violation).

A significant contribution was made by Gibbons, who categorized offenders in terms of certain variables, such as offense patterns, interactional settings, attitudes, and self-images.[1] Clinard and Quinney based their typological construction upon four characteristics: (1) the criminal career of the offender; (2) the extent to which the behavior has group support; (3) correspondence between criminal behavior and legitimate behavior patterns; and (4) societal reaction.[2] Sandhu suggested a tripartite treatment classification based on the offender's containments (weak, modest, adequate), response to treatment (inadequate, moderate, substantial), and suggested treatment intensity (maximum, medium, minimum).

A behavioral classification based on offenses committed by juveniles distinguishes differences in their characteristics a little more effectively:

1. The *violent offender:* murderer, assaultist, and rapist
2. The *property offender:* robber, auto thief, burglar, and larcenist
3. The *authority offender:* runaway and youth beyond control

The violent delinquent generally does not have a long delinquent history, but tends to act impulsively and violently. The property offender generally has a long delinquent history, tends to repeat delinquent acts, and develops a criminal career. The authority offender develops problems of adjustment with parents or other authority figures and tends either to run away from the frustrating situation (flight mechanism) or to rebel against the authority figures (fight mechanism).

THE VIOLENT OFFENDER

Murderer

Persons under 18 commit relatively fewer murders than personal and property offenses. Even so, 12 percent of all murders in the United States are committed by juveniles under the age of 18. The trend, however, is very disquieting: During the years 1960 to 1973, murder arrests of offenders 18 years of age and over increased by 124 percent, while arrests of offenders under 18 years of age increased by 255 percent. Of the juveniles arrested for murder, Negroes account for 62.5 percent, whites for 35 percent, and American Indians for 1.2 percent. Murder is largely a male offense. Of those arrested, 85 percent are males and 15 percent are females.[3]

In 1973 there were an estimated 19,510 murders committed

in the United States. The national murder rate is, thus, 9.3 victims for every 100,000 inhabitants. By population grouping, cities with 250,000 or more inhabitants reported a murder rate of 20.7 victims per 100,000 inhabitants, the suburban areas showed a rate of 5.1, and the rural areas a rate of 7.4. So murder is mostly a big-city phenomenon. A geographical breakdown shows that 44 percent of the murders occurred in the Southern states, 22 percent in the North Central states, 19 percent in the Northeastern states, and 15 percent in the Western states.[4] What follows is an account of murderers generally and not of youthful murderers specifically. However, the characteristics of the two categories are so similar, that the following observations may be said to be true of youthful murderers as well.

A staff report submitted to the National Commission on Violence compared the United States homicide rate with those of European countries in the year 1966. The homicide rate per 100,000 population for the United States was 6.0; for Finland, 2.3; Hungary, 1.9; Australia, 1.5; Canada, 1.3; Austria, 1.1; and England and Wales, 0.7. The same report pointed out the following:

> No doubt industrial society generates awful tensions. No doubt the ever-quickening pace of social change depletes and destroys the institutions which make for social stability. But this does not explain why Americans shoot and kill so many more Americans than Englishmen kill Englishmen or Japanese kill Japanese. England, Japan, and West Germany are, next to the United States, the most heavily industrialized countries in the world. Together they have a population of 214 million people. Among these people there are 135 gun murders a year. Among the 200 million people in the United States there are 6,500 gun murders a year—about 48 times as many. Philadelphia alone has about the same number of criminal homicides as England, Scotland, and Wales combined—as many in a city of two million (and a city of brotherly love, at that) as in a nation of 45 million.[5]

In 1973, as in previous years, firearms predominated as the most often used weapon in homicide in the United States. In the Southern states, firearms were used in more than seven out of every ten murders. Nationwide, 53 percent of the homicides were committed with handguns.[6]

The Circumstances Surrounding Murder The circumstances which result in murder vary from family arguments to felonious activities. A pattern that has continued for years is that murders within the family make up approximately one-fourth of all murder offenses. Over one-half of these family killings involve spouse killing spouse. The remainder are parents killing children and other family killings. In murders involving husband and wife, the man kills his wife in 52 percent of the incidents, and the wife kills her husband in the remaining 48 percent. Thus, the husband and the wife are about equal partners in spouse killings. During 1973, about 7 percent of all murders were the result of romantic triangles or lovers' quarrels.[7]

The Slayer-Slayed Relationships In the majority of cases, the homicide offender and the victim are close relatives, friends, or acquaintances. Their relationships tend to show the following pattern:[8]

Relationship	Percentage
Spouses	15.8
Other family members	8.9
Other primary relationships	9.0
Nonprimary relationships	45.4
Not known or stranger	20.9

The families involved in the killings of their members are generally marked by domestic quarrels, drinking, fighting, beating, heated arguments, and lack of self-restraint. It is somewhat difficult to believe that murder should strike so often among close relatives and members of a family.

Straus asserts that empirical data and relevant theory leave no doubt that violence among family members is so common as to be almost universal. Continuing violence in a nuclear family is a systemic product rather than a product of individual behavior pathology.[9] To Steinmetz and Straus, violence seems as typical of family relationships as love. Family members physically abuse each other far more often than do unrelated individuals. Starting with slaps and going on to torture and murder, the family provides a prime setting for every degree of physical violence.[10] Gil thinks that physical abuse of children is more often an indication of a prevailing pattern of caretaker-child interaction in a given home than an isolated incident.[11] Curtis believes that, theoretically, child beating should result in hostility toward the parents and toward the world. An empirical study of children and adolescents who kill presented the following causative factors:

- Intensification of a family rivalry situation
- Foster-home situations in which the feelings of love are insufficient to curb aggressive tendencies
- Organic inferiority
- Educational difficulty
- The tendency to identify with aggressive parents and to pattern after their behavior[12]

The Victim's Role In personal offenses such as homicide, manslaughter, and assault, the victim has, at times, a very crucial role in determining whether the crime will occur. The victim may provoke an attack by angrily offending the attacker. A derogatory remark, a pungent insult, a sly comment, an open act of brazen infidelity, a questioning of someone's masculinity, or an argument over money, a woman or a man, or children can precipitate homicide. Wolfgang applied the term *victim-precipitated* to those criminal homicides "in which the victim was the first to show and use a deadly weapon, to strike a blow in an altercation."[13] In the Philadelphia study of murder, Wolfgang found that 26 percent of all the murders were victim-precipitated.

Murder Weapons Weapons do not kill; weapons are the means to kill. It is the hand that pulls the trigger that kills. Yet some weapons are more lethal than others. Handguns kill five times more people than knives. Handguns can easily be misused—quite often against one's own family members and friends. Guns are particularly dangerous in the hands of mental incompetents, psychopathic offenders, psychotic criminals, and compulsive killers.

Homicide and the Subculture of Violence Homicide offenders are generally young, members of minority groups, and predominantly males. According to Wolfgang and Ferracuti, these offenders are the products of a subculture of violence, which is found in many societies to varying degrees. Several groups and communities place a premium on physical aggression, vendettas, and an exaggerated sense of honor and prestige. Acts requiring courage, bravado, fearlessness, and recklessness are extolled.

The responses of individuals depend on how deeply they are involved in such subcultures of violence. They respond violently to acts perceived by them as derogatory to their honor. They often settle their arguments and differences by force and violence. When violence is a norm in a subculture, it is imperative to be violent in certain situations. The subcultural demand is so pressing that "restraint from using violence may be a frustrating, ego-deflating, even a guilt-ridden experience."[14] In the words of Wolfgang:

> This subculture is characterized by poor housing, high density of population, overcrowded home conditions, and by a system of values that often condones violence and physical aggression from child-rearing processes to adult interpersonal relationships that sometimes end in criminal slayings.[15]

Finding that most homicide cases occurred on weekends, and that in two-thirds of these cases there had been drinking, Wolfgang adds: "When the socioeconomic group most likely to commit homicide almost simultaneously receives its weekly wages, purchases alcohol, and meets together socially, it is not unlikely that the incidence of homicide should also arise."[16] Wolfgang further notes that about two-thirds of the homicide offenders had a previous arrest record, most often for aggravated assault.

Distinguishing Murderers Can murderers be differentiated in their personal attributes? Even in a subculture of violence, a large majority of persons do not commit any murder—only a small minority do. Do the murderers have different kinds of *life experiences*? In order to answer this question, Palmer made an intensive study of fifty-one murderers in New England. For a control group, he used the nearest-in-age brother of each murderer. The majority of Palmer's fifty-one murderers had either minor or no conviction records. Only about 14 percent of their murders were planned; the rest showed no planning or premeditation.[17] Their parents showed an amazingly low rate of physical separation. Palmer felt that

> The parents of murderers tend to be people who conform rigidly to certain, although by no means all moral codes. One of the codes to which they seem to conform is that married couples will not separate or divorce. They may not get on well, one or both of them may drink heavily, but they stick together.[18]

These families were in the lowest social class in the community. Working intermittently in an unskilled capacity, the murderers led dismal, unprestigious, and frustrating lives.[19] Their mothers were well-meaning but maladjusted individuals.

They were, in many instances, highly repressed about sexual and aggressive matters. As compared to their brothers (who were used as controls), the murderers as a group suffered many more physical and psychological frustrations. *The most significant difference was that while the nonmurderer brother released his frustration through acceptable channels, the murderer used socially unacceptable ways to release his frustration.*[20]

In another study of thirteen murderers, a striking finding was that the attitude of the fathers in all cases was generally hostile. The father was consistently a negative figure (either absent from the family picture or indifferent or overtly rejecting). The murderers suffered from marked feelings of sexual inadequacy, which were reflected in their marital lives. With increasing demands on their social capabilities, they became more angry and tense. At such a time, even a slight insult or provocation triggered the violent surge of rage that resulted in murder.[21] While weighing the reliability of this evidence, we should bear in mind that the number of cases in this study was very small.

Disregard for Human Life Lombroso, who is called the "father of criminology," thought that some offenders are insensitive to the pain they inflict on others. In the same vein, Schilder inquired into the attitudes of murderers toward death and killing. According to him,

> The young slayer does not think about his own death, and the life of the other has no particular significance for him. . . . It almost seems that these "normal murderers," who are not otherwise so badly adapted to their reality, show particular infantile trends in their reaction to life and death. One may say they kill because they do not appreciate the deprivation they inflict upon others.[22]

Psychotic Killers In a minority of cases, the offenders are psychotic killers who start shooting during one of their "spells." Psychotic killers may pick a special category of victims or shoot aimlessly at whoever comes their way. According to Ray, even psychotic murderers tend to kill their own associates.

> Nearly every homicide committed by an insane individual had been preceded by some signs of insanity. Victims of the insane killer were found generally to be intimate associates, not infrequently his own offspring. Most of the insane murderers

exhibited no remorse and freely confessed the deed. The expressed motive for killing generally seems wholly inadequate to the sane individual. The crimes of the insane murderer are generally extremely gory.[23]

About one-third of all psychotic killers are found to have previously been in a psychiatric institution. According to Guttmacher's study, more than one-third of the psychotic group forgot all or part of the crime. The most puzzling thing about such psychotic amnesia is that the offenders remembered the premurder and postmurder events.[24] This naturally raises doubt, in the minds of the police, the investigators, and the courts, about the truthfulness of the offenders' statements. It appears that sometimes offenders may really forget about the traumatic incident of murder, while at other times they may be pretending.

Lamberti and others distinguished another category which they call the *sudden murderer*. They defined him as a patient who

> . . . without any prior pattern of antisocial behavior that might indicate the individual concerned would commit such a crime, suddenly attempted to kill or did kill another person —the crime as a function of the personality of the individual concerned was much more difficult to understand.[25]

According to Lamberti et al., sudden murderers suffer from emotional and social isolation and seem to conceal persistent resentment. They come from cohesive backgrounds where conformity was emphasized.[26] As in most other cases, they may also choose their victims from among friends, relatives, and acquaintances.

Stranger Killers We have seen that in about 20 percent of the murder cases, the offender is a stranger to the victim. This gives rise to three questions:

- Why should a stranger kill?
- What kind of person kills a stranger?
- Under what circumstances does such a person kill?

These killers comprise a very heterogeneous group. In many cases, the offenders are robbers who, when caught, shoot to escape, to do away with victims who could provide evidence against them, or to save their own lives. In other cases, the offenders are mentally deranged. They shoot aimlessly, killing strangers who happen to come their way. The motive in such cases is not clear, and it presents several difficulties in investigation.

There is also the rare case in which a stranger-rapist forces his way into a house to rape and kill. A recent example is that of a person who forcibly entered the living quarters of eight nurses in Chicago, raped them one by one, and killed seven of them. Then there is an occasional murder of a prostitute who is murdered by a sadistic killer, after going through a bizarre ritual which is somehow erotic to the killer.

Forcible Rapist

Forcible rape, as defined by the FBI, is the carnal knowledge of a female through the use of force or the threat of force. During 1973, there were an estimated total of 51,000 forcible rapes. Of the persons arrested for forcible rape, about 20 percent were under 18 years of age, 39 percent were under 21, and 61 percent were under 25. Rape has been increasing at the rate of 10 to 12 percent every year. During the years 1960 to 1973, it increased by 101.6 percent for all offender ages, but 132.3 percent for offenders under 18 years of age.

A crime rate, in its proper perspective, is a victim risk rate, since it gives the number of crimes per unit of population. In 1973, 47 out of every 100,000 females in the United States were reported rape victims. In cities with populations in excess of 250,000, the victim risk rate was 100 rapes per 100,000 females. Of the persons under 18 years of age arrested for rape, 44 percent were white and 54 percent were black.[27]

The Characteristics of a Forcible Rapist The rapist is typically a young man between the ages of 17 and 20 years. Two-thirds of all the rapists arrested are under the age of 25. According to Amir's study, a forcible rapist is generally unmarried and has a low occupational status. He tends to choose his victim from his own race, community, and group. He is likely to use force when he is drunk or if he is involved in group rape. In Amir's study, alcohol was found only in one-third of all the rape cases.[28]

> Alcohol is a factor found to be strongly related to violence used in the rape situation, especially when present in the offender only. In terms of race, it was drinking Negro victims

or the offenders who were involved most often in violent rapes. Also, alcohol was found to be *significantly* associated with sexual humiliation forced upon drinking victims.[29]

What kind of criminal histories do rapists have? According to a Cambridge study, slightly more than half had no previous sex-offense convictions. About one-quarter had one; about 7 percent had two; and 9 percent had three or more previous sex-offense convictions. Rapists do not have a high repeat of sex crimes. Those who are reconvicted are often convicted for a nonsex crime, such as larceny or breaking and entering. By examining the after-conduct of convicted offenders for a period of 4 years, the Cambridge study found that results were more favorable for those convicted of heterosexual conduct.[30] Similarly, Gebhard et al. made a separate characterization of heterosexual aggressors versus minors and heterosexual aggressors versus adults. While the former present a very bleak picture, the latter appear to be relatively normal individuals.

> The aggressors vs. minors may be characterized as irresponsible, aggressive, and amoral young men seeking the gratification of today with little concern for the future. . . . Some of them were not simply thoughtless, hot-blooded young men but were plainly antisocial and criminal.[31]
> The majority of aggressors vs. adults may be succinctly described as criminally inclined who take what they want, whether money, material, or women, and their sex offenses are by-products of their general criminality. Aside from their early involvement in crime, there are no outstandingly ominous signs in their presex-offense histories; indeed, their heterosexual adjustment is quantitatively well above average.[32]

Bernard Glueck also found the rapists of adult females more aggressive, outgoing, and impulsive than other sex offenders; moreover, they were younger and better integrated into the community, though with poorer employment records.[33]

The Circumstances Leading to Rape We have examined the sociological and psychological characteristics of a rapist. However, the usual circumstances precipitating rape also deserve scrutiny. Still more important is the subjective interpretation given to the events by the offender: He may perceive the situation and the behavior of the victim favorable for the commission of rape. Of course, a wide variety of events enter into the perpetration of forcible rape, but from different accounts, and particularly from Amir's study, the following seem to emerge.

The offender, young as he is, has imbibed from his peer group the opportunity, masculinity, and *modus operandi* involved in raping a girl. Most rapes are single rapes, but there are some pair rapes and group or multiple rapes. The initial meeting between the offender and his would-be-victim occurs at the residence of one of them or a street, bus stop, bar, park, or party. Somehow, he reads into the situation the possibility of persuading or coercing the girl to have sexual intercourse. When he conceives this idea, he plans, manipulates and removes the girl to a proper place (if needed). He persuades, cajoles, intimidates, threatens, slaps, and beats her to overcome her resistance. In a minority of cases (about 13 percent), the rapist uses some violence to subdue his victim. He does this mostly to prevent her from screaming and thus attracting the attention of neighbors or passersby.[34]

Amir distinguished the following patterns of forcible rape:

1. Of all 646 rape events, 71 percent were planned rapes; 11 percent were partially planned; and in 16 percent of the cases the offense was an explosive event [page 142].
2. Although planned rapes were characteristic of all rape events, they were mostly connected with pair and group types of rape while explosive rapes were significantly associated with the single type of rape [page 144].
3. Sixty-seven percent of the forcible rapes were indoor affairs and not, as it is believed, mainly dark-alley encounters [page 145]. Fifteen percent of the rapes took place in the auto; and only 18 percent of the rapes took place in open spaces.
4. The rapist inflicted sexual humiliation: fellatio, cunnilingus, pederasty, and repeated intercourse on victims in 27 percent of the rape events [page 159].
5. The victim was kept by the offender in captivity at the scene of the crime after the forced sexual intercourse was complete in 9 percent of the cases. The span of time she was kept in captivity (after the last forceful intercourse) ranges from half an hour to four hours or more [page 175].
6. In 48 percent of the cases, the offender and the victim were acquainted with each other, and in 14 percent of the cases very intimately. Neighbors and acquaintances were apt to commit more brutal rapes [pages 345–346].[35]

Group Rapes

Amir also investigated pair rapes, in which two offenders rape one victim; and group rapes, in which three or more males rape one victim. The group rapes were perpetuated by young offenders who selected young victims of the same age from their neighborhood. These rapes were generally planned and tended to occur during weekend drinking parties. The group-rape offenders generally had a previous arrest record. The group leader initiated the rape and inflicted sexual humiliation upon the victim, and these acts were repeated by other members of the group.[36]

Aggravated Assault

Aggravated assault is defined as an unlawful attack by one person upon another for the purpose of inflicting severe bodily injury. It is usually accomplished with a weapon or other means likely to produce death or serious bodily harm. In 1973, there were an estimated 416,270 aggravated assaults, with a rate of 198 per 100,000 inhabitants. This is about twenty times the homicide rate. In 1973, 26 percent of the serious assaults were committed with the use of a firearm. Such assaults had, in 1973, increased by 63 percent over the 1968 total.

Most aggravated assaults occur within the family unit or among neighbors or acquaintances. The victim-offender relationship, as well as the very nature of the attack, makes this crime similar to murder. Because of the nature of the crime, arrests are frequently made as soon as patrol units respond. However, this type of patrol call is hazardous to the responding officers. From 1962 to 1971, 101 officers lost their lives responding to disturbance-type calls, which frequently involve family arguments.[37]

Among family members, the threat to kill seems to be much more common than the killing itself. In a study by Macdonald of 100 patients who threatened to kill, eight of every ten patients threatened to kill members of their own family. The family members are often reluctant to report such cases until the situation gets out of hand.[38]

> The five to six-year follow-up study of one hundred patients admitted to the hospital because of homicidal threats showed that seven had either taken their own lives or those of others. Four committed suicide and three committed homicide. The incidence of homicide or suicide may be more than 7 percent,

since twenty-three patients have not yet been traced. The study suggests that patients admitted to hospital because of homicidal threats have much higher homicide and suicide rates than the general population.[39]

Macdonald advises that, just as suicide threats are taken seriously, homicide threats should not be taken lightly. Threatened individuals should remain careful, and the police should remain vigilant about the offenders.[40]

There is a very thin line between committers of aggravated assault and murderers. The two types of offenders are very much alike in most respects. If it were not for modern medicine and surgery, many assault offenders would end up being convicted as homicide offenders. The close family (or other) relationship which exists between victims and assailants accounts for the victim's frequent unwillingness to testify for the prosecution. Acquittals and dismissals, therefore, run high, comprising four out of every ten cases.

Roebuck describes another typology of *assaulters* who are also *drinkers*. These people are always ready to fight to prove themselves "real men." The possession of a knife at all times is a must. "Most of their fighting which led to assault charges took place in bars, with male drinking acquaintances and in gambling games with their peers. . . . They displayed little respect for the policeman."[41]

THE PROPERTY OFFENDER

Robber

There were an estimated total of 382,680 robbery offenses committed in the United States in 1973. About one-third of all robberies were committed by persons under age 18; 56 percent, by those under age 21; and 76 percent, by persons under age 25. The youthful robbers frequently acted in groups. Of the persons arrested for robbery, Negroes constituted a majority of 68.5 percent, while 30.4 percent were white. In 1973, 7 of every 100 persons arrested for robbery were females. Armed perpetrators were responsible for 66 percent of the robbery offenses during 1973, while 34 percent were muggings, yokings, or other violent confrontations in which personal weapons were used by the offender to subdue or overcome the victim.

Robbery is primarily a large-city crime. American cities with more than 250,000 inhabitants accounted for two-thirds of all robberies.[42] Robbery strikes everywhere: in the street, commercial house, gas station, residence, chain store, bank, cab, and bus. About 55 percent of all robberies take place in the street.

Robbery is a vicious crime which subjects the victim both to loss of property and to violence or the threat of violence. It is a combination of both property and personal offense. Robbery frequently results in physical injury, and almost always inflicts a psychological injury on the victim. It is perhaps the most fear-provoking crime. It has greatly hampered the free movement of people on the streets in large cities, for either business or pleasure. It has compelled many people to keep themselves confined to their homes in fear.

Robbery is particularly terrifying because the victim is exposed to violence from a criminal who is a stranger. People do face violence from spouses, other family members, friends, and acquaintances, but violence at the hands of strangers has a different character to it. According to the President's Commission on Crime, the fear of crimes of violence is not a simple fear of injury or death but, at bottom, a fear of strangers.[43] When a person shoots his or her own spouse, this is undoubtedly an indication of a family tragedy; but the violence remains within the home. When a stranger robs or kills on the street, this spreads more terror; the whole social order is threatened. Suffering violence at the hands of strangers is much more demoralizing.

> The fear of strangers has greatly impoverished the lives of many Americans, especially those who live in high-crime neighborhoods in large cities. People stay behind the locked doors of their homes rather than risk walking in the streets at night. Poor people spend money on taxis because they are afraid to walk or use public transportation. Sociable people are afraid to talk to those they do not know. . . . The general level of social interaction in the society is reduced. When fear of crime becomes fear of the stranger the social order is further damaged. As the level of sociability and mutual trust is reduced, streets and public places can indeed become more dangerous. Not only will there be fewer people abroad but those who are abroad will manifest a fear of and a lack of concern for each other. The reported incidents of bystanders indifferent to cries for help are the logical consequences of a reduced sociability, mutual distrust and withdrawal.[44]

An extensive analysis of robbery offenders and victims in 1722 cases revealed that 41 percent of the robberies produced no injury at all, while 56 percent produced some injury. According to the Sellin-Wolfgang seriousness-of-crime index, the juvenile robberies were as serious as robberies in general. There was a significant association between robbery and the race and sex of both victim and offender. Negroes and males are involved in far more robberies than their proportions in the general population would indicate. In Philadelphia in the early 1960s, Negroes had more than twice as many victims and three times as many offenders as their proportion in the general population. Normandeau concluded that there is a clear difference between robbery and other crimes of violence in many of the characteristics of victims, offenders, and modus operandi: Robbery resembles offenses against property more than offenses against the person.[45]

Types of Robbery Offenders A wide variety of people are involved in robbery, for different reasons. One factor that is common to all types of robbers is their youth. More than three-fourths of them are under 25 years of age. About one-third of all the robbers who are involved in strong-arm robbery are under age 18. Racially, 66 percent of the robbers are Negroes.[46] Conklin identifies four types of robbery offenders:

> The *professional* seeks money as a source of income, using it to support a hedonistic life style. He plans his robberies in detail and seeks large sums of money. The *opportunist* wants only a little extra money for clothes or partying. He selects vulnerable victims who rarely carry much money. The *addict* prefers other types of theft, but will occasionally rob to get money to buy drugs. His primary interest is in drugs, and if he had a readily accessible free supply, it is likely that he would commit few crimes. The *alcoholic* robber rarely considers how much money he will steal or what he will do with it once he has it. Instead, his intoxicated state sometimes leads him to assault others and to take their money as an afterthought. The four types thus vary in terms of commitment to crime, plans made to carry out the crime, and reasons for committing the crime.[47]

Does the robber operate alone or with accomplices? Studies indicate that more than 66 percent of the robbers do not operate alone, but are assisted by accomplices. However, 72 percent of the bank robbers tend to operate alone. Also, situational spur-of-the-moment robberies are likely to be committed by lone robbers and involve a lone victim.[48] Some robberies require careful and elaborate planning.

Burglar

First, a few words about the magnitude of burglary. An estimated total of 2,540,900 burglaries were committed during 1973. This is 29 percent of the total of all crime index offenses. When viewed as a segment of property crime, burglary is found to comprise 33 percent of the total. Economically, the offense of burglary represents a substantial sum. Victims suffered a loss of $856 million in 1973, with the average dollar loss per burglary being $337.[49]

Young persons under 18 accounted for 54 percent of all arrests for burglary. Females were involved in 5 of every 100 arrests for burglary during 1973. Arrests of whites outnumbered arrests of Negroes by two to one. The arrest of one person may clear up several burglaries.[50] More than 70 percent of the offenders operate with one or more associates. Group members can share their responsibilities: One person can keep watch outside, the other can enter the house, and the two can help each other in carrying heavy pieces of furniture.

According to a crime-specific study done in California, about 43 percent of the burglars had prior records. Of those with prior records, 70 percent had been convicted previously for burglary, and 56 percent for drug violations.[51] This is partial evidence that burglars are career criminals. Those who become career burglars generally start at a relatively young age, between 11 and 12 years old. It should be noted that the maximum number of burglary arrests took place at age 16.

An account of the lifestyles of burglars and their modi operandi can be had from their case histories, autobiographies, and personal interviews. Burglars are, at times, proud of their escapades and like to talk about their "capers" to their peers, friends, spouses, and those interviewers whom they can trust. Some of the common patterns include a beginning, during childhood, with petty theft and a slow graduation to the breaking and entering of unoccupied houses. In order to dispose of the stolen goods, they must know of a fence. Most of them come from broken homes or homes with deviant models (parents or elder siblings who were involved in drinking, prostitution, or crime).

In an analysis of common patterns in the life histories of five burglars, David found alcoholism and gambling among their parents. During their childhood, all were left by themselves, with no supervision or control. All five respondents admitted that they started shoplifting as juveniles. All associated with peers who were involved in similar activities and used drugs. All stole regularly. Some claimed an average of 300 burglaries per year, with an average "income" of $400 to $500 per week. This amount of money was necessary to support their drug habits and gambling (the respondents were in their twenties at the time of the interview).[52] Most juvenile burglars are unmarried. If they get married, they do not have stable marriages.

Like all other professionals, burglars have their specialties. Some residence burglars steal only cash, jewelry, and bankbooks. Others steal cameras, radios, television sets, and record players. Some enter the house through a window or door, and others climb in through the skylight. The author knows of a burglar who would only break into the houses of high dignitaries.

Some have fetishes about their stolen goods. One burglar had a great urge to steal antique clocks, so much that he collected more than 150 clocks in his house. When he had to go to prison, he asked his girlfriend to take care of them. On his release from the prison, he found all of his clocks missing, along with the girl. A Reporter at Large of the *New Yorker* relates:

> Last year, police caught a burglar who specialized in stealing wigs, and this year the produce-market district has had a number of egg burglaries, the theater district has been plagued with wardrobe burglaries, and several interstate trucking firms have complained that it is nearly impossible to ship a load of shrimp to New York City without the trucks being burglarized.[53]

Black distinguishes between the "prowlers" and the more sophisticated burglars who are careful planners. The prowlers, also known as "hit-or-miss" burglars, go out to steal "on the blind." The sophisticated planners have their research done for them through confederates, who are known as "fingers." Some hotel employees act as fingers and pass information concerning hotel guests to burglars.[54] Burglars are constantly on the lookout for opportunities to steal. They sometimes even seek information about a house or apartment and its occupants from delivery people and servants. They may even strike when a house or apartment is occupied—day or night.

Auto Thief

In 1973, 923,000 motor vehicles were reported stolen. The number of auto thefts has increased 19 percent since 1968. A car is stolen every 34 seconds in the United States. Across the nation in 1973, 1 of every 128 registered automobiles was stolen. Regionally, this rate was the highest in the Northeastern states, where 12 cars per 1000 registered vehicles were stolen. It is primarily a large-city problem.[55]

In 1973, 56 percent of the people arrested for this offense were under 18 years of age, and 74 percent were under 21.[56] Of the auto thieves under 18 years of age, 69 percent were white, 29 percent Negro, and 1.2 percent Indian. Auto theft is essentially an offense committed by males: Of the persons arrested, 94 percent were males and 6 percent females. Car thieves can be classified as (1) young boys between 13 and 16 years old who commit no offense but car theft; (2) young boys who combine auto theft with other delinquent activities; and (3) professional auto thieves, mostly adult.

Pure auto thieves are predominantly white boys brought up in better socioeconomic circumstances. They are more joyriders than thieves. The prognosis in their case is generally more hopeful than that of other groups. If they get into difficulty again, it will, in the majority of cases, be because of another car theft.[57] Wattenberg and Balistrieri came up with similar findings when they compared 230 white boys charged with automobile theft with 2544 others in trouble with the Detroit police in 1948. The automobile thieves were more likely to come from relatively favored neighborhoods and to have good social relationships with their peers. They were least likely to be "lone wolves." It was suggested that they readily respond to the values of their immediate associates but disregard the norms of the larger society.[58]

The young boys who combine auto theft with other delinquent activities are quite criminally oriented. Savitz describes this type of auto thief as generally an unmarried male, usually caucasoid, who lives in an urban center and has some history of alcoholism. He is overly responsive to the demands of his peer group and is very often a recidivist.[59]

The professional car thieves, who comprise only a small minority, operate as members of an organized ring. These persons change the identity of the car and transport it to some other state or country for sale. Juveniles are rarely members of such rings.

Larcenist

In 1973, there were 4,304,400 larceny offenses, making up 50 percent of crime index total. The average value of the property stolen in each larceny in 1973 was $140. The total loss to victims was $603 million. Forty-eight percent of those arrested for larceny were under 18 years of age, and two-thirds were under 21. Females comprised 32 percent of all arrests for larceny. Thus, females are involved more in larceny than in any other crime index offense. Arrests of females rose 8 percent in 1973, while arrests of males increased 2 percent. For persons under 18 years, arrests of whites (71 percent) outnumbered arrests of blacks (28 percent) by more than two to one.[60]

Although mostly poor people are arrested, larceny is very common at all ages and in all social classes. The habit of stealing, however, generally shows up early in life, and its roots are often found in childhood. Adolescents may steal in reaction to the pinch of poverty or the opportunity of abundance. They may be tempted to steal by pressing need or just for the fun of it. The motivation may be apparent or hidden in the complexity of the mind. The reasons may be material or nonmaterial—people steal for love, security, and belongingness. The act of stealing may symbolize an attempt to hurt someone and/or punish oneself out of a sense of guilt. If the incidence of theft is limitless, so are its causes.

THE AUTHORITY OFFENDER

Runaway

In 1973, 178,433 persons of age 17 and under were arrested as runaways. There must be many more who were not arrested or who were not even reported to the police. More girls than boys were arrested: 55.5 percent versus 44.5 percent. Racially, a large majority of the runaways (88.2 percent) were white; 10.1 percent were Negro, and 1.2 percent were Indian. While there were 3890 arrests in the age bracket 10 and under, the maximum number of arrests (149,115) were of runaways between the ages of 13 and 16 years.[61]

The Impulse to Wander Wanderlust is not new, and it is not unique to juveniles. The impulse to wander is as old as travelers, explorers, scholars, and tourists. People run away at all ages, driven by economic, social, and political pressures. Wandering is the lifestyle of gypsies and is a part of some religious orders. The difference in the case of juveniles is that, for them, running away from home without the consent of their parents constitutes an offense under the juvenile laws.

The Profile of a Runaway As long ago as the late 1920s, Armstrong did a comprehensive study of 660 runaway boys. She compared them with incorrigibles, other delinquent boys, and nondelinquent boys. Her findings are still valid after half a century. Her runaways were younger, as a group, than the delinquent boys, but the same age as the incorrigible boys. Their families were beset with numerous difficulties: The father was an alcoholic in 17 percent of the families. Overt destructive factors such as immorality, psychoses, and criminality were more frequently present among the mothers of the runaways. The home as a stable environment was unknown to at least 55 percent of the runaways. There was a larger proportion of stepbrothers and stepsisters than in other boys' families.

The boys had a record of 2.33 previous court arraignments and had a relatively larger incidence of orphanage experience. The majority of runaway boys tended to offend alone, unlike boys involved in other delinquent acts. The runaway boys also showed a higher incidence of physical defects such as diseased tonsils, bad ears, and endocrine disorders—mainly caused by neglect.[62]

A recent study characterizes runaway youth (of both sexes) as being impulsive in their decision making and relying heavily on peers without really knowing who they are. They have difficulties in relating to adults, and they feel lonely, friendless, and depressed when in trouble. They have lower than average health, with higher levels of gonorrhea, hepatitis, other infectious diseases, and head injury in the past. About 50 percent of the families of runaways have alcohol problems. Their families move more often and suffer greater disorganization.[63]

A study of runaway girls classifies them in two categories: (1) girls running away from unpleasant homes, and (2) girls running to more exciting places and people. The former category "included those girls who had intrapersonal conflicts as well as family problems that they were unable to resolve."[64] They had a great deal of unresolved anger. The conflicts they experienced surpassed their tolerance levels. Their involvement in the runaway's culture is minimal, and their recidivism rate is lower than that of the other group. Insight-oriented treatment and the use of family therapy can be helpful with this group of girls.[65]

The second group, girls running to exciting places and people, included girls who were pleasure seekers. They were looking for a variety of experiences that were forbidden at home, including sex, drugs, and liquor. Their peers were involved in serious delinquency. They found it difficult to internalize social controls. As a result, their recidivism rate was relatively high. For treatment, it was necessary for them to learn to set limits on their behavior. They needed to learn a sense of responsibility.[66]

What were the juveniles' reasons for running away? Most of the blame was placed on the family. The runaways said they could not tolerate the family situation. The school shares in the responsibility, but to a lesser degree. Some girls ran away with a boyfriend. They liked the adventure of running away.[67] In some cases the youngsters were virtually kicked out by their parents. Armstrong contends: "The argument might be advanced that the runaways are reacting normally to the given situations and inconsistently enough, are held culpable therefore."[68]

What is the impact of running away on the adolescent? A group of runaways were interviewed 1 year after their apprehension. Sixty-six percent believed, in retrospect, that running away had been a positive, growing experience for them. If temporary independence from family and the familiar setting can be used by some adolescents as a positive growing experience, we should consider alternative options for such an experience.[69]

The "Beyond Control" Youth

There are many more girls than boys in this category of delinquency. They form a heterogeneous group which includes youths described as ungovernable, unmanageable, incorrigible, wayward, or predelinquent. Broadly speaking, this category includes youngsters whose behavior is persistently displeasing, defiant, disobedient, sexually promiscuous, and/or threatening.

There is only a vague line separating the juvenile who is beyond control from the juvenile who is a law violator. Several factors influence the decision to classify an offender as one or the other. They include family status, the juvenile's attitudes and delinquent history, the community's attitude, and the like. About one-third to one-half of all juvenile arrests are for behavior beyond control, and the rest are for law violations. Referring to

California juvenile statistics, Green and Esselstyn found that "in probation referrals, twice as many juveniles are referred for law violations as for beyond control behavior. Within the law violator group, there are about eight boys for every two girls."[70]

The principal targets of beyond control behavior are, understandably, authority figures—parents, teachers, employers, law enforcement officers, and probation officers. Many times, such behavior is self-destructive and is directed against the delinquents themselves. The behavior is expressed through running away from home, school truancy, sexual promiscuity, precocity, and sex delinquency.

Green and Esselstyn identify three types of runaway girls: the rootless, the anxious, and the terrified. The rootless girl is an impulsive hedonist, seeking immediate gratification. She drops out of a series of schools and jobs. The anxious girl comes from a problem-loaded family. She runs away for a few hours to seek temporary relief. The terrified girl runs away from the threat of incest at home, or from a family member who may be an alcoholic, mental patient or drug addict.[71]

The truancy from school may be precipitated by boredom, the perceived irrelevancy of the school program or student-teacher hostility. Sexual delinquency starts pretty early among many juveniles but remains invisible, unreported, and unrecognized. A juvenile who is guilty of a sex offense is often not charged for that specific offense, but instead, is charged for "vagrancy, loitering, or immoral or indecent conduct." This would be especially true in those courts which do not want to stigmatize children. Arrests of males under 18 for sex offenses (except forcible rape and prostitution) decreased by 1.7 percent, and of females by 64 percent, from 1960 to 1973. Apparently, there is condonation for juvenile sex offenses.

It appears that there are regional differences in the sex patterns of delinquent boys. Rosenberg and Silverstein, who interviewed several delinquent boys in Chicago, New York, and Washington, found some differences in their sex attitudes. "Acts of aggression connected with sex no doubt are intensified by heavy consumption of alcohol. Sex, liquor, and violence form a gestalt in Chicago not nearly so discernible in New York or Washington."[72]

Some delinquent boys boast about sexual conquests and like to add unnecessary sadism to sex. They behave quite brutally toward their sex partners, with little regard for their girls' wishes. The boys do not bother with birth-control measures, and often make the girls pregnant. When a girl does become an unwed mother, the boys refuse to take any responsibility either for the mother or the child. They are not willing to marry an easy pickup, yet they need a pickup to establish their status among other adolescents. "Among young lower-status adolescent boys, perhaps the most common mode of heterosexual intercourse is the 'gang-shag' or 'gang-bang.' A gang of boys usually knows one or more girls who are easy "pick-ups" for the group who will consent to serial intercourse."[73]

Reiss contends that girls are more readily defined as sex offenders than boys. The girls, when apprehended by police or juvenile authorities, are given physical examinations to determine if they are pregnant or suffering from venereal infection. So the chances are greater for girls to be labeled as sex delinquents,[74] even though boys may be equally promiscuous, or even more so. The sexual activity of delinquent youths is likely to be confined to the physical level, without any emotional involvement or moral commitment.

> Such notions as fidelity and loyalty are out of place. . . . They constrain freedom. . . . Sex there is in abundance but when love rears it ugly head there comes the moment of truth wherein something must give. . . . It is to the great lesson of mankind that they [the youth] should attend: involvement brings liberation, commitment is freedom.[75]

SUMMARY

This chapter classifies offenders into three categories: the violent offender, the property offender, and the authority offender. Of the *violent* offenders, the murderer and the assaultist have about the same characteristics. In one-fourth of all murders, the assailant and victim have a family relationship. In half of these family murders, one spouse kills the other. In about 80 percent of the cases, the slayer and the victim are close relatives, friends, or acquaintances.

The families of homicide offenders are characterized by violence. In about 26 percent of the cases, the victim precipitates a homicidal attack on himself or herself. Most homicide offenders act under the influence of the subculture of violence. The subculture urges them to settle their disputes by violence. Murderers are generally young, members of minority groups, and predominantly males.

Aggravated assault offenders are similar to homicide offenders in many ways. The assaulters who are also drinkers are always ready to fight. The *rapist,* another violent offender, shares some of the characteristics of the assaultist. A forcible rapist is typically a young man, is generally unmarried, has a low occupational status, and tends to choose his victim from his own race, community, or group. A rapist under the influence of drink is more likely to inflict violence on his victim and sexually humiliate her. Group rapes are more likely to take place during weekend drinking parties.

Robbers seem to share the characteristics of both violent offenders and property offenders. The FBI *Uniform Crime Reports* include robbers among violent offenders; many scholars believe robbers have more in common with property offenders. About one-third of all robberies are committed by persons below age 18. Robbery is primarily a large-city crime, which may be why Negroes are involved in this crime to a much greater extent than their population proportion. Juveniles tend to rob in groups, rather than alone. Conklin identifies four types of robbery offenders: the professional who is a sophisticated planner; the opportunist who is not looking for a large sum of money; the addict who must rob to buy drugs; and the alcoholic robber who starts a fight under the influence of drink and commits robbery as an afterthought.

Burglary would seem to be a juvenile offense, since more than half of all burglary arrests are of persons below age 18. Burglars who start their delinquent careers in their early teens often become career criminals. Most burglars start with petty theft and then graduate to breaking and entering houses. Like most career criminals, they establish contacts with fences, fellow burglars, bonding agents, and lawyers. Burglars tend to develop patterns of burglary, special modi operandi, and preferences for stealing specific articles.

Auto theft is another popular juvenile property offense. Car thieves can be divided into three categories: (1) young boys who are joyriders; (2) boys who combine car thefts with other crimes; and (3) professional car thieves. *Larcenists* steal for many diverse reasons.

Among the authority offenders (status offenders), there are *runaways* and *youth beyond control.* Runaway boys come from unstable homes, rely heavily on the advice of their peers, and make decisions impulsively. One study classifies runaway girls as either running away from an unpleasant home or running to more exciting places. Girls in the latter category are looking for sex, drugs, and liquor. The youth beyond control category is a heterogeneous group consisting of incorrigible, ungovernable, and defiant children. These children tend to strike against authority figures who have not treated them well. They show their defiance in many ways, one of which is flouting existing sex norms and experimenting with new sex styles.

Discussion Questions

1. How do you account for the higher murder rate in the Southern states?
2. What is the role of handguns in the increasing rate of murder?
3. What can we do to reduce violence in the American family?
4. Differentiate between single and group rapists with regard to their personal characteristics and group orientation.
5. What are the sociological conditions in a large city that account for a high rate of robbery?
6. What is the role of the fence in burglary?
7. Do you think that runaways should be handled by juvenile authorities?

Glossary

Amnesia A lack of memory, generally or of specific experiences.

Authority Offender A juvenile who flouts and rebels against the legitimate authority of a parent, guardian, teacher, or any other lawful authority.

Crime Index Offenses The offenses of murder, forcible rape, robbery, aggravated assault, burglary, larceny, and motor vehicle theft are used to establish an index in the Uniform Crime Reporting Program to measure the trend and distribution of crime in the United States. The crime index offenses were selected as a measuring device because, as a group, they represent the most common local crime problems. They are all serious crimes, either because of their nature or because of the frequency with which they are committed.

Empirical Data Data based on experience, observation, or experimentation.

Exhibitionist A person who intentionally and compulsively exposes his or her sex organs for the purpose of seeking attention.

Fetish An erotic craving for an object, such as a glove, or a part of the body.

Internalization A psychoanalytical mechanism through which one incorporates something in his or her mind at a deep level. It is a process of adoption of another person's values, ideas, or norms wholeheartedly.

Kleptomania A persistent urge to steal, usually associated with sexual excitement.

Latent Attitudes Hidden dispositions which are dormant but can become manifest if the circumstances are conducive to their manifestation.

Mean (Statistical) A measure of average values. Mean is calculated by adding all the values and dividing it by the number of cases.

Modal (Statistical) The most common value in a series. Modal pertains to a mode.

Modus Operandi A manner or way of working, usually applied to criminal activities.

Negativism Persistent resistance to positive suggestions made by other persons.

Peer Group A group of equals who have close relationship.

Predatory Vandalism Irresponsible destruction of property, involving plunder.

Predelinquent A youngster who is on the way to delinquency but has not yet become delinquent. He or she may have truanted from school once or twice or may be associating with delinquent peers, but has not committed a delinquent act.

Footnotes

[1] Don C. Gibbons, *Society, Crime, and Criminal Careers*, Prentice-Hall, Englewood Cliffs, N.J., 1973, pp. 233–251.

[2] Marshall B. Clinard and Richard Quinney, *Criminal Behavior Systems: A Typology*, Holt, New York, 1967, pp. 4–8.

[3] Federal Bureau of Investigation, *Uniform Crime Reports for the United States—1973*, U.S. Government Printing Office, Washington, D.C., pp. 128, 131–134.

[4] Federal Bureau of Investigation, p. 6.

[5] Donald J. Mulvihill et al., *Crimes of Violence, A Staff Report Submitted to the National Commission on the Causes and Prevention of Violence*, vol. 11, U.S. Government Printing Office, Washington, D.C., 1969, pp. xxvii–xxviii.

[6] Federal Bureau of Investigation, p. 6.

[7] Federal Bureau of Investigation, p. 10.

[8] Donald J. Mulvihill et al., p. 217.

[9] Murray A. Straus, "A General Systems Theory Approach to a Theory of Violence between Family Members," *Social Science Information*, vol. 12, no. 3, pp. 105–125, 1973.

[10] Suzanne K. Steinmetz and Murray A. Straus, "The Family as Cradle of Violence," *Society*, vol. 10, no. 6, pp. 50–56, 1973.

[11] David G. Gil, *Violence Against Children: Physical Child Abuse in the United States*, Harvard, Cambridge, Mass., 1970, p. 108.

[12] George C. Curtis, "Violence Breeds Violence—Perhaps?" *American Journal of Psychiatry*, vol. 120, no. 4, pp. 386–387, 1963.

[13] Marvin E. Wolfgang, "Victim-Precipitated Criminal Homicide," *Journal of Criminal Law, Criminology and Police Science*, vol. 48, no. 1, p. 2, June 1957.

[14] Marvin E. Wolfgang and Franco Ferracuti, *The Subculture of Violence*, Tavistock Publications, London, 1967, p. 263.

[15] Marvin E. Wolfgang, "A Sociological Analysis of Criminal Homicide," *Federal Probation*, vol. 25, no. 1, p. 50, March 1961.

[16] Marvin E. Wolfgang, p. 52.

[17] Stuart Palmer, *A Study of Murder*, Thomas Y. Crowell, New York, 1960, pp. 21–22.

[18] Stuart Palmer, p. 26.

[19] Stuart Palmer, p. 37.

[20] Stuart Palmer, p. 181.

[21] Joseph W. Lamberti et al., "The Sudden Murderer," *Journal of Social Therapy*, vol. 4, no. 2, 1958, reprinted in Marvin E. Wolfgang, editor, *Studies in Homicide*, Harper & Row, New York, 1967, pp. 179–192.

[22] Paul Schilder, "The Attitude of Murderers Toward Death," *Abnormal and Social Psychology*, vol. 31, 1936, pp. 362–363.

[23] Isaac Ray, *Treatise on the Medical Jurisprudence of Insanity*, 5th ed., Little, Brown, Boston, 1871, p. 289, in Marvin E. Wolfgang, editor, p. 115.

[24] Manfred Guttmacher, "The Normal and the Sociopathic Murderer," in Marvin E. Wolfgang, editor, pp. 115–116.

[25] Joseph W. Lamberti et al., p. 179.

[26] Joseph W. Lamberti et al., pp. 190–192.

[27] Federal Bureau of Investigation, pp. 13, 126, 134.

[28] Menachem Amir, *Patterns in Forcible Rape*, University of Chicago Press, Chicago, 1971, pp. 337–340.

[29] Menachem Amir, p. 340.

[30] Cambridge Department of Criminal Science, *Sexual Offenses*, Macmillan, London, 1957, p. 300.

[31] Paul H. Gebhard et al., *Sex Offenders: An Analysis of Types*, Harper & Row, New York, 1965, pp. 175–176.

[32] Paul H. Gebhard et al., pp. 205–206.

[33] Bernard C. Glueck, editor, *Final Report*, Research Project for the Study and Treatment of Persons Convicted of Crimes Involving Sexual Aberrations, 1952–55, p. 15, cited in Walter C. Reckless, *The Crime Problem*, 4th ed., Appleton Century Crofts, New York, 1967, p. 237.

[34] Menachem Amir, "Patterns of Forcible Rape," in Marshall B. Clinard and Richard Quinney, editors, *Criminal Behavior Systems*, Holt, New York, 1967, p. 64.

[35] Menachem Amir, *Patterns in Forcible Rape*, pages as noted (with permission of the publishers).

[36] Menachem Amir, pp. 343–344.

[37] Federal Bureau of Investigation, *Uniform Crime Reports for the United States—1971*, U.S. Government Printing Office, Washington, D.C., p. 12.

[38] John M. Macdonald, "The Threat to Kill," *American Journal of Psychiatry*, vol. 120, no. 2, p. 128, 1963.

[39] John M. Macdonald, *Homicidal Threats*, Charles C Thomas, Springfield, Ill., 1968, p. 109.

[40] John M. Macdonald, pp. 87–91.

[41] Julian B. Roebuck, *Criminal Typology*, Charles C Thomas, Springfield, Ill., 1967, p. 165.

[42] Federal Bureau of Investigation (1973), pp. 15–17.

[43] President's Commission on Crime, *The Challenge of Crime in a Free Society*, U.S. Government Printing Office, Washington, D.C., 1967, p. 52.

[44] President's Commission on Crime, p. 52.

[45] Andre Normandeau, "Violence and Robbery: A Case Study," *Acta Criminologica*, vol. 5, pp. 13–106, Montreal, 1972.

[46] Federal Bureau of Investigation (1971), p. 18.

[47] John E. Conklin, *Robbery and the Criminal Justice System*, Lippincott, New York, 1972, pp. 77–78.

[48] National Institute of Law Enforcement and Criminal Justice, *The Crime of Robbery in the United States*, U.S. Government Printing Office, Washington, D.C., 1971, p. 13.

[49] Federal Bureau of Investigation (1973), pp. 19–22.

[50] Federal Bureau of Investigation (1973), p. 22.

[51] State of California, *Crime-Specific Burglary Prevention Handbook*, Office of Criminal Justice Planning, Sacramento, May 1974, p. 124.

[52] Pedro R. David, editor, *The World of the Burglar*, University of New Mexico Press, Albuquerque, 1974, pp. 1–11.

[53] Susan Black, "Burglary-I" *The New Yorker*, December 7, 1963, pp. 63–128.

[54] Susan Black, pp. 63–128.

[55] Federal Bureau of Investigation (1971), pp. 26, 28.

[56] Federal Bureau of Investigation (1973), p. 28.

[57] Irwin Schepses, "Boys Who Steal Cars," *Federal Probation*, vol. 25, no. 1, p. 62, 1961.

[58] William W. Wattenberg and James Balistrieri, "Automobile Theft: A 'Favored-Group' Delinquency," *American Journal of Sociology*, vol. 57, no. 6, p. 579, May 1952.

[59] Leonard D. Savitz, "Automobile Theft," *Journal of Criminal Law, Criminology and Police Science*, vol. 50, p. 142, 1959–60.

[60] Federal Bureau of Investigation (1973), pp. 23–26.

[61] Federal Bureau of Investigation (1973), pp. 131, 134.

[62] Clairette P. Armstrong, *660 Runaway Boys, Why Boys Desert Their Homes*, Richard G. Badger, Boston, 1932, pp. 170–80.

[63] Department of Health, Education, and Welfare, Office of Youth Development, *Youth Reporter*, May 1975 (Publication OHD/OYD 75–26030).

[64] Louise E. Homer, "Community-based Resources for Runaway Girls," *Social Casework*, vol. 54, no. 8, p. 474, 1973.

[65] Louise E. Homer, p. 477.

[66] Louise E. Homer, pp. 475, 479.

[67] Louise E. Homer, p. 477.

[68] Clairette P. Armstrong, p. 148.

[69] M. C. Howell et al., "Reminiscences of Runaway Adolescents," *American Journal of Orthopsychiatry*, vol. 43, no. 5, pp. 851–853, October 1973.

[70] Nancy B. Green and T. C. Esselstyn, "The Beyond Control Girl," *Juvenile Justice*, vol. 23, pp. 13–19, November 1972.

[71] Nancy B. Green and T. C. Esselstyn, pp. 13–19.

[72] Bernard Rosenberg and Harry Silverstein, *The Varieties of Experience*, Blaisdell, Waltham, Mass., p. 63, 1969.

[73] Albert J. Reiss, "Sex Offenses: The Marginal Status of the Adolescent," *Law and Contemporary Problems*, vol. 25, no. 2, p. 312, Spring 1960.

[74] Albert J. Reiss, p. 314.

[75] Henry Miller, "On Hanging Loose and Loving: The Dilemma of Present Youth," *Journal of Social Issues*, vol. 27, no. 3, pp. 41, 42, 46, 1971.

Delinquents, Police, and Detention

The police have an important and complex role in the control and prevention of delinquency. For control, it requires that a police officer

- Exercise great restraint in apprehending a delinquent.
- Use very sound judgment in choosing the most appropriate of the several possible dispositions of each case.

Similarly, for preventive work, an officer must

- Befriend the youngsters on the street.
- Divert their energies to lawful activities.
- Generate, in the youngsters, a respect for the law.

For both control and preventive work, the police officer needs a generic ability and skills in the area of *human relationships*.

POLICE-JUVENILE ENCOUNTERS

Police encounters with youths are crucial. A youth being questioned by a police officer may already be on the way to becoming a delinquent. However, whether the youngster actually does become one depends to a large extent on the officer's attitude.

> A patrol officer may suspect that a crime has happened or is about to happen. Or he may believe the juvenile's conduct is offensive, insolent, or in some other way improper. On such occasions, the policeman has a relatively great range of choices. He can pass by. He can stop for a few words of general banter. He can ask the juveniles their names, where they live, where they are going. He can question them about what has been happening in the neighborhood. He can search them, order them to disperse or move on. . . . He can send or take them home,

where he may warn their parents to keep them off the street.[1]

A police encounter may become a historic event in the destiny of a youth. With the prevailing antagonism against the police, an unduly harsh police officer can further harden the youth's anti-police attitudes. The police officer's attitude is influenced by several personal and situational factors: background, training for youth problems, past experiences with delinquent youth, the orientation of the police department, and, perhaps most important, the youth's demeanor. An angry retort, a heated comment, or a defiant attitude on the part of the youth will not be of help. It may evoke harshness from the police officer.

A recent study has shown that most police work with juveniles stems from citizen complaints. Of a total of 281 juvenile-police encounters studied, 72 percent were citizen initiated. Only 28 percent were initiated by police on patrol. In view of this evidence, police work with juveniles should be regarded more as a response to citizen requests than as being initiated by the police themselves.[2]

Encounters with Gang Members

Piliavin spent 18 months observing and interviewing police officers and juvenile officers on daily patrols in Oakland and San Francisco. Werthman collected data on gang members in a series of taped interviews with fifty-six core members of eleven delinquent gangs and jacket clubs. Among other observations, they noticed that the gangs develop territorial claims to the streets on which they "hang around," and where they perform most of their daily activities.

> Activities such as poker games, arguments, lovemaking, drinking wine, and serious reading of comic books and newspapers are considered uniquely appropriate in this [street] setting. As a rule, gang members use street corners for behavior that most ordinary adolescents would confine to a house or a car.[3]

The patrol officer whose beat is on the same street also lays claim to the territory. With this duality of claims, there are occasional territorial disputes. Most often, though, there are tacit compromises between the gang members and the patrol officer on duty. Sometimes, the local community is willing to indulge the gang members to an extent. Then the patrol officer will usually overlook some disorderly and even rowdy behavior on the street, as long as the gang members stay within limits and live by their own code. If they exceed their limits, then the officer intervenes to remind the gang members of the violation. If they stray toward a neighboring hostile territory, then the officer asks them to return to their home territory. There is always a possibility of a fight in the "enemy" territory, and both the gang and the patrol officer know it.

Both parties recognize that the police officer must maintain order—which is in the best interest of the gang members and other residents. "A 'good cop' must try to order the life of an ethnic lower-class community from within by holding people such as gang boys to their own ideals, however little these ideals may be reflected in behavior."[4] Similarly, a good juvenile officer is not a trouble raiser, but rather a moderator, an arbitrator trusted by different sections of the community.

Many confessions are made to juvenile officers, and they carry many secrets. They use their contacts and all available information to solve crimes. For instance, by reviewing carefully the lists of previous offenders and their offenses, the juvenile officer may, at times, find a clue to the identity of an offender in a particularly troublesome case. Juvenile officers also make their own lists. The patrol officer also looks for more visible indicators of potential problems such as a youth's dress, companion, marital status, and means of support.[5] Such careful scrutiny may or may not be justified.

Police Disposition

The police have wide discretion in the disposition of juvenile cases. A police officer will often simply talk with a juvenile on the street, and then dismiss the youth with a verbal warning. Such contacts are casual and brief. In other cases, the arresting officer or juvenile specialist may want to do some further questioning, or to check the youth's records. The officer may then take the youth to the station house. Even when a youth has been taken into custody for a relatively serious offense, the police can choose any one of a large variety of dispositions.

> The dispositions available to the police range from outright release, usually to the parents, to referral to the juvenile court. Court referral may mean citation, filing of a complaint, or physical removal of the child to detention awaiting formal ac-

tion. Between those extremes are referral to community resources selected by the officer and station adjustment, by which is meant the juvenile's release on one or more conditions. The term station adjustment, as used here, implies an effort by the police to control and change the juvenile's behavior.[6]

In some police departments, when station adjustment is under consideration, informal hearings are scheduled. Police departments have been advised to have written standards for release and for referral under station adjustment, in the form of a manual for the guidance of their youth divisions. Station adjustment can result in a youth's "release with reprimand, imposition of direct sanction, referral to a social service or similar community resource, or referral to the court."[7]

Like casual police-juvenile contacts on the street, station adjustment is affected by several sociopersonal and situational factors. They include the present offense, past delinquent history, status of the juvenile as a probationer or parolee, and the juvenile's affiliation with a gang, reputation in the community, and demeanor. The Task Force Report on Juvenile Delinquency and Youth Crime states:

> Another imponderable is demeanor—the juvenile's behavior and apparent attitude towards the police. By policy a denial of involvement requires a court referral in some jurisdictions. Some police officers seem to feel that a denial of guilt or a defiant attitude indicates an uncooperative youth, one who will not be amenable to treatment. Such a youth is considered a greater risk to the community if released, and police prefer to have that judgment made by the court. A similar rationale may account for referrals of juveniles whose parents are defensive about their misbehavior or resent police intrusions. Some experienced juvenile specialists, in fact, regard the parents' attitude as more significant than the child's.[8]

The demeanor of the apprehended juvenile is considered to be a major determinant in 50 to 60 percent of the juvenile cases. Cooperation with the police is positively associated with admonishment and release (the least severe disposition), and an uncooperative attitude is markedly associated with arrest (the most severe disposition).[9] The relationship is mutual: respect begets respect. While delinquency is often a product of social judgment made by the police officer, the youth's own behavior contributes to that judgment.

When station adjustment is the course of action, the police can impose any reasonable condition, such as perfect school attendance, job training, staying away from a gang, or some sort of curfew. This practice of stringent though informal discipline is called *grounding* in Kansas City. The youth must dress conventionally and study at home for a minimum prescribed period each day. These conditions are gradually relaxed. A high degree of success is claimed for this program.[10]

A large majority of apprehended juveniles are diverted away from the juvenile justice system through alternative dispositions made by the police department. The Task Force on Delinquency and Youth Crime reports two large cities where, in 1965, 66 to 70 percent of the official police contacts with juveniles were handled by station adjustment. That is, the disposition was made at the level of the police department, without formally referring the case to a juvenile court. Nationally, such intradepartmental handling by police has been reported to occur in 45 to 50 percent of all juvenile contacts. This includes station adjustment, even for offenses as serious as involuntary manslaughter, rape, serious assault and battery, armed robbery, burglary, and other felonies.[11] Since this extensive pre-judicial disposition of cases necessitates the collection of various kinds of information, the President's Commission on Crime of 1967 recommends the temporary employment of case aides.

> In cases where information on the child is needed, it should be sought through home visits as well as from official records, and the police should be aided, or replaced, by paid case aides drawn from the neighborhood within the police district and selected for their knowledge of the community and their ability to communicate easily with juveniles and their families.[12]

The commission has further recommended that the police should make use of the youth services bureau for appropriate services and thus restrict direct referral to juvenile courts.

Analyzing the police records in four communities, Goldman found very wide variations in the rates of arrest and court appearances in these communities. He found that these variations reflected varying relations between the police and the community. In general, the police respond to the community's attitude to delinquency. Where there is an impersonal relationship between the police and the public, the court referral rate is high and indiscriminate. On the other hand, where there is a personal, face-to-face relationship between the police and the public, the court referral rate is low, and there is more discrimination with respect to the juvenile's sex, race, and seriousness of offense.

The differential selection of offenders for official action is also influenced by the attitude of the police officer toward the offender, the juvenile court, and the role of a police officer. An officer's attitude toward different juvenile offenses is colored by his or her childhood and career experiences. A high degree of criminal sophistication, evidenced when a juvenile uses burglar tools, criminal jargon, a gun, or planning or premeditation, is generally considered an immediate cause for court referral. Police officers view the juvenile courts unfavorably if the courts are unfair to the police or overlenient with offenders. The disposition of cases is also affected by the pressure of political groups or other special interest groups.

JUVENILE INVESTIGATION UNITS

Some larger police departments have juvenile investigation units. In smaller departments, these juvenile duties may be assigned to a few officers, chosen because they show a special aptitude for working with youngsters. These special units are known by different names, the most popular being *juvenile aid bureau* and *youth aid bureau*.

The bureau staff should possess the special skills, training, and experience needed to handle juveniles. It should include women, to handle girls and small boys. Both experienced patrol officers who have performed well with juveniles and new recruits may be assigned to the bureau. Experienced officers who need formal education should take college courses, and recruits fresh from college should be given beat experience. Both groups should receive some inservice training. Pertinent college courses include criminology, juvenile delinquency, the philosophy of police work with children, interviewing, juvenile-police relations, and juvenile laws. The inservice training should include experience with arrest procedures, the updated special procedures of the juvenile court, the nature of the community, the history and general makeup of groups in the area, the laws of evidence, the maintenance of records, and the rights of children.

The juvenile aid bureau is responsible for most matters pertaining to juveniles: investigation and adjustment of cases, referral to the court, protection of children, frequent inspection of places that attract youth, and prevention of delinquency. If a patrol officer makes an arrest, the case should generally be handed over to a juvenile officer. Juvenile officers should be friendly but firm with arrested youths.

Juvenile aid bureaus have definitely improved police service to juveniles. One deputy commissioner of police listed several improvements which took place during the 6 years in which a bureau operated in his jurisdiction:

1. A very noticeable depreciation in recidivism.
2. A better identification of the pre-delinquent through prevention patrols, and prevention programs.
3. A marked improvement in the police-family relationships, resulting in better mutual respect.
4. The reduction of unnecessary petitioning, and the establishment of a more effective and sophisticated petitioning process.
5. A better understanding of the complex forces which are at work in juvenile delinquents from minority group homes.
6. The development of a more professional attitude between the police and related social agencies.
7. Last, but not least, a greater deterrent effect on youth than ever could not have been realized without J. A. B.'s specialized services.[13]

POLICE-JUVENILE RELATIONS

Search, seizure, arrest, and admonishment have their place in the law-and-order complex. However, lasting peace and order develop through an informal and friendly relationship among the police, the juveniles, and the community. For well-informed and better police work, better police-community relations are needed. An improved relationship is vital to the control and prevention of delinquency. The 1967 President's Commission on Crime was convinced that "if such subjects as the use of stop-and-frisk or police policies toward juveniles were openly and fully discussed by representatives of the police and the community, much misunderstanding and mutual antipathy could be avoided."[14] There has to be an open dialogue between the police and juveniles, juvenile gangs, their families, and other citizens' groups.

Community-Relations Machinery

The police and the community each have problems related to juvenile delinquency. For mutual understanding, and to stimulate action aimed at solving these problems, the police should have an active community-relations unit, and there should be an advisory committee at the community level. The President's Commission on Crime recommends the establishment of these two bodies.

Community relations must be both a staff and a line function. Police departments in all large communities should have community-relations machinery consisting of

- A headquarters unit that plans and supervises the department's community-relations programs
- Precinct units, responsible to precinct commanders, that carry out the programs

Such machinery is a matter of the greatest importance in any community that *has a substantial minority population.*

There should be a citizens' advisory committee in each police precinct in a minority-group neighborhood. The committee should meet regularly with police officials to work out solutions to problems of conflict between the police and the community. It is crucial that the committee represent all parts of the community, including those elements who are critical or aggrieved.[15]

The headquarters community-relations unit should be commanded by a high-ranking experienced officer. This officer should be responsible directly to the chief, and should sit on the departmental policymaking board. The unit should conduct continuing research into citizens' attitudes toward, or conflicts with, the police; it should evaluate the department's performance in the light of this research. It should plan and supervise the work of the precinct units, and formulate the community-relations responsibilities and duties of all the department's officers and officials.[16]

The Task Force Report on Police recommends that community-relations officers be assigned to precinct and to special squads. Preferably, the precinct community-relations officer should have staff responsibility to the precinct commander. The object is to ensure that community relations permeates every aspect of police activity.[17]

Most of the community-relations effort will be focused on the prevention and control of juvenile delinquency. (Thus, the community-relations unit and the juvenile aid bureau have a lot in common. They will often find themselves supplementing each other's work.) Most police programs in the area of community relations aim at befriending the community and its juveniles. Naturally, during this process, the parties concerned come to know each other better. This, in turn, leads to an improved police image in the community, promotes public understanding of the police role, and thus generates more respect for law. The police get more support from the community in the solution of crime, control of riots, and prevention of delinquency and crime.

Police Efforts

School children make up the most suitable population with which to start such a program. Police officers have often been guest lecturers at public schools. Now, though, uniformed officers have, at some schools, assumed full-time faculty status or have become counselors. Recent police efforts to improve the attitude of junior high school students toward law and law enforcement have met with some success.

From 1965 to 1968, Portune did a study, known as the Cincinnati Police-Juvenile Attitude Project, with 1000 junior high school students. He administered the attitude-toward-police scale to all the students, and then split them into two groups—an experimental group and a well-matched control group. The experimental group were given special instruction on law and law enforcement in their social studies curriculum. After 6 weeks of instruction, the experimental group showed a significant change in a favorable direction, while the control group showed no change. Portune concludes: "Hopefully, the largest and quickest gains can be made between the ages of twelve and sixteen, between the time the American youth becomes an individual personality and the time he reaches the age of overt activism."[18]

A few other school studies showed favorable results. In an attempt to reduce alienation between youth and the police, the Michigan Department of State Police has, for several years, operated a police-school liaison program. In this program, a police officer serves as an unofficial counselor to students and as a resource person, while maintaining his or her primary identification as a law enforcement officer.

Portune lists the following standard police programs that influence youth attitudes when they are designed to be pleasant, stimulating, and rewarding for the youngsters involved:

1. Bicycle safety inspection
2. Traffic safety programs
3. Self-defense programs
4. Police athletic leagues
5. Junior police organizations
6. Police-youth discussion groups
7. Security assignments at dances and athletic events
8. Field trips by youth to police centers[19]

The central theme in all these programs is to promote interaction between youth and the law enforcer, and thus to generate among youth a respectful attitude toward law. The police athletic league (PAL) program has been singularly successful throughout the nation. Youth-police athletic meets always have some friendly carryover affect to street encounters. Junior police organizations invite youths to voluntarily participate in some police activities. Even the hiring and paying of youths as an auxiliary force has proved to be worth much more than its cost in dollars. During the race riots of the 1960s, "youth patrols" entered the riot-torn areas, dispersed crowds, and asked the rioters to "cool it." These "Teens-on-Patrol" were not armed, of course, but they provided good support for the police.[20]

Citizens' Advisory Committees

A police department can feel the pulse of the community through neighborhood advisory committees. These committees also afford affected groups (youths and minorities) an opportunity to air their grievances, provided such groups are properly represented. Citizens' committees can also serve as a bridge between the police and the community.

Citizens' committees have had an erratic history. They did not work effectively for many years, because of half-hearted cooperation from the police and the lack of representation of ordinary citizens. It is very important that the segments of society that are in conflict with the police are represented on these committees. New York City has precinct youth councils, with adequate representation of youth from minority groups.

The police need to keep avenues of communication open with the kinds of people who harbor the greatest hostility toward them, who most need an escape valve for their antagonisms, real or imagined, and who have the most to say about police practices on the street. This is important not only to influence these people, but also to give the department an accurate picture of the attitudes of persons on the street. All too often, community relations units do not have this knowledge and therefore cannot realistically plan or program for meeting community problems.

Persons who are hostile may be argumentative, disruptive, or otherwise difficult to deal with. Allegations may be made which are, or which appear to be, radical or irresponsible. However, this free discussion allows the committees to become vehicles for meeting conflict head-on in a controlled forum. The possibility of unpleasantness at a meeting is obviously preferable to leaving these confrontations to the streets.

Such meetings do have the potential for dispelling myths and pointing up problems about police practices. But those attending need to have confidence that they will get honest answers to such urgent questions as: Under what circumstances are Negroes stopped in white neighborhoods? Why are late strollers stopped so often for questioning? Why are juveniles told to move on? How are areas selected for saturation patrols? Complaints, whether or not they have basis, should be solicited and seriously considered; for as long as they are expressed in rumors, they will create friction. Relatively high-ranking officers should be present to give authoritative answers and to take steps to alleviate abuses when this is necessary.[21]

It is a sad fact that hard-core delinquents do not care to belong to such committees, and they do not attend the meetings. They have to be reached individually, on the street.

One viewpoint holds that the police should leave social work to the social workers, and they should concentrate more fully on activities that are directly related to combating crime. However, this viewpoint seems to be a minority one. A commission survey of police officers found that over 65 percent believe that juvenile officers should try to find jobs for older juveniles who come to their attention. Moreover, 43 percent of the officers thought that what they liked most about police work was the "feeling that comes from helping people." And 70 percent placed this feeling among their top three sources of job satisfaction.[22] In this context, an English author says: "The friendliness, confidence, respect, trust and affection that they receive from the people are almost the sole basis of the power and efficiency of the police of Britain."[23]

TEMPORARY DETENTION

Juveniles arrested for minor offenses can be released to their families or to foster homes. A juvenile who does not have a suitable home to go to may be lodged temporarily in a *shelter*. Dependent and neglected children are generally sent to shelters, as are suspected delinquents who do not require secure custody. Delinquents who have committed serious offenses, and who cannot be released without endangering the community or their own safety, have to be detained securely. Pending court disposition, the most reasonable place in which to detain these delinquents temporarily is the *juvenile detention home*. Since not every county has a juvenile detention home, a juvenile is quite often taken to a *local jail*. Statutory provisions require that juveniles be kept separate from adult detainees. Detention decisions are made by the juvenile court. However, in an emergency the police can hold a juvenile in a *police lockup* for up to 24 hours if the youth is arrested on a weekday or 48 hours or so if the youth is arrested during the early part of the weekend pending the receipt of court orders. Brief descriptions of these detention arrangements are given below.

Police Lockup and Local Jail

Children cannot be detained by the police for more than 48 hours. Police departments are advised to resort to lockup only when absolutely essential, and to keep the detention period to the minimum. A county or city jail is no place for juveniles. If juveniles must be temporarily committed to a jail for holding or under judicial order, they definitely must be segregated and constantly supervised. The California Welfare and Institutions Code requires the youth authority to conduct an annual inspection of each jail or lockup that was used to confine any minor under the age of 18 for more than 24 hours. If a jail falls short of the minimum jail standards, the youth authority can declare that jail unsuitable for the confinement of minors until the unsuitable conditions are remedied.[24]

It is generally recognized that jail confinement can be psychologically destructive. For this reason, children under 14 years of age are not normally jailed. However, because of the utter lack of alternatives in many jurisdictions, many juveniles are confined to jails temporarily. "Children are also placed in makeshift detention facilities which are virtually child jails. These so-called detention homes often consist of a barred room in a county court house, or home for the aged, or in other institutions."[25]

Juvenile Detention Center

The juvenile detention center is, in some ways, the counterpart of the local jail in the adult criminal justice system. The difference is that there are fewer juvenile detention centers than local jails. Not every county has enough juvenile detention cases to justify having a juvenile detention center. Since these institutions are quite expensive, only a big county can operate one independently. However, several smaller counties can group themselves together to operate a joint juvenile detention center. It has been suggested that a population of 250,000 produces about 300 juvenile detention cases annually. This would justify the operation of a twelve- to fifteen-bed center for an average stay of 14 days.[26]

In 1971, there were 303 juvenile detention centers in the United States, almost all of them with facilities for holding both males and females. About half of them held fewer than twenty-five inmates; seventy-nine centers had populations of twenty-five to forty-nine inmates; and fifty centers had capacities of from fifty to ninety-nine children. The average daily population of all the detention centers was 12,186, and the average per capita operating expenditure was $7541 per inmate per year.

A majority of juvenile detention centers are administered by local rather than state governments. Most of the children held by local jurisdictions are placed in detention centers.[27] A study sponsored by the U.S. Department of Health, Education, and Welfare strongly recommends that regional juvenile detention care should be the responsibility of the state, and not of local jurisdictions. This recommendation is made on the basis of economics and the efficiency of service.[28]

Since the average length of stay of a juvenile in a center is only 11 days, the center staff should not be expected to devise an elaborate rehabilitative program. However, it is the responsibility of the staff to see that the detention experience is not destructive to the juvenile. Detention should not advance a child along the road to criminality. But, by the same token, juveniles arriving at a detention center are often willing to speak openly about their recent offenses. They may thus be amenable to counseling. Counselors or probation officers may be able to reach them, before they begin to defend their deviant behavior. During counseling sessions, the center staff must be careful not to infringe upon the juveniles' constitutional rights, as their cases will still be in the courts.

The center staff should be well trained, and paid according to their education and experience. The staff can be ably assisted by volunteers, some of whom could be professionals—trained teachers, counselors, social workers, psychologists, crafts instructors, athletic coaches, and clergymen. All vounteers should be approved by the advisory board of the center. The center should have referral arrangements with those social agencies in the community which might be of assistance to the juveniles. Even though a detention center itself cannot offer a long-term rehabilitative program, it can help to place the juveniles with social agencies that can render aid on a long-term basis.

The detention center has certain advantages over the training school. It is smaller in size in most cases, and it is located much closer to the community, quite often in the center of the community. Occasionally, the detention center and the juvenile court are located in the same building, along with the juvenile intake unit, the district attorney, and the public defender. This concentration of services expedites the disposition of cases and reduces the detention period. Juvenile Center, in Tulsa, Oklahoma, claims that this type of arrangement allows them to dispose of cases in an average period of 5 days.

The center should provide both inside and outside recreational areas, and a common area where boys and girls may spend some time together. Individual rooms should be pleasant, adequately furnished, and homelike, rather than cold and hostile.

Shelters

Youth shelters, like juvenile detention centers, provide temporary care for juveniles awaiting court disposition. In contrast to detention centers, however, shelters are not primarily designed for incarceration. They usually are not physically restrictive. Shelters supply broad child welfare services, for dependent and neglected children as well as suspected delinquents.

According to the 1971 national survey, there were only 18 shelters, with a population of 363 children, in the United States. One-third of the residents were females, and the average length of stay was 20 days. Thus, shelters provide only temporary protection and serve only a very small population. At the time of the census, public shelters held less than 1 percent of all persons being held in public juvenile facilities.[29]

Most of the children lodged in shelters actually do need shelter. They have been abandoned, neglected, mistreated, or sexually exploited. In some cases, their families are not willing to receive and accept them; in other cases, juvenile authorities are unwilling to send these children back to parents who may be unfit to care for them. Unlike detention centers, shelters are noncustodial. Being open institutions, they should have more interaction with the community. Children residing in shelters should be able to continue to attend school without undue interruption.

SUMMARY

The police officer has a vital role in the prevention of delinquency and the control of delinquents. One important skill that a police officer must use in encounters with juveniles on the street is the ability to relate to youth. Unduly harsh handling of delinquents can increase, rather than control, the incidence of delinquency. The officer must use professional discretion in determining, at the time, whether or not to consider an act as delinquent.

The officer's discretion is influenced by several factors, the most important of which is the demeanor of the juvenile. Defiance on the part of the suspected delinquent, or a lack of cooperation from parents, will naturally have an adverse effect. The National Advisory Commission on Criminal Justice Standards and Goals has set a number of police standards. Given below is Standard 9.5, concerned with juvenile operations.

The chief executive of every police agency immediately should develop written policy governing his agency's involvement in the detection, deterrence, and prevention of delinquent behavior and juvenile crime.

1. Every police agency should provide all its police officers with specific training in preventing delinquent behavior and juvenile crime.

2. Every police agency should cooperate actively with other agencies and organizations, public and private, in order to employ all available resources to detect and deter delinquent behavior and combat juvenile crime.

3. Every police agency should establish in cooperation with courts written policies and procedures governing agency action in juvenile matters. The policies and procedures should stipulate at least:

a. The specific form of agency cooperation with other governmental agencies concerned with delinquent behavior, abandonment, neglect, and juvenile crime;

b. The specific form of agency cooperation with nongovernmental agencies and organizations where assistance in juvenile matters may be obtained;

c. The procedures for release of juveniles into parental custody; and

d. The procedures for the detention of juveniles.

4. Every police agency having more than 15 employees should establish juvenile investigation capabilities.

a. The specific duties and responsibilities of these positions should be based upon the particular juvenile problems within the community.

b. The juvenile specialists, besides concentrating on law enforcement as related to juveniles, should provide support and coordination of all community efforts for the benefit of juveniles.

5. Every police agency having more than 75 employees should establish a juvenile investigation unit, and every smaller police agency should establish a juvenile investigation unit if community conditions warrant. This unit:

a. Should be assigned responsibility for conducting as many juvenile investigations as practicable, assisting field officers in juvenile matters, and maintaining liaison with other agencies and organizations interested in juvenile matters; and

b. Should be functionally decentralized to the most effective command level.[30]

The staff of the juvenile investigation unit should have the special training needed to deal with juveniles. Police departments that have used juvenile investigation units are happy with the success of these units. A meaningful juvenile-police relationship is essential to delinquency prevention and reduction. The police department should have a community-relations unit in its structure, should invite citizens' advisory committees to engage in a continuing dialogue, and should solicit mutual cooperation. The police should also promote activities that involve the participation of both youth and the police.

When youths are apprehended but cannot be released to their families immediately, they may have to be lodged temporarily in a youth shelter (or in a juvenile detention center, if secure custody is required). The role of the police in intake and detention is prescribed by the National Advisory Commission on Criminal Justice Standards and Goals in Standard 8.1, as follows:

> Each juvenile court jurisdiction immediately should take the leadership in working out with local police agencies policies and procedures governing the discretionary diversion authority of police officers and separating police officers from the detention decision in dealing with juveniles.
>
> **1.** Police agencies should establish written policies and guidelines to support police discretionary authority, at the point of first contact as well as at the police station, to divert juveniles to alternative community-based programs and human resource agencies outside the juvenile justice system, when the safety of the community is not jeopardized. Disposition may include:
> *a.* Release on the basis of unfounded charges.
> *b.* Referral to parents (warning and release).
> *c.* Referral to social agencies.
> *d.* Referral to juvenile court intake services.
> **2.** Police should not have discretionary authority to make detention decisions. This responsibility rests with the court, which should assume control over admissions on a 24-hour basis.

When police have taken custody of a minor, and prior to disposition under Paragraph 2 above, the following guidelines should be observed.

1. Under the provisions of Gault and Miranda, police should first warn juveniles of their right to counsel and the right to remain silent while under custodial questioning.

2. The second act after apprehending a minor should be the notification of his parents.

3. Extrajudicial statements to police or court officers not made in the presence of parents or counsel should be inadmissible in court.

4. Juveniles should not be fingerprinted or photographed or otherwise routed through the usual adult booking process.

5. Juvenile records should be maintained physically separate from adult case records.[31]

Discussion Questions

1. If police discretion is so crucial in dealing with juveniles, what kind of people would you want as police officers? What kind of inservice training should they have?
2. What are some of the pressures under which a patrol officer works on the street?
3. Describe some of the cooperative police programs in effect at the high school in your community. How could you improve those programs if you were working with the police department?
4. Statistics show that most delinquent girls are not much of a danger to their community. Why, then, should they be detained in juvenile detention centers pending the disposition of their cases?
5. What kind of programs should detention centers offer, in view of the fact that the average stay in a shelter or detention center is only 2 to 3 weeks?

Glossary

Case Aide Assistant to the caseworker. A case aide may collect information on the juvenile's family, school, and peers, and relay this to the caseworker. A probation aide may help the probation officer in a similar way.

Citation An order or summons notifying or directing a defendant to appear before a competent authority.

Community-Relations Unit A managerial section which attempts to promote understanding and cooperation between the agency unit and the community.

Disposition (of Cases) A decision made by a lawful authority which fulfills the ends of justice by correcting a wrong done, settling a dispute or conflict between parties, and prescribing a course of treatment for the convicted person.

Incarceration The imprisonment of a person in a security institution.

Jail An institution generally holding persons who are undergoing their trial without bail. It also holds convicted offenders who are sentenced to short terms of imprisonment up to one year.

Jurisdiction (of a Person, Group, Agency, Institution) The legal powers vested in a certain person, body, or agency to govern, legislate, administer law, act, or exercise lawful authority.

Jurisdiction (of Territory) The geographical limits or territory within which any particular power may be exercised.

Juvenile Intake Unit A department, generally organized under the juvenile court, to receive and screen all children and youths referred to the court. This unit tries to divert as many youngsters as possible away from the juvenile justice system.

Juvenile Officer The police officer who works with the juvenile aid bureau.

Police Encounter Initial interaction between the police officer and the person who is stopped by the former for questioning.

Police Officer The patrol officer who is in direct contact with the youth in the street.

Precinct A subdivision of a larger territory, usually established for governmental, administrative, or police purposes.

Pre-judicial Disposition Determination of a juvenile case without referring the case to a juvenile court.

Reprimand A public and formal expression of criticism or disapproval administered to an offender by a competent authority.

Self Incrimination The charging of oneself with a crime.

Station Adjustment Informal disposition of a juvenile case at the level of the police department, without formally referring the case to a juvenile court.

Footnotes

[1] President's Commission on Crime, *The Challenge of Crime in a Free Society*, U.S. Government Printing Office, Washington, D.C., 1967, p. 78.

[2] National Advisory Commission on Criminal Justice Standards and Goals, *Corrections*, U.S. Government Printing Office, Washington, D.C., 1973, p. 249.

[3] Carl Werthman and Irving Piliavin, "Gang Members and the Police," in David J. Bordua, editor, *The Police*, Wiley, New York, 1967, p. 58.

[4] Carl Werthman and Irving Piliavin, p. 66.

[5] Carl Werthman and Irving Piliavin, pp. 78–87.

[6] President's Commission on Crime, *Task Force Report: Juvenile Delinquency and Youth Crime*, U.S. Government Printing Office, Washington, D.C., 1967, p. 12.

[7] President's Commission on Crime, p. 13.

[8] President's Commission on Crime, p. 13.

[9] President's Commission on Crime, p. 12.

[10] President's Commission on Crime, p. 13.

[11] President's Commission on Crime, p. 12.

[12] President's Commission on Crime, *The Challenge of Crime in a Free Society*, p. 82.

[13] John P. Finnerty, "Juvenile Aid Bureau—They Really Work," in Dan G. Pursuit et al., editors, *Police Programs for Preventing Crime and Delinquency*, Charles C Thomas, Springfield, Ill., 1972, p. 185.

[14] President's Commission on Crime, *The Challenge of Crime in a Free Society*, p. 101.

[15] President's Commission on Crime, pp. 100–101.

[16] President's Commission on Crime, p. 101.

[17] President's Commission on Crime, *Task Force Report: The Police*, U.S. Government Printing Office, Washington, D.C., 1967, passim pp. 151–152.

[18] Robert Portune, *Changing Adolescent Attitudes Toward Police*, W. H. Anderson, Cincinnati, 1971, p. viii.

[19] Robert Portune, p. 71.

[20] Robert Portune, pp. 85–86.

[21] President's Commission on Crime, p. 157.

[22] President's Commission on Crime, p. 162.

[23] Charles Reith, *A Short History of the British Police*, Oxford University Press, Fair Lawn, N.J., 1948, p. 112.

[24] State of California, *Minimum Jail Standards,* Board of Corrections, Sacramento, Calif., p. 25.

[25] U.S. Department of Health, Education, and Welfare, *State Responsibility for Juvenile Detention Care* (authored by John J. Downey), U.S. Government Printing Office, Washington, D.C., p. 2.

[26] U.S. Department of Health, Education, and Welfare, pp. 8–9.

[27] U.S. Department of Justice, Law Enforcement Assistance Administration, *Children in Custody: A Report on the Juvenile Detention and Correctional Facility Census of 1971,* U.S. Government Printing Office, Washington, D.C., 1974.

[28] U.S. Department of Health, Education, and Welfare, pp. 9–10.

[29] U.S. Department of Justice, p. 4.

[30] National Advisory Commission on Criminal Justice Standards and Goals, *Police,* U.S. Government Printing Office, Washington, D.C., 1973, p. 221.

[31] National Advisory Commission on Criminal Justice Standards and Goals, *Corrections,* p. 264.

The Juvenile Court

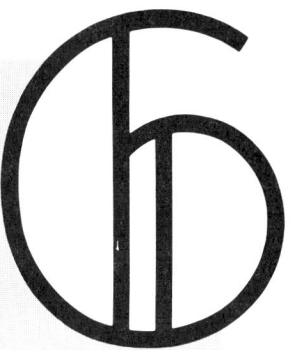

Juvenile courts are judicial tribunals that deal in special ways with young people's cases. Their importance can be judged from the fact that one in every nine children will be referred to a juvenile court before his or her eighteenth birthday. For boys alone, this ratio rises to one in every six. It is apparent that the responsiblity for meeting the problems of crime rests most heavily on these judicial institutions.

The juvenile court originated around the turn of the century with a philosophy and practices vastly different from those of the criminal courts. Juvenile courts substitute procedural informality for the adversary system, emphasize investigation of the juvenile's background in deciding upon dispositions, and rely heavily on the social sciences for both diagnosis and treatment.[1] Recently, juvenile courts have come under attack from the Supreme Court, on the basis that the courts were denying children their constitutional rights. Historic Supreme Court decisions have restricted the discretion of the juvenile courts, and thus have greatly altered the operation of those courts.

DEVELOPMENT OF THE IDEA OF A JUVENILE COURT[2]

The juvenile court owes its origin to several historic movements. Some believe it is a descendant of the English chancery court, which traditionally protects the property rights of children. When the English legal system was transplanted to the United States, the chancery court's activities were extended to include the protection of minors from personal as well as property injury.

Another opinion holds that the beginnings of the juvenile court were present in the English common law. Under the common law, a child under 7 years of age was incapable of felonious intent. A child between 7 and 14 years of age was assumed to be similarly incapable, unless it could be shown that the child understood the consequences of his or her actions. A somewhat different view of the court's origin is that the juvenile court is not a descendant of chancery, but rather was created by special statutes.

The nineteenth century was characterized by reforms in the treatment of both adult and juvenile offenders. Immigration and industrialization were attracting people to the cities by the thousands. The resulting overcrowding and disruption of family life led to increases in vice, crime, and all the other destructive influences of rapid urbanization. Truancy and delinquency rose rapidly. With a growing concern about environmental influences came the desire to rescue children and restore them to a healthful, useful life. This gave rise to the penitentiary, reformatory, and parole for adult offenders, along with the house of refuge, probation, and the juvenile court for the juvenile offender.

The humanitarian efforts of feminists, penologists, and philanthropists also helped in the birth of the juvenile court. Members of the Chicago Women's Club, Hull House Group, Catholic Visitation and Aid Society, and Chicago Bar Association worked actively to get a bill passed to authorize the first juvenile court in Illinois in 1899. By 1925, almost every state had juvenile courts. Today there is a juvenile court act in every American jurisdiction.

Although juvenile court practices differed widely from place to place, there were some common features. Hearings were supposed to be informal and nonpublic; records were confidential; a probation staff was appointed; and children were detained separately from adults. A new vocabulary symbolized the new order: *petition* instead of complaint, *summons* instead of warrant, *initial hearing* rather than arraignment, *finding of involvement* rather than conviction, and *disposition* instead of sentence. The physical surroundings were considered important too: They should seem less imposing than a courtroom, with the judge seated at a desk rather than behind a bench. This gave the judge a parental and sympathetic, but authoritative and sobering appearance.

The goals of the juvenile court were to investigate, diagnose, and prescribe treatment. The court was not to adjudicate guilt or fix blame. The offender's background was more important than the facts of a given incident. Lawyers were unnecessary. Adversary tactics were out of place, for the mutual aim was not to contest or object, but to determine the best treatment plan for the child.

PHILOSOPHY OF THE JUVENILE COURT

There seem to be three important parts to the philosophy of the juvenile court:

1. The state is the father of the children (parens patriae).
2. Working on the principle of parens patriae, the juvenile court acts in the best interests of the child.
3. While protecting the interests of the child, the juvenile court also safeguards society.

Parens Patriae

The concept of parens patriae has guided the juvenile courts ever since the inception of these courts in America. *Parens patriae,* a latin phrase, suggests that the state is the higher or ultimate parent of all children within its borders. Through this doctrine, in England, all English children are wards of the crown. A child who is mistreated or grossly neglected by his or her natural parents may be removed from the custody of the parents. The state then assumes guardianship of the child and provides the needed protection, care, and guidance. In America, the authority of parens patriae is vested in the juvenile court.

The Supreme Court pointed out that the doctrine of *parens patriae* does not assure children a "right to liberty," but merely promises them a "right to custody."

> The right of the state, as parens patriae, to deny to the child procedural rights available to his elders was elaborated by the assertion that a child, unlike an adult, has a right "not to liberty but to custody." He can be made to attorn to his parents, to go to school, etc. If his parents default in effectively performing their custodial functions—that is, if the child is "delinquent"—the state may intervene. In doing so, it does not deprive the child of any rights, because he has none. It merely provides the "custody" to which the child is entitled. On this basis, proceedings involving juveniles were described as "civil" not "criminal" and therefore not subject to the requirements which restrict the state when it seeks to deprive a person of his liberty.[3]

This custodial and protective function of parens patriae extended the court's jurisdiction to include persons in need of supervision (PINS) and minors in need of supervision (MINS).

Occasionally, a question arose about the wisdom of including these persons, who had committed no offense, along with delinquent children. But, because the juvenile court was supposed to be the protector of all children, it continued to handle these children along with delinquent children.

There were some doubts and misgivings about placing delinquents and nondelinquents together and giving them more or less the same treatment. It was most irritating to the nondelinquent children, who protested against the "punitive" treatment given them when they were charged with no offense. In consequence, some states revised their juvenile court laws to distinguish between juvenile delinquents and PINS, and yet retain the jurisdiction of the court over both categories.

The New York Family Court Act (1963) discriminates between the delinquent and a noncriminal misbehavior:

> a) "Juvenile delinquent" means a person over seven and less than 16 years of age who does any act which, if done by an adult, constitutes a crime.
> b) "Persons in need of supervision" means a male less than 16 years of age and a female less than 18 years of age who is an habitual truant or who is incorrigible, ungovernable or habitually disobedient and beyond the lawful control of parent or other lawful authority.[4]

The Illinois Juvenile Court Act (1966) created the category of "minor otherwise in need of supervision." (The "otherwise" means for reasons other than delinquency. Delinquency is defined as a violation or attempted violation of a federal or state law, municipal ordinance, or court order.)

> Those otherwise in need of supervision include (a) any minor under 18 years of age who is beyond the control of parents, guardian, or other custodian; and (b) any minor subject to compulsory school attendance who is habitually truant from school.[5]

The category of "neglected minor" (also a "person in need of supervision") includes, besides those children endangered by parental inattention or abandonment, "any minor under 18 years of age . . . whose environment is injurious to his welfare or whose behavior is injurious to his own welfare or that of others."

Present-day feelings are that PINS and MINS should not be

referred to juvenile courts at all. The National Advisory Commission on Criminal Justice Standards and Goals has given a clear mandate: "Under no circumstances should children be referred to court for behavior that would not bring them before the law if they were adults."[6] This standard, when implemented, will erode the custodial or preventive aspect of parens patriae. It will, incidentally, also cut the courts' work load in half.

Best Interest of the Child

The juvenile courts act in the best interest of the child. In the disposition of a case, the child's best interest is the supreme consideration. Undeniably, some element of punishment or deterrence can be found in many decisions. However, much thought is given to the child's safety, care, well-being, improvement of physical and mental health, academic and vocational training, and healthy development of social attitudes.

Knowing that natural parents provide the most normal home for a child, the courts try their best to keep children with their parents. However, if the parents are incompetent, the child is sent to a foster home. If an adequate home that meets the child's needs is not available, the child is sent to a group home. In their decisions, the courts make every effort to see that the youth's schooling or vocational training is not interrupted. If necessary, the child is referred to appropriate agencies in the community.

The court's approach is remedial and rehabilitative. Realizing that a court appearance can be very stigmatizing for a youngster, the court tries to protect the youth's identity and delinquency record. When a child appears before the court several times, the court attempts to revise and redesign its dispositional plan to fit the child's circumstances, rather than "give up" on the child. If a court acts harshly at times, it is the harshness of a kind parent who disciplines the child in the child's best interest.

Protection of Society

Juvenile courts also protect the community through temporary detention of certain youths, transferring them to adult courts, or diverting them to nondestructive activities. The courts help families by bringing about compromises between delinquent children and their families. The courts resolve conflicts between youths and their school teachers. The courts provide some services under their own auspices, including diagnostic and treatment services. The courts also refer juveniles to other agencies and, in some cases, even buy services for the youths. Unlike adult courts, juvenile courts also become involved in prevention programs.

THE JUVENILE COURT IN OPERATION

According to the Task Force Report on Juvenile Delinquency and Youth Crime of 1967, there are approximately 2700 courts hearing children's cases. The structure of the juvenile court varies among—and even within—states. Relatively few are separate, independent courts. Most are part of a circuit, district, superior, county, common pleas, probate, or municipal court system. In a few jurisdictions, family courts have been established to deal with both children's and domestic relations cases.

Jurisdiction

The jurisdiction of the juvenile courts generally extends to cases of delinquency, neglect, and dependency. In addition, children's courts may deal with other types of actions involving children: adoption, termination of parental rights, appointment of a guardian, rescue of children from persons contributing to their delinquency, and nonsupport. In some states, major offenses such as capital crimes are excluded from juvenile court jurisdiction. In other states, the jurisdiction of the juvenile court is concurrent with that of the criminal court in more serious offenses. Only rarely are there written criteria to guide the judge in deciding whether or not to waive the juvenile court's jurisdiction in a particular case.[7] Many state statutes, before 1966, required no hearing or findings on the issue of waiver. This situation has since been ruled upon by the Supreme Court [in *Kent v. United States,* 383 U.S. 541 (1966), discussed later in this chapter].

The county is the geographical area served by most juvenile courts in the United States. However, the jurisdictional unit may also be a town, city, borough, or judicial district. If a single county cannot afford a separate juvenile court, two or three counties may combine to operate a joint juvenile court and related agencies. The county is the conventional unit of local government and of many private organizations. Its use as the

jurisdictional area for the court thus has obvious advan[...]
the coordination of the court's work with that of other agencies
interested in child welfare.[8]

Intake Services

The intake services screen cases referred to the juvenile court by the police and by public and private agencies. The object of the screening is to determine whether the court should take action in a given case or whether the matter should be referred elsewhere. The juvenile court intake is court-sanctioned and preadjudicatory. Even in cases diverted at intake, the court may maintain its followup and counseling functions.

In most states, probation officers do the intake processing; in other states, a specialized staff of *intake counselors* does the screening. The larger court systems have separate intake sections or departments with specially trained staffs. The smaller courts rely on primary screening by the police, schools, and other agencies.[9] According to the 1966 Children's Bureau statistics, more than half of all delinquency cases are disposed of without formal petition. Semiurban jurisdictions seem to rely more heavily than others on nonjudicial handling; 58 percent of their cases do not reach the court, as compared with 51 percent in urban jurisdictions and 40 percent in rural jurisdictions.[10]

Intake and Dispositional Choice

The options at intake include outright dismissal, referral to another community agency, informal supervision by the probation staff, detention, and filing of a petition. There is, thus, much room for the use of discretion on the part of the intake staff (and the possibility of misuse). Also, in the absence of written guidelines for the intake staff, their decisions may lack consistency and uniformity. This may be beneficial in the sense that each case is decided on its own merits, and there are no stereotyped decisions. But as the concept of parens patriac recedes in importance, pre-judicial dispositions will have to become more formalized. Otherwise, they could deprive many children of due process of law. The importance of formal guidelines in guarding against abuse is becoming more widely recognized. The new standards proposed by the National Commission on Juvenile Intake Services will be discussed later in this chapter.

Diagnostic Services, Informal Adjustment

Many times, the intake staff and the juvenile court require some sort of diagnostic services to help in finding a suitable disposition for a case. Evaluation tools generally include personality, aptitude, and intelligence tests and, in special cases, psychiatric or medical tests. If these services are not available in the juvenile diagnostic center, the court may have to purchase these services from other agencies. Occasionally, these tests may indicate that brain damage, schizophrenia, mental retardation, venereal infection, or speech or hearing difficulties have contributed to a child's delinquency.

Informality pervades most court activities: there are informal adjustment, informal probation, informal disposition, informal supervision, unofficial probation, counsel and advice, and consent decrees. These informal services are rendered to children without the filing of petitions, and with the consent of the parties concerned. In some jurisdictions, court referees periodically review informal decisions. A recent analysis has shown that approximately half of the cases handled informally were closed as successful—the children and their families experienced no further difficulties.[11]

Informal Probation

In cases considered suitable for such supervision, a probation officer can request that the court place the child under the officer's supervision for *informal probation*. The probation officer does not file a petition until after the child has had some informal treatment. If the child shows signs of improvement during the course of the informal probation, the case is closed. This saves the child the stigma of a delinquent record, as no formal petition was filed.

Opponents of informal probation object to the possibility of legal double jeopardy. That is, violation of the probation rules can result in a dual charge—the probation violation plus the original charge. The National Advisory Commission on Criminal Justice Standards and Goals has supported the idea of informal probation, provided the child's constitutional rights are protected and the informal probation does not exceed a reasonable limit. They also suggest that a petition on the original complaint should not be allowed after an agreement has been worked out with all parties involved.[12]

Consent Decrees

A consent decree is a formal order for casework supervision or treatment to be provided either by the court staff or by some other agency. It is negotiated by the court staff and approved by the judge with the consent of the parents and child. The consent decree provides an intermediate approach for cases too serious for informal handling but not grave enough for formal probation or institutionalization. It also helps to ease the case load of the court.

The consent decree serves to protect the public and the youngster, and eliminates the stigma associated with a finding of delinquency. There is no official pronouncement of delinquency, and the youth is not removed from his or her home.[13]

Probation Officer

The probation officer works closely with the juvenile court judge. The probation officer investigates the juvenile's all-important social history; serves at times as an intake counselor; presents the case in the court; helps write probation contracts; supervises and counsels youths; makes referrals; acts as a broker between the probationer and agencies in the community; writes progress reports; and reports back to the court. The probation officer is often asked to oversee juvenile detention centers, supervise youth shelters, and manage court-attached diagnostic and treatment centers (clinics, camps, halfway houses, and group homes). The officer's salary is seldom commensurate with this heavy load of responsibilities, so there is a high rate of probation staff turnover.[14]

Procedural Justice

Prompted by their original humanitarian philosophy, the juvenile courts tended to avoid the rigorous formalities of the criminal courts. The objective of the juvenile courts was to understand the children and help them adjust to themselves and their environment. Punishment for wrongdoing, the rationale of criminal law, was foreign to juvenile court philosophy. Hence, there was no need for the traditional criminal procedures designed to shield an accused innocent from punishment. These procedures were destructive to the child.

The juvenile courts were more interested in the pattern of prior behavior and social circumstances of the child than in the present offense. The proceedings were civil rather than criminal; they were addressed to the salvation rather than the punishment of the child. The courts therefore conducted hearings in an informal manner, paying little attention to due process of law. However, this philosophy came under attack, on the basis that the courts were not protecting the constitutional rights of juveniles. The reasons for this dissatisfaction with the original philosophy of the courts include the following:

1. The juvenile court is inclined to ignore the facts of a particular instance of misconduct. Instead, it decides cases on the basis of past conduct and other extraneous factors. A child deserves judicial consideration of the alleged facts, and should be allowed every opportunity to cross-examine witnesses and offer a defense. This becomes most important when the court might possibly intervene in the life of the juvenile by ruling in favor of detention.

2. Adjudication as a delinquent by the juvenile court stigmatizes a youth and is a disadvantage in several respects. The juvenile court, in an attempt to rehabilitate, could actually make the situation more difficult for a youth.

3. The efforts of the juvenile court have not been able to lead delinquents to the promised healthy and constructive life. Youths get neither regenerative treatment nor legal protection; they are losers on both counts.

4. Despite the juvenile court's good intentions, elements of deterrence, condemnation, and incapacitation are visible in decisions made by the court. Children punished by the juvenile court should not be deprived of due process of law. Also, the children do not see the all-powerful and arbitrary exercise of authority by judges and probation officers as an aid in their rehabilitation; they see this as coercion and punishment.

The Use of Evidence

It has been suggested that adjudication hearings and disposition proceedings should be kept separate from each other. The social history compiled by the probation officer and the intake counselors should not bias the adjudicatory hearing in any way.

The social history should be available to the judge at the disposition hearing. The child (and counsel) may be provided with the summary, but not with the rest of the report.[15]

Privacy and Confidentiality

Proponents of public scrutiny and openness in the juvenile court have questioned whether or not privacy and confidentiality should be maintained and, if so, to what extent. The Task Force on Juvenile Delinquency and Youth Crime maintains:

> Exclusion of the general public from the juvenile court hearing rests on the justification that a private hearing "contributes to a casework relationship, and avoidance of the spectacle of a public criminal trial." Communications between court and child tend to be distorted by the presence of large audiences. In many cases publicity tends itself to constitute a form of punishment.[16]

Most courts allow the press to attend juvenile proceedings and leave the reporting to the good sense of the press. Many newspapers handle news affecting juveniles very responsibly. They have developed their own code of ethics, which includes withholding the names of delinquents except in cases of major crimes.

The judge generally decides whether or not to release confidential information. There is evidence that many courts release information concerning juveniles to the military and to private employers. The Task Force Report on Juvenile Delinquency suggests that legal reports should be available only to official criminal justice agencies (police, courts, and corrections). Social reports often contain extremely personal information and investigators' subjective interpretations. They would be available only to probation departments, mental health clinics, and other social agencies dealing with the delinquent.[17]

Self Incrimination

Before the Gault decision in 1966, most courts had held that the constitutional privilege against self incrimination need not be available to the parties in juvenile proceedings, except where

168 Juvenile Delinquency

there was a possibility of criminal prosecution. The basis for this view was that, by definition, juvenile proceedings are not criminal proceedings. As we shall see later in this chapter, the Supreme Court held that a child has the right to remain silent, especially when facing commitment to a state institution.

Intake officers and youth services bureaus need to take statements if they are to make informed decisions on whether or not to file petitions. The New York Family Court Act provides that the information in such statements may not be admitted in evidence at an adjudicatory hearing.[18]

Trial by Jury

There are no jury trials in juvenile courts. To date, no one has asked that juvenile cases be tried by jury. A jury trial brings no advantage to the juvenile, but would bring the disadvantage of formality to the trial; whatever informality remains in the juvenile court would vanish. Juries are not very popular these days, even in adult criminal trials.

Appeal

Juvenile court dispositions are very rarely appealed. By and large, the juvenile court system has operated without appellate surveillance. Appeals improve the system in many ways by rectifying errors and injustices. Now that counsels are engaged, the number of appeals will probably increase. Since appeals are to be based on court records, court proceedings will have to be more carefully recorded.[19]

Detention

According to the Task Force Report on Juvenile Delinquency and Youth Crime, two-thirds of all juveniles apprehended in 1965 were admitted to detention facilities. The youths were held for periods ranging from a few hours to several days. The average length of stay was 12 days. The report recommends that temporary detention, pending a detention hearing, should be restricted to cases in which it is clearly necessary to protect the youth or the community. The law should require that a detention hearing be held within 48 hours of initial detention. Every effort should be made to find alternatives to detention. Parents and other responsible relatives should be located; group homes should be used for temporary detention, if feasible.[20]

Notice, Counsel

The right to be notified of the charge and the right to counsel will be discussed in the context of the Supreme Court decisions.

SUPREME COURT DECISIONS

For more than sixty-five years, the juvenile courts were unchallenged in their procedures. Then, in the middle 1960s, the juvenile courts received a severe jolt when the Supreme Court criticized their decisions as arbitrary and neglectful of due process of law. The courts were taken to task for depriving children of their constitutional rights and for failing to do anything to rehabilitate them. The Supreme Court decisions of the 1960s not only disparaged the parens patriae role of the juvenile courts, but also pointed out the ineffectiveness of the courts' decisions and the inefficiency of the entire juvenile justice system.

The Supreme Court advised the juvenile courts to give judicial procedures precedence over the parens patriae function. These procedures are the basis of American freedom; they are therapeutic if they are administered fairly. One would expect that, in a society like America, with its emphasis on freedom, the juvenile courts would be asked to exalt children's constitutional guarantees over their right to custody and protection. And the 1960s, being an era of civil rights, was the proper time for Supreme Court decisions such as those that follow.

Kent v. United States[21]

Kent, the petitioner, was arrested at the age of 16 in connection with charges of housebreaking, robbery, and rape. As a juvenile, he was subject to the exclusive jurisdiction of the District of Columbia Juvenile Court. However, that court could, after "full investigation," waive jurisdiction and remit him for trial to the U.S. District Court for the District of Columbia. The Juvenile Court did waive its jurisdiction over Kent and hand him over to the U.S. District Court for trial as an adult. The petitioner's counsel then filed a motion in the Juvenile Court. The motion requested, of the court,

1. A hearing on the question of waiver
2. Access to the Juvenile Court's social service file, which had been accumulated on petitioner during his probation for a prior offense

The social service file was an important document, as it was going to be used in consideration of the waiver.

The Juvenile Court did not rule on these motions. It entered an order waiving jurisdiction and noting that this was done after the required "full investigation." Kent was tried by the District Court and convicted as an adult on six counts of robbery and housebreaking. He was acquitted on two rape counts by reason of insanity. He was sentenced to serve 5 to 15 years on each of six counts, with a total of 30 to 90 years in prison.

The petitioner pled that the Juvenile Court procedure leading to waiver and the waiver order itself were invalid. The Supreme Court held that the Juvenile Court order waiving jurisdiction and remitting petitioner for trial in the District Court was invalid.[22] In lay terms, the court also held that the Juvenile Court's latitude in determining whether to waive jurisdiction is not without legal restraints. The juvenile court must satisfy the basic requirements of due process and fairness and must comply with the statutory requirement of "full investigation." The parens patriae philosophy of the juvenile court is not an invitation to procedural arbitrariness.

Morris A. Kent, Jr., first came under the authority of the Juvenile Court in 1959, at age 14, for several housebreakings. He was placed on probation and, during the probation supervision, court officials accumulated a social service file on Kent. In 1961, Kent entered the apartment of a woman. He took her wallet and raped her. Three days after this incident Kent was taken into custody by the police. Kent was 16 years old and, therefore, subject to the exclusive jurisdiction of the Juvenile Court. At police headquarters Kent admitted his involvement in the alleged offense. He was detained at the receiving home for almost a week. During this period, Kent's counsel arranged for his examination by two psychiatrists and a psychologist. Kent was certified to be a "victim of severe psychopathology" and was recommended for hospitalization for psychiatric observation.

Justice Fortas delivered the opinion of the Supreme Court. The judges observed that our system of law does not allow a result of such tremendous consequence to be reached without ceremony—without a hearing, without the effective assistance of counsel, without a statement of reasons.[23] The judges lamented the fact that the juvenile courts were unable to implement their philosophy of protection and rehabilitation, and that they did not give children their legal rights during trials. The children were getting a raw deal on both counts.

> There is much evidence that some juvenile courts lack the personnel, facilities and techniques to perform adequately as representatives of the State in a parens patriae capacity, at least with respect to children charged with law violation. There is evidence, in fact, that there may be grounds for concern that the child receives the worst of both worlds: that he receives neither the protections accorded to adults nor the solicitous care and regenerative treatment postulated for children.[24]

The Supreme Court also ruled that the social records of the child, relevant to waiver proceedings, must be made available to the child's counsel. The right to counsel is not enough; counsel must be given the opportunity to function effectively.

The Gault Case[25]

Briefly, the facts of this case are as follows: On June 8, 1964, Gerald F. Gault, age 15, and a friend, Ronald Lewis, were taken into custody by the Sheriff of Gila County, Arizona. The police action was taken as the result of a verbal complaint by the boys' neighbor, Mrs. Cook, concerning a telephone call made to her in which the caller or callers made lewd or indecent remarks. It was alleged that the contents of the call were of the irritatingly offensive, adolescent, sexual variety. At the time Gerald was picked up, his mother was at work and his father was out of town. On her return from work, Gerald's mother went to the detention home, where Deputy Probation Officer Flagg, who was also superintendent of the detention home, told Mrs. Gault "why

Jerry was there." The probation officer said that a hearing would be held in juvenile court the following day.

Officer Flagg filed a petition with the court on the hearing day. It was not served on the Gaults. The petition made no reference to any factual basis. It pled for a hearing and an order regarding "the care and custody of the said minor." Mrs. Cook, the complainant, was not present at the hearing. No one was sworn, and no transcript or recording was made. At a subsequent hearing on June 15, the judge committed Gerald to the state industrial school as a juvenile delinquent, "for the period of his minority" (that is, until age 21), unless sooner discharged by due process of law. Arizona law does not permit appeals in juvenile cases.

The use of vulgar, abusive, or obscene language in the presence of or hearing of woman or child is a misdemeanor according to the Arizona Criminal Code. The penalty specified in the criminal code, which would apply to an adult, is a fine of $5 to $50 or imprisonment for not more than 2 months. For the same offense, Gerald Gault (who was already under a 6-month probation order at the time of the alleged phone call) was ordered to be committed to an institution for a period of about 6 years.

In August, 1964, a petition for a writ of habeas corpus was filed with the Supreme Court of Arizona. It was dismissed. The Gaults took the matter to the Supreme Court of the United States, challenging the validity of the juvenile code of Arizona on its face or as applied in this case. They contended that, contrary to the due process clause of the Fourteenth Amendment, the juvenile was denied the following basic rights when he was taken from the custody of his parents and committed to a state institution:

1. Notice of the charges
2. Right to counsel
3. Right to confrontation and cross-examination
4. Privilege against self incrimination
5. Right to a transcript of the proceedings
6. Right to appellate review

While fully appreciating the historic intent, philosophy, and benevolent practices of the juvenile courts, the Supreme Court criticized the omission of due process of law. The judges stressed that procedure is an essential ingredient of law, and that only through due process is it possible for the truth to emerge. The Supreme Court noted that a juvenile court's unbridled discretion, however benevolently motivated, is frequently a poor substitute for principle and procedure. The Supreme Court incisively judged that the paternal advice of the juvenile court judge can be seen by a youth as very unfair when it is devoid of procedure. The judges emphasized the necessity for fairness, impartiality, and orderliness in juvenile court procedures. They felt that the essentials of due process could be more impressive and more therapeutic to youth than the paternal approach of the juvenile court.

Turning to the specific issues raised in this case, the judges gave the following rulings.

Notice of Charges The Supreme Court ruled that, to comply with due process requirements, notice of charges and hearings must be given sufficiently in advance of scheduled court proceedings so that a reasonable opportunity to prepare will be afforded, and it must "set forth the alleged misconduct with particularity."

Right to Counsel The appellants had charged that the juvenile court did not advise Gerald or his parents of their right to counsel. They also charged that the court proceeded with the hearing, the adjudication of delinquency, and the order of commitment in the absence of counsel for the child and his parents.

The juvenile court argued that "the parents and the probation officer may be relied upon to protect the infant's interests." The Supreme Court judges did not agree: If probation officers arrest a child, initiate proceedings, file the petition, and testify against the child, they cannot act as counsel for the child. According to the Supreme Court, a juvenile needs the assistance of counsel to cope with problems of law; to make skilled inquiry into the facts; to insist upon regularity within the proceedings; and to ascertain whether there is a defense and to prepare and submit it. The Supreme Court held that the assistance of counsel is essential for the determination of delinquency.

> We conclude that the Due Process Clause of the Fourteenth Amendment requires that in respect of proceedings to determine delinquency which may result in commitment to an institution in which the juvenile's freedom is curtailed, the child and his parents must be notified of the child's right to be

represented by counsel, retained by them, or if they are unable to afford counsel, that counsel will be appointed to represent the child.[26]

Confrontation, Self Incrimination, Cross-Examination The appellants complained that they were denied the rights of confrontation and cross-examination in the juvenile court hearings, and that the privilege against self incrimination was not observed. The juvenile court judge testified in the habeas corpus proceeding that Gerald admitted making "some of the lewd statements . . . [but not] any of the more serious lewd statements." There was conflict and uncertainty among the witnesses as to what Gerald did or did not admit. The Supreme Court observed that Gerald and his parents were not advised that he did not have to testify or make a statement, or that an incriminating statement might result in his commitment as a delinquent. The judges were not happy with the conditions under which Gerald made his partial confession.

The judges held that, in the absence of a valid confession, and in the absence of sworn testimony and the opportunity for cross-examination, an order for commitment to a state institution could not be sustained.

THE JUVENILE COURT AFTER THE GAULT DECISION

Many judges were slow to adopt the rulings of the Supreme Court in the Gault and Kent cases. Some judges did not care to read these decisions for 2 to 3 years. However, the mandates of the Supreme Court could not be ignored for long. The emphasis on fact-finding increased, and so did representation by counsel.[27] The reputation of the juvenile courts was somewhat tarnished when they were dubbed "kangaroo courts," but they emerged somewhat wiser. At this time, they must protect the children as their chief guardian, while observing all judicial and constitutional procedures.

THE COURT'S VULNERABILITY: EXTERNALLY[28]

In a consultant's paper written for the Task Force on Juvenile Delinquency and Youth Crime, Vinter perceives the juvenile court as a most vulnerable institution in the judicial system. Several forces and conditions affect the court's ability to achieve its potential. First, let us look at some of the external forces hampering the court in its functions.

Too Many Masters to Serve

The juvenile court has complex relationships with other organizations at both the local and state levels. In the words of Vinter:

> [The juvenile court's] basic mandates are defined by the legislature, its proceedings can be reviewed and supervised by higher courts, and its operations are partially subject to fiscal and administrative decisions of various agencies, such as state welfare departments. . . . Much of its financial support is provided or curtailed by local government; and the judge usually occupies his position by consent of the local electorate. . . . Both law and voter must be served by court performance.[29]

Inferior Status of the Court

The juvenile court does not enjoy a superior status in the hierarchy of courts. It is neither regarded well by lawyers nor respected highly by the welfare professions. Ambitious persons in these two professions do not aspire to judgeships in the juvenile courts. The court's low salaries and low esteem attract very few qualified personnel. Only devoted staff members stay with the court.

Too Many Demands

The juvenile court has to adjudicate according to juvenile statutes, yet ensure that none of the legal rights of the children are violated. The police, the schools, and other agencies in the community expect a judge to mete out exemplary punishments to delinquents and uphold public order. Yet the judge is also supposed to protect children and act in their best interest. "The court is expected simultaneously to preserve the institution of law, to enhance the legitimate interests of its clients, especially those of children, and to serve the welfare of the community while protecting public order."[30]

Court's Dependence on Outside Agencies

For case referrals, the juvenile court must depend upon several social agencies, such as welfare departments, children's aid societies, drug abuse centers, children's hospitals, psychiatric clinics, the YMCA, group homes, schools, and churches. This referral process involves the court in several reciprocal obligations. The referring agency may expect the juvenile court to consider its wishes in deciding the case. These mutual obligations could damage the judicial process and neutralize the doctrine of parens patriae.

THE COURT'S VULNERABILITY: INTERNALLY

The juvenile court attempts to be both a judicial and a service organization. This duality of roles is partially responsible for some of its internal problems.

Chronic State of Overload

There is an imbalance between the court's resources and the volume of cases it has to handle. Intake departments try to deflect and divert many cases to reduce the court's case load. Youths processed by the court present a wide range of problems, but the court does not have at its command the same range of dispositional alternatives.

Faulty Recording System

According to Vinter,

> Systems for the recording, retention, retrieval, and usage of information are antiquated and less than reliable, usually depending only on manual techniques. . . . Much information is retained only in heads of workers and is never reported, while important decisions are sometimes unrecorded.[31]

Computerized court processing technology should be given a trial.

The Stigma

The stigma of court disposition is real, no matter how the court attempts to hide it. In smaller communities, as one judge observed, "Everyone knows about juvenile court cases anyway." Lemert says:

> Such stigma, represented in modern society by a "record," gets translated into effective handicaps by heightened police surveillance, neighborhood isolation, lower receptivity and tolerance by school officials, and rejection of youth by prospective employers.[32]

The Armed Forces are definitely allergic to delinquency records, and so are many other employers. These records are not easily expunged.

Hurried Trials

Murphy, who was the chief attorney with the Juvenile Office of the Legal Aid Society in Chicago, tells us how juveniles were made to admit their "offenses" in 2- to 5-minute conversations between a college student employed by the public defender's office and the parents of the child. The juvenile defendant had little to say.

> Since there are so many cases to be heard, the nine judges hearing them are under great pressure either to hasten trials into summary, ten-minute affairs or to talk the attorney representing the children into pleading them guilty in exchange for probation. . . . On a hot uncomfortable day, or on a day when the judges are in a hurry to get away to the golf links or the political clubhouse, it can be hard indeed to receive a fair, unhurried trial.[33]

If this is the situation in Chicago, it is no better in Los Angeles, where the average time given to a juvenile case was reported to be 3 minutes.[34]

THE FUTURE OF THE JUVENILE COURTS

The juvenile delinquency case load has doubled in 10 years. In 1960, there were 510,000 delinquency cases disposed of by juvenile courts; in 1970, there were 1,125,000.[35] The National Advisory Commission on Criminal Justice Standards and Goals believes that major reform of juvenile justice is needed. It was pointed out that a delinquent child most often reflects a family in trouble—a family burdened with problems. The commission recommended that jurisdiction over juveniles be placed in a family court which should be a division of a trial court of general jurisdiction. The family court should have jurisdiction over all legal matters related to family life, including delinquency, neglect, support, adoption, custody, paternity actions, divorce, annulment, and assaults involving family members. Dependent children—those needing help through no fault of their parents—should be handled outside the court system.

The commission also recommends that family courts have authority to order the transfer of certain juveniles for prosecution in the adult courts, but only after a full and fair hearing.[36] The juvenile should have all the rights of an adult criminal defendant except that of trial by jury.

The Task Force on Juvenile Delinquency and Youth Crime takes a very grave view of those youths whose conduct is a threat to the community. It advises the court to take stern measures in the interest of protecting society.

> The juvenile court, like other courts, is therefore obliged to employ all the means at hand, not excluding incapacitation. . . . While rehabilitative efforts should be vigorously pursued in deference to the youth of the offenders, the incapacitative, deterrent, and condemnatory aspects of judgment should not be disguised.[37]

A 1963 survey made by the National Council of Juvenile Judges found that, in large cities, 71 percent of the judges had received law degrees. But in other areas the educational background of the judges was not adequate to the responsibilities they were entrusted with. Almost 75 percent had been elected to office.[38] The judges of tomorrow will have to be well trained, both in law and in the behavioral sciences. Juvenile courts will also have to involve themselves in evaluative research on a continual basis. They will have to see what works and what does not work. It will be helpful to maintain proper records for research, engage in longitudinal studies, and assess the effectiveness of different programs.

SUMMARY

Some believe the juvenile court is a descendent of the British Chancery; others give credit for this humanitarian idea to the American mind. Whatever its ancestry, the court is supposed to act as the kindly parent of all children in the state. The modus operandi of the juvenile court is different from that of the criminal court. It includes informality and emphasis on protection rather than on prosecution, therapeutic socialization rather than sentencing, and education and training rather than punishment. Ideally, the best interest of the child is very close to the court's heart.

The juvenile intake services screen cases to determine if a petition to the juvenile court should be filed against a delinquent youth. More than half the cases receive pre-judicial disposition. Intake services are vital to the efficient operation of the court. To bring about some uniformity and consistency in intake decisions, the National Advisory Commission on Criminal Justice Standards and Goals has recommended the following standards.

> Each juvenile court jurisdiction immediately should take action, including the pursuit of enabling legislation where necessary, to establish within the court organized intake services operating as a part of or in conjunction with the detention center. Intake services should be geared to the provision of screening and referral intended to divert as many youngsters as possible from the juvenile justice system and to reduce the detention of youngsters to an absolute minimum.
>
> 1. Intake personnel should have authority and responsibility to:
> a. Dismiss the complaint when the matter does not fall within the delinquency jurisdiction of the court or is so minor or the circumstances such that no intervention is required.
> b. Dismiss complaints which seem arbitrary, vindictive, or against the best interests of the child.
> c. Divert as many youngsters as possible to another appro-

priate section of the court or to alternative programs such as mental health and family services, public welfare agencies, youth service bureaus, and similar public and private agencies.

2. Intake personnel should seek informal service dispositions for as many cases as possible, provided the safety of the child and of the community is not endangered. Informal service denotes any provision for continuing efforts on the part of the court at disposition without the filing of a petition, including:
a. Informal adjustments.
b. Informal probation.
c. Consent decrees.

3. Informal service dispositions should have the following characteristics:
a. The juvenile and his parents should be advised of their right to counsel.
b. Participation by all concerned should be voluntary.
c. The major facts of the case should be undisputed.
d. Participants should be advised of their right to formal adjudication.
e. Any statements made during the informal process should be excluded from any subsequent formal proceeding on the original complaint.
f. A reasonable time limit (1 to 2 months) should be adhered to between date of complaint and date of agreement.
g. Restraints placed on the freedom of juveniles in connection with informal dispositions should be minimal.
h. When the juvenile and his parents agree to informal proceedings, they should be informed that they can terminate such dispositions at any time and request formal adjudication.

4. Informal probation is the informal supervision of a youngster by a probation officer who wishes to reserve judgment on the need for filing a petition until after he has had the opportunity to determine whether informal treatment is sufficient to meet the needs of the case.

5. A consent decree denotes a more formalized order for casework supervision and is neither a formal determination of jurisdictional fact nor a formal disposition. In addition to the characteristics listed in paragraph 3, consent decrees should be governed by the following considerations:
a. Compliance with the decree should bar further proceedings based on the events out of which the proceedings arose.
b. Consummation of the decree should not result in subsequent removal of the child from his family.

c. The decree should not be in force more than 3 to 6 months.
   d. The decree should state that it does not constitute a formal adjudication.
   e. No consent decree should be issued without a hearing at which sufficient evidence appears to provide a proper foundation for the decree. A record of such hearing should be kept, and the court in issuing the decree should state in writing the reasons for the decree and the factual information on which it is based.
6. Cases requiring judicial action should be referred to the court.
   a. Court action is indicated when:
      (1) Either the juvenile or his parents request a formal hearing.
      (2) There are substantial discrepancies about the allegations, or denial of a serious offense.
      (3) Protection of the community is an issue.
      (4) Needs of the juvenile or the gravity of the offense makes court attention appropriate.
   b. In all other instances, court action should not be indicated and the juvenile should be diverted from the court process. Under no circumstances should children be referred to court for behavior that would not bring them before the law if they were adults.

Under the supervision of the court, review and monitoring procedures should evaluate the effectiveness of intake services in accomplishing the diversion of children from the juvenile justice system and reducing the use of detention, as well as appropriateness and results of informal dispositions.

7. Predetention screening of children and youths referred for court action should place into their parental home, a shelter, or nonsecure residential care as many youngsters as may be consistent with their needs and the safety of the community. Detention prior to adjudication of delinquency should be based on these criteria:
   a. Detention should be considered a last resort where no other reasonable alternative is available.
   b. Detention should be used only where the juvenile has no parent, guardian, custodian, or other person able to provide supervision and care for him and able to assure his presence at subsequent judicial hearings.
   c. Detention decisions should be made only by court or intake personnel, not by police officers.

d. Prior to [the] first judicial hearing, the juvenile ordinarily should not be detained longer than overnight.
   e. Juveniles should not be detained in jails, lockups, or other facilities used for adults.[39]

Traditionally, the juvenile court has not been very particular about due process of law: The court was relaxed about laws of evidence, a youth's privilege against self incrimination, the right to notice, the right to counsel and appeal. Then historic Supreme Court decisions found fault with the parental role of the juvenile court and pointed out that youngsters were getting neither badly needed rehabilitation nor fair trials. They were getting the worst of both worlds. The Supreme Court ordered that the juvenile court, acting as parens patriae, must protect children's legal rights. As a result of these decisions, juvenile trials may come to resemble adult trials, in spite of the fact that the juvenile courts do not like to treat their wards as criminals.

Vinter perceives the juvenile court as having both external and internal problems. The juvenile court has to please several masters: local and state government officials, higher courts, service agencies, and voters. The court combines both the judicial and social work functions, yet it does not command much respect among either lawyers or social workers. For a variety of reasons, the court is dependent upon several agencies in the community. These dependencies interfere with the independent judicial role of the court. The court is chronically overloaded and has to meet conflicting demands.

Discussion Questions

1. What are the differences between the philosophy and practices of the juvenile court and those of the criminal court?
2. Do you sense any conflict between the roles of the court as parens patriae and as the dispenser of justice?
3. Do you think that PINS and MINS should be referred to juvenile courts? If not, how should they be handled?
4. What are some of the pre-judicial dispositions made by intake staffs?
5. The juvenile court is sometimes criticized for failing to rehabilitate juveniles. Has the adult court done any better?

6. What is the impact of the Supreme Court decisions on the workings of the juvenile court?
7. What do you believe is the future of the juvenile court?

Glossary

Adjudication The giving or pronouncing of a judgment, decree, or decision in a case; also the decision itself.

Adjudicatory Hearing Hearing given for pronouncing a judgment.

Adversary The opposing party in a court action.

Appeal In general terms, a resort to a higher court.

Arraignment The procedure for bringing a prisoner to court to answer an indictment.

Attorn To direct.

Borough A local governmental subdivision, approximately equivalent to a town or city.

Certiorari A writ calling for the records of an inferior court trial.

Circuit Court Courts whose jurisdiction extends over several counties or districts.

Common Pleas Court A court having general original jurisdiction in civil suits. In American law, the court of common pleas has jurisdiction for trials of fact and law according to the principles of common law.

Consent Decree A court judgment entered by consent of the parties. It is not properly a judicial sentence, but is in the nature of a solemn contract between two parties.

County Court In American law, an ordinary court of record with jurisdiction extending over civil cases, persons and estates coming within legal guardianship. It also has a limited criminal jurisdiction.

Court of Chancery A court of equity. Equity is a branch of remedial justice administered by certain tribunals, distinct from the common-law courts.

Disposition Hearing A preliminary examination held by a juvenile court which decides the proper course of action to be taken (probation supervision, commitment to an institution, or treatment by a psychiatric agency, etc.).

District Court A court of the United States having a territorial jurisdiction over a district. It has powers over all penal and criminal matters cognizable under the laws of the United States.

Due Process of Law The administering of justice fairly and properly in accordance with the rules and principles established by the law of the land. Among other things, this includes adequate opportunities for hearing of the accused, presentation of defense by the accused, and protection of fundamental and legal rights.

English Common Law The ancient law of England, both written and unwritten, based on custom and statute.

Felonious Intent Design, resolve, or determination to commit a felony. A felony is a crime of atrocious nature which could be punished with a sentence above one year.

House of Refuge An institution established in New York in 1824, (later spreading to other states) used to incarcerate minors guilty of criminal offenses. The managers of houses of refuge believed strongly that children could be reformed by early instruction and discipline.

Informal Adjustment The informal disposition of certain cases by the intake workers. These cases generally do not warrant official action by the court; the intake workers may use their judgment and discretion in making a disposition.

Informal Probation One of the several nonjudicial methods of handling juvenile cases coming to the attention of the court. When a probation officer wishes to reserve judgment regarding the necessity for filing a petition until after a child has had the opportunity for some informal treatment, the child can be placed on informal probation by the court.

Longitudinal Study A study of individuals over a period of time.

Petition In the context of juvenile delinquency, a written request by a person to a juvenile court for a hearing of the case and a redressing of the wrong.

Probate Court A court having jurisdiction over the estates of minors, including the appointment of guardians.

Psychopathology The systematic investigation of morbid mental conditions.

Self Incrimination The charging of oneself with a crime.

Superior Court A court of general or extensive jurisdiction as distinguished from the lower ranking courts.

Footnotes

[1] President's Commission on Crime, *Task Force Report: Juvenile Delinquency and Youth Crime,* U.S. Government Printing Office, Washington, D.C., 1967, p. 11.

[2] President's Commission on Crime, pp. 2–4.

[3] *In re Gault,* in *United States Reports,* vol. 387, p. 17, 1966.

[4] New York Family Court Act, par. 712 (1963), in President's Commission on Crime, p. 26.

[5] Illinois Juvenile Court Act, par. 702–3 (1966), in President's Commission on Crime.

[6] National Advisory Commission on Criminal Justice Standards and Goals, *Corrections,* U.S. Government Printing Office, Washington, D.C., 1973, p. 267.

[7] President's Commission on Crime, p. 4.

[8] Robert G. Caldwell, "The Juvenile Court: Its Development and Some Major Problems," *Journal of Criminal Law, Criminology and Police Science,* vol. 51, no. 5, p. 496, 1961.

[9] National Advisory Commission on Criminal Justice Standards and Goals, p. 251.

[10] Ted Rubin and Jack F. Smith, *The Future of the Juvenile Court,* consultants' paper for the Joint Commission on Correctional Manpower and Training, Washington, D.C., 1968, p. 26.

[11] National Advisory Commission on Criminal Justice Standards and Goals, p. 254.

[12] National Advisory Commission on Criminal Justice Standards and Goals, p. 255.

[13] National Advisory Commission on Criminal Justice Standards and Goals, p. 255.

[14] President's Commission on Crime, p. 6.

186   Juvenile Delinquency

[15] President's Commission on Crime, p. 35.

[16] President's Commission on Crime, p. 38.

[17] President's Commission on Crime, pp. 38–40.

[18] President's Commission on Crime, p. 38.

[19] President's Commission on Crime, p. 40.

[20] President's Commission on Crime, p. 36.

[21] *Kent v. United States,* in *United State Reports,* vol. 383, pp. 541–565.

[22] *Kent v. United States,* pp. 552–564.

[23] *Kent v. United States,* p. 556.

[24] *Kent v. United States,* p. 556.

[25] *In re Gault,* pp. 1–81.

[26] *In re Gault,* p. 41.

[27] David B. Johnson, "A Contemporary View of the Gault Decision," *Journal of Crime and Corrections,* vol. 1, pp. 17–23, Spring 1973.

[28] Robert D. Vinter, "The Juvenile Court as an Institution," Appendix C, in President's Commission on Crime, pp. 84–90.

[29] Robert D. Vinter, pp. 84–85.

[30] Robert D. Vinter, p. 85.

[31] Robert D. Vinter, p. 88.

[32] President's Commission on Crime, p. 92.

[33] Patrick T. Murphy, *Our Kindly Parent . . . the State,* Viking, New York: 1975, pp. 8–9.

[34] President's Commission on Crime, p. 94.

[35] National Advisory Commission on Criminal Justice Standards and Goals, Juvenile Delinquency Interdepartmental Council, *Standards and Goals for Juvenile Justice,* Law Enforcement Assistance Administration, Washington, D.C., p. 7.

[36] National Advisory Commission on Criminal Justice Standards and Goals, pp. 8–9.

[37] President's Commission on Crime, pp. 2, 9.

[38] President's Commission on Crime, p. 6.

[39] National Advisory Commission on Criminal Justice Standards and Goals, *Corrections,* pp. 266–267.

Juvenile Probation and Aftercare

Juvenile probation holds a very important position in the juvenile justice system. Every year it affects the lives of several hundred thousand new juveniles in the United States; cumulatively, juvenile probation covers many more youths. Some of these young persons are under probation supervision intermittently until they are 21 years of age.

The probation officer in the juvenile justice system has a much broader role than the probation officer in the adult system. The duties of the former include:

- Apprehending juveniles
- Investigating their cases
- Participating in the intake process
- Presenting cases in the court
- Acting both as prosecutor and defense attorney in the juvenile court
- Consulting with the court in the disposition of cases
- Supervising clients
- Giving aftercare

In some cases, the probation officer is also the superintendent of the youth shelter or juvenile detention center, as in the Gault case.

A child placed on probation is allowed to stay in the community, usually at home, subject to the supervision and guidance of a probation officer. The Task Force on Corrections defines probation in the following words:

> Juvenile probation, which permits a child to remain in the community under the supervision and guidance of a probation officer, is a legal status created by a court of juvenile jurisdiction. It usually involves (a) a judicial finding that the behavior of the child has been such as to bring him within the purview of the court, (b) the imposition of conditions upon his continued freedom, and

(c) the provision of means for helping him to meet these conditions and for determining the degree to which he meets them. Probation thus implies much more than indiscriminately giving the child, "another chance." Its central thrust is to give him positive assistance in adjusting in the free community.[1]

Dispositions based on probation are often criticized as leniency. However, the court takes several factors into consideration. For example, a juvenile court sent two girls, one charged with shoplifting and the other with truancy, to a training school. But one boy charged with manslaughter was placed on probation. When these seemingly anomalous decisions were criticized in public, the facts were revealed. The two girls had so many problems that the close custodial care and social reeducation available only in training school were essential ingredients in their treatment. The background of the boy charged with manslaughter showed so many assets that any disposition other than probation could have been disastrous.

HISTORICAL DEVELOPMENT

Most of the mechanism of juvenile probation has been developed in the present century. However, its roots run back through a considerable number of years. In England, specialized procedures for dealing with youthful offenders emerged as early as 1820. Then, magistrates adopted the practice of sentencing youthful criminals to 1 day in prison, followed by conditional release under the supervision of their parents or master. Later on, this supervision was supplied by police officers, and then by volunteer and philanthropic organizations.

Mathew Davenport Hill, Recorder of Birmingham, believed that the individual was not wholly corrupt, and there was reasonable hope of reformation, if a guardian could be found kind enough to take charge of the young convict. Hill claimed that only 16 percent of the probationers had been brought back to the court during his 17 years of experience. That was an impressive rate of success. Young offenders were also bailed out on recognizance. Clergymen and volunteers provided both the supervision and the counseling.[2]

In the United States, criminologists tend to trace the development of probation to the work of John Augustus in the city of Boston, beginning in 1841. Augustus, a Boston bootmaker, bailed out a common drunkard and salvaged him from his miserable plight. Encouraged by his initial success, Augustus supervised about 2000 persons during a period of 18 years. He expanded his efforts to cover children, women, and offenders of many types. Augustus' work after his death was carried on by the Boston Children's Aid Society, the Society of St. Vincent de Paul, and other organizations. The success rate was claimed to be high, and only first offenders and minor recidivists were served by probation supervision.[3]

In 1869, Massachusetts provided by law for the appointment of a state agent to be attached to the Board of State Charities. The agent was authorized to attend the court hearings of children, find them suitable homes, and visit them periodically. The latter half of the nineteenth century was characterized by a growing concern for dependent, neglected, and mistreated children. When the juvenile court came into being at the turn of this century, it prepared the way for juvenile probation. In fact, each contributed to the growth of the other, as they were interdependent institutions.[4]

In the early nineteenth century, probation was the product of humanitarian, charitable, and moralistic movement. Volunteers brought material relief to the probationer, who was considered a victim of the vicious environment. However, after World War I, probation workers were greatly influenced by the psychiatric and psychoanalytic theories advanced by Freud, Adler, Jung, and Rank. Their empasis shifted to a narrow preoccupation with the individual and his emotional dynamics. Caseworkers trained in schools of social work came into prominence and were considered more suitable for probation work. Because of the low salaries, very few of them were attracted to correctional work or to probation jobs. In the 1970s, probation workers do not rely much on psychoanalytical explanations. Instead, they try to utilize community agencies in rendering a variety of services aimed at reintegrating the offender into the family, school, job, and community.

GOALS AND FUNCTIONS

Goals

According to the Task Force on Corrections, the main purpose of the total correctional structure is to promote the welfare and security of the community. Within this overall goal, the specific assignment of juvenile probation includes (1) preventing repetitions of delinquent behavior and (2) diverting youths to more constructive activities to enable them to achieve their potential as productive citizens. Thus, the central services of probation are directed to the child and often to the family. However, in some jurisdictions, probation departments are also assigned responsibilities in delinquency prevention programs. Probation officers know the needs of juveniles; their expertise is put to use in community plans to reduce delinquency.[5]

Functions

The modern probation department has three central functions, and sometimes several auxiliary ones. Its central services are (1) intake and screening, (2) social study and diagnosis, and (3) supervision and treatment.

Intake and Screening As noted earlier, the probation officer holds preliminary discussions of the case with the child, the family, and the referring source. Their object is to determine whether there is a legal basis for court intervention or whether the problem can be better resolved by using the services of some other community resource.[6] This screening process proceeds under the general guidance of the juvenile court, with the help of the court referee, where available. The intake staff does its best to keep as many youngsters as possible out of court.

Social Study and Diagnosis During both investigation and treatment, the probation officer has to make a thorough study of the youth's physical, social, and emotional condition. The officer collects this information through visits to the youth at home, and by interviewing the youth's family and teachers or employers. Another source of information is correspondence with and phone calls to various social agencies.

Of particular importance are the youth's personal attitude toward the delinquency, the acceptance or rejection of the youth by the family, and the reaction of the community. Of equal importance is the availability of needed youth services in the community.

Such a study involves the awesome task of predicting human behavior. The focal concern is the probable nature of the child's response to the necessary demands of society. Will he or will he not be able to refrain from offending again if permitted to continue to reside in the free community? An even more complicated question is: What will be his adjustment under the various possible conditions of treatment—i.e., if he is returned home without further intervention, or if he is provided differing sorts of community supervision and service, or if he is confined in an institution? Only by illuminating such questions can the social study be of value to the court's dispositional decision.[7]

These diagnostic studies are very complicated. The decision made on the basis of these studies is, of course, extremely important in the life of the affected youth. Officials making such decisions should be professionally educated, with sound inservice training, and well versed in interviewing, diagnosing, and counseling.

Supervision and Treatment The Task Force on Corrections points out three major elements of effective supervision: surveillance, service, and counseling. The officer must keep in touch with the child, the child's family and school, and other persons to ensure that the probation plan is being carried out.[8] The child must be made aware of his or her responsibilities as a member of society. The supervision should be constructive in its outlook.

The officer should put the child and the child's family in contact with the appropriate agencies. It is a sad fact that needy families are either ignorant of agencies that could be of help, or too indifferent to make use of them. After making the referrals, the officer should check that the client is keeping appointments with these agencies. Counseling should involve both the child and the family. If the youth is peer oriented, it may be appropriate in some cases to include peers in the counseling—that is, to consider using group counseling sessions.

Large departments frequently perform certain auxiliary tasks. They operate mental health clinics providing diagnostic and, sometimes, treatment services for children referred to the court.

Some administer a variety of other treatment services, which may include foster home programs, forestry camps, group homes, and other residential or nonresidential treatment facilities.

ORGANIZATION OF PROBATION SERVICES

Juvenile probation services are organized in each state in one of the following ways:

1. A centralized, statewide system.
2. A centralized county or city system, the services of which are strengthened and supported by state supervision, consultation, standard setting, recruitment, assistance with inservice training and staff development, and partial state subsidy of the local department.
3. A combination of the above systems, with the more populous and prosperous jurisdictions operating their own departments and with service being provided by the state in the other areas.[9]

Of the three organizational types, a well-coordinated state plan appears preferable for many states. Such a pattern

1. Permits the recruiting of qualified staff and the provision of centralized or regional inservice training and staff development programs
2. Permits staff reassignment from area to area in response to changing conditions
3. Assures uniform standards and practices[10]

County and city systems are organized mainly according to two patterns. In the prevalent pattern, the probation services are administered by the court itself or by a combination of courts. In the other, these services are provided to the court by an administrative agency, such as a probation department established as a separate arm of the local government. A survey reveals that, in two out of every three states, probation is administered by the courts, as shown in the table on page 193.

Those who favor administration by the courts argue that probation officers appointed by a judge make a better team for that judge. Those who oppose this pattern object that it leads to inbreeding and the exclusion of progressive workers. They also note that the court is often too busy to administer and supervise the

Probation administered by	Number of states
Courts	32
State Department of Public Welfare	7
State correctional agencies	5
Other state agencies	4
Other agencies or combination of agencies	2

probation system; as a result, both the court's judicial functions and probation work suffer. Those who favor entrusting probation work to a separate administrative agency strongly believe that proper recruiting, inservice training, assignments, transfers, promotion, and retirement comprise too big a task for the court.

A juvenile probation system can be improved by the appointment of a carefully selected citizens' advisory committee. The functions of such a committee should include (1) giving the system the benefit of citizens' expertise and (2) constant interpretation to the community of the problems and needs of the probation department. The committee should include representation from business and industry, organized labor, the bar, medicine (including psychiatry), the social services, education, religion, and other pertinent community forces.[11]

State subsidies can be helpful in improving the salaries of the staff and in staff development. In such cases the state usually reserves the right to set standards in regard to staff qualifications, salaries, and performance. A state agency can also provide consultation services and staff training, and collect statewide statistics.

PROBATION OFFICERS

One condition that is essential to the success of juvenile probation is to have qualified probation officers. The Task Force on Corrections suggests two sorts of qualifications:

> First, officers performing the basic probation function should possess the highest personal attributes. They should have emotional and intellectual maturity, ability in interpersonal relations, positive value systems, and dedication to the service of others. Second, they should have the training and experience that will supply the knowledge and skill necessary for their enormously complicated work. Since their tasks include diagnosis and treatment, they must have professional training in these functions.[12]

The Task Force on Corrections prefers a master's degree in one of the social or behavioral sciences: sociology, psychology, criminology, corrections, social work, or a related field. If a sufficient number of candidates with master's degrees are not available, then the minimum qualifications should be (1) a bachelor's degree in the social sciences and (2) some graduate work in one of the sciences mentioned above or 1 year of paid, full-time experience under professional supervision in a recognized social agency. The Task Force on Corrections regrets that only a few agencies maintain the preferred educational standard, and not many maintain the recommended minimum standard. This clearly suggests the necessity for extensive use of inservice training and other staff development tools in probation departments.

On-the-Job Training

There are several levels of on-the-job training. It begins with an *orientation* program for new workers, to help them become acquainted with the agency's rules, procedures, and policies. The orientation should consist of 80 to 120 hours of lectures, discussions, and workshops, and about as much apprenticeship with an experienced colleague. The supervisor must consult with the new worker on diagnosis and supervision. Without this help, it is difficult for the untrained worker to translate the training program into practice.[13]

This should be followed by a *continuing inservice training program*, carefully designed to meet the varying needs of staff at different levels. Because of the growing state of knowledge, *refresher courses* should be arranged after a suitable length of time. The topics for discussion could include important court decisions, new legislation, the rights of probationers, social change and new behavioral patterns, youth movements, new research, and staff development. Those who would like to attend a university to continue their education or for specialized training should be given educational leaves. Those who are interested in making special visits to exemplary projects should be given all possible help.

Service Conditions

Surveys have shown that the salaries of probation officers and their supervisors are not high enough to attract competent staffs with the required qualifications. No wonder that 37 percent of the agencies indicated lack of staff as their chief obstacle to effective juvenile probation service.[14] About half the states provide their probation officers with civil service or merit system coverage. The probation system should provide reasonable security to its employees. However, it should be competitive enough so that it does not stagnate or shut itself off from new thought and new blood.

REFEREES

Some courts employ referees to assist the judges and, at times, officiate in their place. Referees' decisions are subject to confirmation or reversal by the judge. Often the referees are probation officers assigned to hear cases. Children's Bureau standards require that referees be members of the bar with legal experience, and that the office of referee be distinct from the probation staff. Training in social work is considered valuable but no more essential to referees than to judges.[15]

There have been other quasijudicial substitutes for the juvenile court. In 1953, juvenile conference committees came into existence in New Jersey. They act as referees, hearing and disposing of cases of alleged delinquency. Such committees are composed of magistrates, probation officers, police and school representatives, and other public-spirited laypersons interested in child welfare. In establishing these boards, an effort was made to secure the aid of citizens with experience in social work, particularly probation personnel, rather than lawyers.

Cases requiring commitment to institutions are excluded; they must be dealt with by the court. These committees combine and apply the wisdom and resources of the community to solve the problems of maladjusted youths who do not require official court action. The juvenile conference committees have had quite a bit of success: Out of 3929 cases heard in fourteen counties, there were only 355 recidivists. They are considered a valuable adjunct to the juvenile court in New Jersey.[16] We shall shortly see that Sweden has similar organizations, called child welfare boards.

CASE LOAD SIZE

The size of the case load assigned to the probation officer is important both for social study and for supervision. The Task Force on Corrections is concerned that an officer with a disproportionately heavy case load may make only cursory inquiries and could definitely harm some children. A heavily overworked probation officer can provide only meaningless supervision.

> If probation supervision is attempted under circumstances that make possible only superficial contact with the child and the family, it is worse than meaningless, for the child subjected to it may become convinced that the officer, who to him represents conforming society and its institutions, may readily be duped or hoodwinked, is unaware of him as an individual human being, or simply is not much interested in him.[17]

What is the optimum size of the case load? The American Correctional Association has suggested some standards: "A workload of 50 units, computed on a rating of one work unit for each probationer supervised, and five work units for each pre-sentence investigation completed and written in a given month is recommended as the maximum for a probation officer."[18] This standard is minimal. A fifty-unit case load allows an average of 1 hour per month for face-to-face confrontation with the child. The Task Force on Corrections regretfully remarks, "Obviously, one hour a month is not enough time in which to reshape defective attitudes and behavior."[19]

The determination of an appropriate case load size has been the subject of prolonged investigation in several jurisdictions. The evidence suggests that it is not the number of cases that counts, but the quality of supervision given to the probationers. Clients have varying supervision needs. It has been suggested that those probationers who need minimum supervision may be handled in a larger case load. However, Adams is of the opinion that larger case loads may be appropriate in dealing with adult offenders, but small case loads are more suitable for juveniles. Juveniles need more attention, care, and guidance than adults.

It has been further suggested that the earlier a delinquent receives therapy, the greater the return on the therapeutic effort.[20] How much supervision (number of counselor-client contacts in a month) one needs is not easy to decide. Most clients are given maximum supervision until they show that they do not need intensive supervision but can do with minimum supervision and guidance.

SUPPORTING SERVICES

Probation supervision or counseling cannot be very effective in a vacuum; a probation counselor needs a wide variety of supporting services. These services include the Volunteers in Probation, foster families, group homes, psychological and psychiatric services, experimentation and research centers, and youth service bureaus. Japan uses volunteers very actively in assisting the overworked probation officer. The volunteer may be a family friend or a member of the probationer's family.

In America, foster homes are frequently used for those children who cannot adjust in their own homes or whose own homes cannot meet their needs. Adolescents who are in the process of achieving emotional emancipation from parents or parental figures fit better in a small, open group home. A group home offers youths the satisfactions of a peer society.

Psychological and psychiatric services are vitally important to the diagnosis and continuing treatment of some children. These services are, however, inadequate, and the Task Force on Corrections is unhappy about it.

> The length of the waiting list usually makes the clinic of dubious value to the child, who cannot be helped unless he becomes involved in the treatment process at the point of crisis. Commonly, also, the clinical service builds up in the child, through diagnosis, an awareness of the need for and some expectation of treatment, and then it frustrates the entire process by failing to provide any form of continuing treatment. Frequently, even when a psychiatric resource is available, diagnostic and not treatment services are called on.[21]

Only a few departments maintain an experimentation and research arm. Some of these departments use innovative methods: supplementing the individual case work approach with group work or help-each-other methods.

> Juvenile Delinquency is commonly a group experience . . . therefore efforts to change delinquent behavior should focus primarily on a group like that within which the individual operates. A number of group counseling methods have been employed but the method called guided group interaction has been used most extensively.

The general strategy of guided group interaction calls for involving the offenders in frequent, prolonged, and intensive discussions of the behavior of individuals in the group and the motivations underlying it. Concentrating on participants' current experiences and problems, the approach attempts to develop a group "culture" that encourages those involved to assume responsibility for helping and controlling each other. The theory is that the offender-participants will be more responsive to the influence of their fellow offenders, their peers, than to the admonitions of staff, and less likely to succeed in hoodwinking and manipulating each other.[22]

This is borne out by the author's own experience as a caseworker. When he himself could not bring about a change in the attitudes of a delinquent, he often invoked the help of a peer of that delinquent. The peer-helper frequently had better success. It has been suggested that, in this helping process, the helper and the helped profit from each other. Reissman contends:

While it may be uncertain that people receiving help are always benefited, it seems more likely that the people giving help are profiting from their role. . . . Various reports point to improvement in the givers of help rather than the recipients. . . . Perhaps, then, social work's strategy ought to be to devise ways of creating more helpers! Or, to be more exact, to find ways to transform recipients of help into dispensers of help, thus reversing their roles, and to structure the situation so that recipients of help will be placed in roles requiring the giving of assistance.[23]

The probation officer's best counseling efforts will have only limited results, unless the officer makes full use of those community sources of help that are available to a youth. Community agencies are the probation officer's best tools. The officer must make the best possible use of these agencies, should get to know the appropriate workers at these agencies, and should refer clients to the agencies when they can be of help.

Unfortunately, the average probation officer is not very community oriented. Probation officers tend to be oriented more to their own agency, and to confine their activities to the supervision of probationers. However, they must be made aware that the battle for reintegration and rehabilitation is fought in the community.

If there is a principal need facing probation as a system, it is the need for a greater range of treatment facilities. As such facilities develop, the probation officer will probably be engaged more as a liaison man between the court and other agencies and he will be less responsible for personally inducing change in offenders. This means that professional training for probation workers would have to stress increasingly the utilization of community resources and mechanisms for fitting the delinquent into neighborhood and community programs, and especially the new opportunities now being made available through such projects as the Neighborhood Youth Corps.[24]

DIVERSION AND CIVIL COMMITMENT

Adult diversion is described as any of several procedures designed to provide an accused or convicted offender with an alternative to traditionally prescribed correctional actions. As discussed in previous chapters, juvenile diversion is much wider in scope than adult diversion and is used at several levels: on the street, at the police station, and by the juvenile intake unit and the juvenile court.

The juvenile court itself was a diversion from the criminal court, when it came into being around the turn of the century. However, the juvenile offender status assumed responsibility for a very large spectrum of behavior (from loitering to habitual truancy, smoking cigarettes to setting fires, sexual irregularities to prostitution, begging to stealing, growing up in idleness to association with an immoral person, and more). Thus, it became imperative to divert a part of this behavior to noncriminal channels. In other words, diversion was necessary to decriminalize, in practice, behavior that had been criminalized unnecessarily in the statutes. Diversion was also necessary to relieve the severely overcrowded juvenile justice system. There were other compelling reasons: avoidance of stigma, curtailing delinquent careers, provision of needed services, and reduction of recidivism.

In spite of all the merits of diversion, there have been some criticisms. One major criticism is that if diversion depends on nonregulated discretion, officials are likely to use this discretion arbitrarily and indiscriminately. This situation is now being remedied by the formulation of well-considered standards. Some of these standards are given later, in the summary.

Another objection is that civil commitment, when substituted for criminal commitment, is likely to be unproductive and, at times, as harmful as criminal commitment. This is especially true when an institution merely confines patients and is unable to offer needed services. Examples are alcoholic rehabilitation centers, drug abuse centers, psychiatric clinics, and institutions for sexually disturbed persons which may not have the resources to cure alcoholics, drug users, and psychiatric and sex offenders. There is also a legal criticism that civil commitment, when used for diversion, may not adequately safeguard the legal rights of the individual. Civil commitment may also, at times, display all the harmful effects of criminal commitment.

It has been suggested that the major consideration in civil commitment should be the juvenile's *helplessness* or *dangerousness*. Civil commitment is desirable if it will help a sick or disabled child, or if it will protect the populace from a dangerous delinquent. If neither of these conditions is present, civil commitment does not have much meaning.

> Society cannot have it both ways. If a deviant behavior or condition is to be defined as not criminal then it would seem that an individual should not be compelled to accept treatment for that condition or behavior unless the condition is ruled inherently dangerous, and he should not be committed for other reasons except on a determination that he himself is dangerous or helpless.
> If society decides that certain nondangerous offenders should be diverted from the criminal justice system, then it should not be satisfied with the substitution of measures which differ only in their description as "nonpenal" or "treatment."[25]

Youth service bureaus have been recommended as a major alternative to social control by the criminal justice system. The stated purpose of these bureaus is to facilitate the diversion of children from judicial processing to social services. "Society should broaden its definition of acceptable behavior rather than merely extend its control efforts to include treatment and provision of services."[26] Some diversion should result in simple release from any system of intervention or control.

JUVENILE AFTERCARE

Juvenile aftercare is defined as the release of a child from an institution at a time when that child can best benefit from release and from living in the community under the supervision of a counselor. Although juvenile aftercare started in the early nineteenth century, it did not become an integral part of juvenile rehabilitation until the late 1950s. In the opinion of many observers, it is less adequate than its counterpart, adult parole. The beginning of juvenile aftercare smacks of slavery.

> Aftercare originated in New York and Pennsylvania, where houses of refuge indentured child inmates to work in private homes for several years. The child's daily regimen rarely included anything but work. Total responsibility for the child was vested in the family that undertook to feed and clothe him, and it was the family that determined when he had earned his freedom. This form of post institutional treatment persisted for over half a century.[27]

The practice resembles that of farming out adult prisoners. Juvenile aftercare is relatively one of the weakest areas in juvenile justice. It is not uncommon for 250 adolescents to be assigned to a program staffed by only two or three aftercare counselors located at the state capital or at a training school. The counselors may be hundreds of miles from the communities where the juveniles are supposedly under supervision.[28]

There are several kinds of organizational patterns for the management of aftercare. Aftercare is administered by a lay board, a public welfare agency, or the training school itself. The training school staff members know the juveniles and their preparation for aftercare better than the members of other organizations. Thus, their opinions on aftercare should be given greater credence. The boy-girl ratio among aftercare supervisees is four to one. Many of these youths remain under probation or parole supervision until age 21, unless discharged earlier. The average length of aftercare supervision tends to be about 1 year.[29]

PAROLEES' RETURN TO THEIR COMMUNITIES

In his incisive study of male juvenile parolees, Arnold throws light on how they returned to their individual friends and peer groups on their release from the training school. They had fewer friends during the postinstitution period than during the preinstitution period. Parolees who lost their individual friends showed a higher rate of parole failure.

More important than individual friends to juvenile parolees were their peer groups. A peer group, according to Arnold, was made up of three or more friends who "hung around" together. The parolees were very anxious to maintain their status in their peer groups; a loss of status in the group was conducive to parole failure. Loss of status in a small group was more damaging to the boys than loss of status in a larger group.

The rate of interaction between parolees and their group peers was lower during the aftercare supervision. Most of their friendships had been made during early adolescence. The boys found it more difficult to establish new friendships during middle and late adolescence. Those who developed an interest in girls, work, or staying out of trouble tended to drift away from both the group and delinquency. Making friendships and forming groups is a phenomenon of age; groups dissolve during late adolescence.[30]

About half the youngsters released from training school rejoined their groups. The other half were not able to return to their groups for several reasons, including dissolution of the group, intervention of parents, and voluntary isolation. However, the allure of the gang was evident in all cases. If a parolee was welcomed by both the parents and the peers, the peers won.[31]

Arnold explained the successes and failures of juvenile parole on the basis of the social psychology of the peer group. Group members involve themselves in delinquent acts only occasionally and intermittently. They engage in delinquent activity when certain criminogenic forces are present. The criminogenic forces are generated when the members perceive a problem which they decide to solve through a delinquent act at the suggestion of the prestigious members.

> At least three elements must be present in a situation if delinquency is to occur: the perception that there is a problem to be solved, the perception that a delinquent act could solve this problem, and the perception that one's valuable peers favor the exercise of this delinquent solution.[32]

In Arnold's study, half the parolees committed another offense at an average age of 15 years and 9 months and became recidivists. In spite of their attachment to the group, the recidivists had more difficulty adjusting to their peers than the nonrecidivists. The former often conflicted with their peers, and there was relatively greater instability in their relationships. Status conscious as they were, the recidivists reacted adversely to their loss of status. So, recidivists were more likely than nonrecidivists to belong to groups to which it was difficult to adjust. After a long delinquent history, these groups were shrinking and disintegrating.

Thus, the kind of group that a youth belonged to was fateful for that youth. The question that arises is, "What makes the future recidivist choose a group that offers difficulties of adjustment?" Arnold has not grappled with this issue. He observed that the recidivists had received less effective antidelinquent teaching than the nonrecidivists from their families, friends, and teachers. (This sounds like Sutherland's differential association theory.) The recidivists, more than the nonrecidivists, liked to maintain interaction with groups of longer delinquent history. Arnold asserts that recidivism of parolees is a product and property of the group, and not a personality characteristic of the individual parolee. This may be a debatable issue, but there is no denying the fact that the influence of the group is pervasive.[33]

SUPPORT FROM PARENTS

The parents of parolees studied by Arnold had unstable marriages. Their families were matriarchal, because the children tended to lean on the mother for emotional support. The father was vested with authority as long as he lived with the family and provided a steady income. In Arnold's words,

> Scarcely any of [the parents] over twenty-five years of age had lived with only one mate. The terms "marriage" and "divorce" were used loosely to refer to establishing and breaking liaisons with particular mates more often than they were to refer to formal ceremonies. In the marital relation and in the rearing of children, wives were subordinate, but husbands had no control over women's social life with other women. The fathers' (not the step-fathers') authority over their children was "final" and to be exercised only when the mothers "gave up." The marital relationships were broken whenever one of the mates decided that the other mate was not acting as he should and/or whenever one of the mates found someone else he liked better. Promiscuity was condemned, but serial monogamy was the rule.
>
> Discipline was severe, obedience to orders was expected to be immediate, and corporal punishment was almost the only disciplinary technique considered effective. When the children

were outside the home, however, almost no supervision was undertaken—parents rarely knew where their children were or what they did.[34]

In their studies, the Gluecks found that parental roles were greatly impaired in delinquents' families. This was the result of alcoholism and poor work habits, and it led to a number of difficulties for the children. The children generally did not receive proper affection, socialization, and supervision.[35] A male child often identifies with the father. But if the father can only present a model of sickness or criminality, the child looks for a model elsewhere, outside the family. A staff report to the National Commission on the Causes and Prevention of Violence observes that the parents of delinquents tend to be more punitive, neglectful, and inconsistent, and less warm and affectionate, than the parents of nondelinquents.[36]

The point here is that the probation or aftercare officer should apply therapy to the entire family unit, rather than to the child alone. Each family has some hidden strengths which can be tapped. It is the author's observation that the families of delinquent children only rarely make use of the social resources in their community. They either do not know of these resources or are too apathetic to make use of them. Given proper information and incentive, they may seek and use those resources.

A family that has visited their youngster in the institution regularly and has written to him or her quite often will also take good care of the child during the aftercare period. Because "absence makes the heart grow fonder," the relationship between the family members and the youngster tends to improve during the early aftercare period. However, if the parents place severe restraints on the youth's freedom, the relationships soon begin to sour.

WHO SUCCEEDS OR FAILS?

The relative effectiveness of the different correctional practices is still in doubt (studies show positive, neutral, and negative results). However, some subjects are more likely than others to show greater success with conventional probation or parole supervision. As measured by the recidivism rate, subjects with the following personal and social characteristics show success and failure as noted.

Those Who Succeed

The characteristics favoring success can be separated into the following categories:

Social Maturity Relatively older age; also relatively older age at the onset of delinquency
Shorter Criminal History Relative freedom from previous delinquent or criminal commitment; staying away from delinquent gangs; involvement in nonproperty rather than property offenses
Stability Either continuing with education or working steadily after release; married; released to rural area; family support

This list is by no means complete. The characteristics relate with success regardless of the type of correctional setting, community based or institutional.

Those Who Fail

The reverses of the characteristics listed above contribute to failure and recidivism:

Social Immaturity Relatively younger age; also younger at the onset of delinquency
Longer Criminal History Relatively longer criminal record; involvement in property offenses; greater participation in a delinquent gang
Instability Staying idle; staying away from school and work; single; released to a larger city in a socially and economically disadvantaged segment of society; some element of personal anomie[37]

EFFECTIVENESS STUDIES

It is very difficult to make reliable statements about the effectiveness of correctional practices used to supplement probation or parole supervision. There are several studies that show positive, neutral, and negative impacts for different correctional practices. In view of the contradictory findings, one has to be careful in making conclusive statements, although the majority of the findings are either neutral or negative.

Attempts have been made from time to time to survey a

handful of treatment studies; many seem to indicate, pessimistically, that nothing works in corrections. More recently, a monumental survey of existing treatment-evaluation studies was undertaken at the behest of the Governor's Special Committee on Criminal Offenders, for the state of New York. This survey was made by Lipton, Martinson, and Wilks; their findings pertaining to juvenile probation and parole are extracted below.[38]

Case Load Size

The size of the probation officers' case load may not have a direct effect on the parolee.

> There is no convincing evidence that small case loads have a "treatment" effect—that is, that they alter the behavior of parolees. However, changes in case load size may produce system effects that influence the success and failure rates of parolees without necessarily altering their behavior. This may come about because parole agents alter their behavior, particularly their use of revocation and suspension. [page 149]

Group Counseling

Counseling of offenders in groups, rather than individually, may be beneficial.

> There is some evidence that group counseling with offenders in the community has a favorable impact on recidivism particularly when combined with field supervision. Long-term gains have yet to be demonstrated. [page 229]

Personality Change

There does not seem to be any link between treatment and personality or changes in personality.

> It is not clear why it should be anticipated that probation or its component operations (for example, counseling, surveillance) should produce attitude and personality changes in general, or particular changes as measured by the available tests or why attitude and personality change among probationers would be considered beneficial. Research findings have

not conclusively indicated that possession of certain attitudes or personality traits is directly linked (or even indirectly linked) to specific criminal behavior. [page 402]

There is no consistent relationship between intensive parole programs and psychological change as measured by psychological tests utilized. Sometimes psychological tests showed improvement while behavior deteriorated, sometimes the reverse occurred, in some cases there was congruence between the two criterion measures. [pages 422 to 423]

A number of decisions must be made before we can evaluate the impact of correctional experiments. Among the questions to be answered are:

- What do we want to achieve with our correctional subjects?
- How should we measure the changes?
- Does the treatment applied have the ingredients needed to effect the desired change in the subject?

We should, meanwhile, go on analyzing the results of different treatment programs as applied to different types of delinquents in different settings by change agents (therapists) with different skills. Hopefully, this will build up a body of correctional knowledge.

JUVENILE JUSTICE: INTERNATIONAL PERSPECTIVE

A look into the methods of delinquency control in other countries reveals both similarities and differences. The comparison here focuses on four countries—Japan, India, the Soviet Union, and Sweden—which present a wide cultural diversity. Both Japan and India are traditional societies with strong family controls. Yet Japan's fast growing rate of delinquency is the product of affluence; India's low rate of delinquency and particularly the nature of its delinquency reflect a culture of poverty. Japan's juvenile justice system is greatly influenced by the American system; India's system was designed by the British. The Soviet society bases the treatment of children on communistic principles. Sweden prefers a pragmatic approach which is inclined more toward welfare than toward the judiciary.

Japan[39]

In Japan, all persons under 20 years of age are legally juveniles. Larceny is the major offense of children aged 14 to 15 years. At age 18 to 20 years, motoring offenses and offenses of violence begin to add up. College students stage violent protest rallies, both on the campus and in other prominent places in the cities.

The juvenile justice system resembles the American system and may have been inspired by it to some extent. There is, however, a greater reliance on the use of the benign influence of family and friends. To make a thorough investigation into cases referred to the family court, the court may place juveniles on tentative probation. This allows the probation officer to observe the juveniles in the community. The probation officer collects information from the juveniles, their guardians, and other persons relevant to their cases, and then brings the data to the court.

The Japanese can be quite severe with dangerous and recalcitrant youths: 13 percent of their cases are referred to the public prosecutor for criminal prosecution. As in many other affluent societies, there is a growing trend toward involvement of young persons from the middle class. Also, a good part of Japanese delinquency is peer sponsored: 31.4 percent of juvenile delinquents have cooffenders.

The use of probation supervision is a popular mode of court disposition. Many youths are kept under probation or parole supervision until they reach age 20; the minimum period of supervision is 2 years. Volunteers work in close cooperation with professionals. Each volunteer is assigned two persons to supervise and counsel. The rate of success is about the same as in America: 24 percent of the juvenile probationers and 41 percent of the juvenile parolees commit further offenses. However, the government of Japan tries its best to enlighten society on matters pertaining to delinquency and crime. In the month of July every year, the Japanese engage themselves in a campaign of crime prevention and purification of society.

India

Juvenile delinquency was not a major problem in India until recently. Even today, it is mostly an urban problem, not a rural problem. India's juvenile justice system exists as a separate entity only in the large cities; in smaller towns, many children are still handled by the police and the adult courts. In Bombay, New Delhi, Madras, and Calcutta, juveniles are handled by special police units; juvenile courts are often presided over by female judges; and probation officers are of both sexes.

Probation officers are overworked, underpaid, and ill equipped. It is difficult to visit juveniles at their homes when the only available transportation is a bicycle. There are very few supporting agencies in the community. However, an intact loving family compensates for the lack of many other agencies. The extended family and close relatives spread their wings over the child, to insulate the child against any further delinquency.

The reform schools, which have quite reasonable programs by Indian standards, provide some schooling, training in handicrafts, medical treatment, recreation, and counseling. There is hardly any follow-up after release from reform school. The recidivism rate is not, however, high. Except for the pickpockets, most youths tend to stabilize after one or two law violations. Female delinquency is very low as compared to that in affluent industrial societies.

Soviet Union[40]

In the Soviet Union, juvenile delinquents under the age of 14 are dealt with exclusively by commissions on juvenile affairs. The commissions are extensively involved in the prevention of delinquency and, to a lesser extent, in the correction of delinquents. Any lawbreaker between the age of 14 and 16 whose violation does not involve criminal responsibility also falls under the primary jurisdiction of the commissions. After the age of 16, a juvenile becomes "responsible" in criminal law for all his or her acts, and thus falls under the jurisdiction of the adult courts.

The courts refer many minors to the commissions when they do not wish to make a judicial disposition. Court proceedings are supposed to have an educative effect on juveniles. The court appoints experts—teachers, psychologists, doctors, and others—to assist the court and serve as people's assessors. In many areas, however, qualified assessors are in short supply.

The courts tend to commit about 50 percent of the referred youths to labor colonies for juveniles; the rest are placed on probation, fined, or "socially censured." Commitment to a juvenile colony is for a period of 3 years, although about 80 percent of the inmates are paroled after about a year. Juveniles between the ages of 14 and 16 are kept in the community under the threat of suspended sentences. Older adolescents may end up in adult corrective labor colonies.

Sweden[41]

In Sweden, delinquents under 18 years of age are handled by child welfare boards. There are no juvenile courts, and the authority of the child welfare boards is supreme. These boards, however, are not courts, and they do not impose fines or punishment. Juvenile probation is rarely used with adolescents below 18 years of age. The juvenile justice system is not nearly as rigidly structured as ours. While America is trying to formalize juvenile justice procedures to do away with the tyranny of discretion, Sweden tends toward discretion as a means of staying away from judicial procedures.

> Child care, according to the Child Welfare Act, is so organized that it is primarily in the hands of local boards, whose members are elected by the communal administrations, who in return are elected by the voters of the communes. Each child welfare board is, by and large, charged with the task of seeing that children and youth within its jurisdiction may grow up under favorable conditions and receive suitable nurture. The work of such boards is not limited to asocial young people; it includes needed assistance to those having shown no asocial tendencies. The boards are not courts, for there are no juvenile courts in Sweden or the other Scandinavian countries. There is no requirement that a jurist be a member of a board, but the Act recommends it if a suitable candidate is available. Furthermore, a board may engage a jurist as secretary or expert. The boards are much less than courts bound in their work by legal formalities. There is no prosecutor who presents a case against anyone before a board. When a board makes a decision that infringes upon someone, the decision may be appealed to State authorities of a courtlike character, and decisions that more seriously infringe upon someone's liberty cannot be executed until they have been approved by a State authority. These authorities also exercise control in other ways over the work of the boards and lend them assistance.
>
> One of the functions of the boards is to take measures against children and youths who act in an asocial manner and therefore are in need of corrective measures. The measures

may consist of advice and warnings, probation, placement in a foster home and commitment to an institution for education and training. A criminal act by the youngster is neither a prerequisite, nor a sufficient reason for taking a measure. The decisive element is instead the recognized need for remedial action. It is, of course, obvious that the need is often demonstrated by the youngster's criminal act. Remedial measures may be taken by the board if the person has not reached his 18th birthday, but under certain conditions they may be applied to older youths not yet 21 years of age.

It should be clear from what has just been said that public child care is entirely divorced from the system of prosecution and court action and from the authorities executing the sentences of courts. However, judicial authorities may allow child welfare boards to take action in criminal matters.[42]

Anyone below 18 years of age who is prosecuted in court and found guilty is handed over to the child welfare board of the district for appropriate disposition. If the welfare board is not able to deal with the case, then the court can impose sanction for the crime. Similarly, the prosecutor must consult the board before deciding to prosecute a youth under 18 years of age. Very often, the prosecutor will drop the case and let the child welfare board take over.

It is difficult to say whether or not the Swedish methods are more successful than ours. Their rate of recidivism is almost as high as that of the United States. Regardless of recidivism, this is the way they want to treat their youth. Ever since the mid 1960s, drug addiction among youth and adults in general, and among the institutionalized population in particular, has been on the increase.

Similarly, the Swedes are greatly concerned about their drunken drivers, and law enforcers take a serious view of them. During a visit to Sweden, the author was told that those who drive irresponsibly on the roads behave in the same fashion in other situations. For the care of alcoholics and alcohol abuse, local temperance boards are created under the authority of a special statute. These boards take measures against those who abuse alcoholic beverages. The measures consist, among other things, of advice, warnings, probation, and commitment to an institution for alcoholics.

The Swedes make use of residential centers (probation hostels) for their probationers—mostly at the beginning of probation and at other emergent occasions. The emergent situation for a probationer could be a sudden loss of job, loss of residence, financial difficulty, or the like. Most probationers have to spend the first month of their probation at the center to make necessary arrangements for a job, training, and a place to live. This residential stay is utilized to collect information on the probationers and to get to know them better.

Every society faces an increasing rate of delinquency, and every society tries to criminalize as few of its children as possible. All nations try to protect the neglected, the dependent, and children in need of supervision. At the same time, they want to protect society from the more dangerous and criminally inclined youth. While the two Asian societies discussed above have juvenile courts, the two European nations do not.

SUMMARY

Probation, which was started by John Augustus as a humanitarian movement, is today considered an essential alternative to incarceration. It occupies an important place in corrections because, for some youths, correction can occur only in the community under the guidance of a probation officer.

The functions of a probation officer in the juvenile system encompass a wider range than those of a probation officer in the adult system. The former is responsible for investigation, intake, diversion, case presentation, supervision, and even aftercare. For such an awesome responsibility, the probation officer should not only be well educated, well trained, and professionally experienced, but also should be a person of great warmth, devotion, and capacity for establishing constructive relationships.

Diversion is an essential procedure. In order to guard against abuses, the National Advisory Commission on Criminal Justice Standards and Goals has drafted the following standards:

> In appropriate cases offenders should be diverted into noncriminal programs before formal trial or conviction.
>
> Such diversion is appropriate where there is a substantial likelihood that conviction could be obtained and the benefits to society from channeling an offender into an available noncriminal diversion program outweigh any harm done to society by abandoning criminal prosecution. Among the factors that should be considered favorable to diversion are: (1) the

relative youth of the offender; (2) the willingness of the victim to have no conviction sought; (3) any likelihood that the offender suffers from a mental illness or psychological abnormality which was related to his crime and for which treatment is available; and (4) any likelihood that the crime was significantly related to any other condition or situation such as unemployment or family problems that would be subject to change by participation in a diversion program.

Among the factors that should be considered unfavorable to diversion are: (1) any history of the use of physical violence toward others; (2) involvement with syndicated crime; (3) a history of antisocial conduct indicating that such conduct has become an ingrained part of the defendant's lifestyle and would be particularly resistant to change; and (4) any special need to pursue criminal prosecution as a means of discouraging others from committing similar offenses.

Another factor to be considered in evaluating the cost to society is that the limited contact a diverted offender has with the criminal justice system may have the desired deterrent effect.[43]

Where the diversion program involves significant deprivation of an offender's liberty, diversion should be permitted only under a court-approved diversion agreement providing for suspension of criminal proceedings on the condition that the defendant participate in the diversion program.[44]

Juvenile aftercare (parole) marks an important step in releasing the juvenile to the community at the appropriate time, when the youngster can profit more from the community than the training school. Given the usual attraction of the group, most parolees like to return to their gangs. Those who lose status in the gang are so affected that they have a greater tendency to recidivate. The recidivists experience greater difficulty in adjusting to their peer groups.

What works and what does not work is an unanswered question in corrections. A large case load is inefficient, but a small case load does not yield any better results, in terms of recidivism. The number of meetings does not seem to matter; what goes into the worker-client meeting is really important.

Different forms of counseling have been tried with probationers. Group counseling has produced some beneficial results. Generally, youths who exhibit more stability and social maturity and shorter criminal histories show lower recidivism.

An analysis of the juvenile systems of different societies reveals several similarities and dissimilarities. Some societies handle their delinquents judicially, through juvenile courts; others handle them administratively, through special commissions.

Discussion Questions

1. How do the roles of probation officers in the juvenile and adult court systems differ?
2. What can we do to make our probation officers more community oriented?
3. List the social agencies in your community. Then note how each of them could be helpful to juvenile probationers.
4. If a parolee revokes his or her aftercare, can he or she be sent back to the training school? If so, who decides it?
5. What are some of the strengths and failings of the family? How can we add to the family strengths?
6. Do you believe that juvenile courts or special commissions should deal with juveniles? Why?
7. What can we do to improve the effectiveness of aftercare?

Glossary

Aftercare Process of official supervision of inmates after their release from an institution.

Bail on Recognizance Release of persons from legal custody subject to the condition that they make themselves available to the court upon call. The accused generally must furnish a written bond with agreement to fulfill the conditions imposed by the court.

Case Load In the context of juvenile delinquency, the number of delinquents constituting the workload of a counselor or probation officer for counseling, guidance, and supervision at a given time.

Civil Commitment A disposition by which a person is assigned to a noncriminal institution, such as a drug abuse center or a detoxification center.

Client (in Casework) A counselee.

Criminalize To hold a certain behavioral act as criminal in nature and to pass legislation to that effect. Decriminalization involves the removal of criminal sanctions from a certain behavioral act.

Criminogenic Pertaining to the development of criminal behavior.

Psychiatric Having to do with psychiatry, a branch of medicine dealing with the prevention, diagnosis, and treatment of mental illness. Also, certain personal problems.

Psychoanalytic Having to do with psychoanalysis, a technique for investigating human motivations.

Recognizance An obligation, agreed to and recorded before a court, to perform some act, such as appear before the court, pay a debt, or keep the peace.

Referee A court official to whom a case pending in a court is referred by the court to take testimony and report thereon to the court.

Referral The act of directing a client to some other person or agency (usually for help).

Social Reeducation Rehabilitation; the act of restoring lost social functioning through training.

Surveillance Supervision.

Suspension of Sentence Either not sentencing a prisoner after a conviction, or withholding the execution of a sentence that has been pronounced. Usually, the suspension is subject to some condition, such as the good behavior of the convicted person.

Footnotes

[1] President's Commission on Law Enforcement and Administration of Justice, *Task Force Report: Corrections*, U.S. Government Printing Office, Washington, D.C., 1967; p. 130. For this section, the author relied on this document.

[2] Paul W. Tappan, *Crime, Justice, Correction*, McGraw-Hill, New York, 1960, p. 542.

[3] Paul W. Tappan, pp. 543–544.

[4] President's Commission on Law Enforcement and Administration of Justice, p. 131.

[5] President's Commission on Law Enforcement and Administration of Justice, p. 131.

Juvenile Delinquency

[6] President's Commission on Law Enforcement and Administration of Justice, p. 131.

[7] President's Commission on Law Enforcement and Administration of Justice, p. 132.

[8] President's Commission on Law Enforcement and Administration of Justice, p. 132.

[9] President's Commission on Law Enforcement and Administration of Justice, p. 134.

[10] President's Commission on Law Enforcement and Administration of Justice, p. 134.

[11] President's Commission on Law Enforcement and Administration of Justice, p. 135.

[12] President's Commission on Law Enforcement and Administration of Justice, pp. 136–137.

[13] President's Commission on Law Enforcement and Administration of Justice, p. 137.

[14] President's Commission on Law Enforcement and Administration of Justice, p. 139.

[15] United Nations, Department of Economic and Social Affairs, *Comparative Survey of Juvenile Delinquency*, part I, North America, New York, 1958, p. 32.

[16] United Nations, pp. 43–44.

[17] President's Commission on Law Enforcement and Administration of Justice, p. 139.

[18] American Correctional Association, *Manual of Correctional Standards*, 3d ed., Washington, D.C., 1966, p. 98.

[19] President's Commission on Law Enforcement and Administration of Justice, p. 140.

[20] Stuart Adams, "Some Findings from Correctional Caseload Research," *Federal Probation*, vol. 31, no. 4, p. 49, 1967.

[21] President's Commission on Law Enforcement and Administration of Justice, p. 140.

[22] President's Commission on Law Enforcement and Administration of Justice, p. 38.

[23] Frank Reissman, "The 'Helper,' Therapy Principle," *Social Work*, vol. 10, no. 2, pp. 27–28, 1965.

[24] Stanton Wheeler et al., "Juvenile Delinquency: Its Prevention and Control," consultants' paper in President's Commission on Law Enforcement and Administration of Justice, *Task Force Report: Juvenile Delinquency and Youth Crime*, U.S. Government Printing Office, Washington, D.C., 1967, p. 423.

[25] National Institute of Mental Health, *Diversion from the Criminal Justice System*, Center for Studies of Crime and Delinquency, Rockville, Md., 1971, p. 9.

[26] National Institute of Mental Health, p. 25.

[27] President's Commission on Law Enforcement and Administration of Justice, pp. 149–150.

[28] President's Commission on Law Enforcement and Administration of Justice, p. 151.

[29] President's Commission on Law Enforcement and Administration of Justice, pp. 151–152.

[30] William R. Arnold, *Juveniles on Parole*, Random House, New York, 1970, pp. 54–61.

[31] William R. Arnold, p. 99.

[32] William R. Arnold, p. 115.

[33] William R. Arnold, pp. 111–123.

[34] William R. Arnold, pp. 27–28.

[35] Sheldon Glueck and Eleanor Glueck, *Family Environment and Delinquency*, Houghton Mifflin, Boston, 1962, pp. 137–140.

[36] James S. Campbell, "The Family and Violence," in James Campbell et al., *Law and Order Reconsidered*, a staff report to the National Commission on the Causes and Prevention of Violence, vol. 10, U.S. Government Printing Office, Washington, D.C., 1969.

[37] Daniel Glaser, *The Effectiveness of a Prison and Parole System*, Bobbs-Merrill, Indianapolis, 1964, pp. 36–52; William R. Arnold, pp. 107–132.

[38] Douglas Lipton, Robert Martinson, and Judith Wilks, *The Effectiveness of Correctional Treatment*, Praeger, New York, 1975.

[39] Government of Japan, *Summary of White Paper on Crime 1969*, The Research and Training Institute of the Ministry of Justice, Printing Bureau, Tokyo, 1970, pp. 41–56.

[40] Walter D. Connor, *Deviance in Soviet Society*, Columbia, New York, 1972, pp. 122–129.

[41] Ministry of Justice, *The Penal Code of Sweden*, Stockholm, 1965, pp. 15–18.

[42] Ministry of Justice, pp. 16–17.

[43] Juvenile Delinquency Interdepartmental Council, *Standards and Goals for Juvenile Justice*, U.S. Government Printing Office, Washington, D.C., p. 19.

[44] Juvenile Delinquency Interdepartmental Council, p. 20.

Juvenile Institutions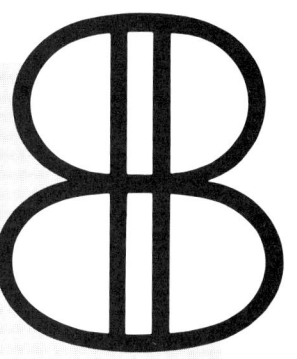

The story of juvenile institutions is the story of a dream that has not come true. The problems of youth are not new to American society. When the children of the poor and the new immigrants were running about in the streets of New York, New Yorkers shut them up in a house of refuge and were relieved to think that the problem of unruly youth had been solved. That was in 1825, when we relied heavily on juvenile institutions.

Today, in the mid 1970s, we find that juvenile institutions have failed to reduce crime. Recidivism rates, imprecise as they may be, are notoriously high. The younger the children are when they enter an institution, the longer they are institutionalized, and the farther they progress into the criminal justice system, the greater is their chance of failure.[1] The National Advisory Commission on Criminal Justice Standards and Goals states:

> Institutions do succeed in punishing, but they do not deter. They protect the community temporarily, but that protection does not last. They relieve the community of responsibility by removing the young offender, but they make successful reintegration unlikely. They change the committed offender, but the change is more likely to be negative than positive.[2]

The facts are very clearly in favor of diversion and community programs. As community programs expand, major institutions for youthful offenders face an increasingly difficult task. These programs remove from the institution the most stable individuals, who previously had a moderating influence on others' behavior.

HISTORY OF INSTITUTIONS: AN UNFULFILLED PROMISE OF REFORM

We have already seen, in Chapter 1, how Americans in the early nineteenth century started to rely heavily on penal institutions as an instrument of reform. Strangely, they thought of a correctional institution not only as an instrument of reform for the incarcerated, but also as a model of reform for the entire society in disorder. The expectation of achieving social reforms from these institutions was too unrealistic. There was an intense faith in the rehabilitative powers of a carefully designed environment in a house of refuge.

The early part of the nineteenth century was the era of discovery of institutions. The first house of refuge was founded by New York philanthropists in 1825. The first penitentiary in the Pennsylvania prison system was built in 1840. The ideas for the penitentiary and the house of refuge were conceived about the same time. Several states had houses of refuge by 1850. These houses were designed to be places of strict discipline, orderliness, and obedience. The primary task of the institution was to teach discipline and respect for authority. The children were kept under unrelenting supervision until they were reduced to a state of "cheerful submission." The managers of the houses of refuge wanted ever-increasing authority to deal with the children without any interference from families. The children were whipped for flimsy reasons, even for bed wetting.[3]

However, emphasis soon shifted from repressive correction to mere custodianship. This resulted mainly from overcrowding by a large variety of juvenile inmates with a still larger diversity of problems. Also, the second generation of reformers was not happy with the harsh treatment meted out to the youth. "The most serious and disturbing objection was to the discipline of the refuge. Critics believed it was harsh and senseless, sometimes indistinguishable from the corrections in the state penitentiary."[4]

Reacting to these pressures, the superintendents became content with merely "running the ship smoothly." They forgot all about rehabilitation. The promise of reform remained unfulfilled.

Since then, the houses of refuge have been succeeded by industrial schools and training schools. The labels have been changed, but there has been little change in the program content of these institutions. To the harsh, repressive, disciplinary approach were added industrial, educational, and religious programs.

Religious programs, as one would expect, were more prominent in sectarian schools. With the advent of Freudian theories, the psychoanalytical and casework approach became more prominent. Some of these juvenile institutions acquired an educational orientation, complete with campuses, halls, libraries, deans, teachers, and graduation ceremonies. Other institutions copied the model of a therapeutic community, though only a few succeeded in acquiring the real character of a therapeutic community. Some smaller centers have experimented with innovative practices.

Except for some of the therapeutic and experimental communities, most of these institutions have not impressed the experts. There is a growing disenchantment with juvenile correctional institutions after their 150 years of existence. Massachusetts has already done away with them. The National Advisory Commission's report, *Corrections*, says:

> It is no surprise that institutions have not been successful in reducing crime. The mystery is that they have not contributed even more to increasing crime. . . . Concentrated efforts should be devoted to long-range planning, based on research and evaluation. Correctional history has demonstrated clearly that tinkering with the system by changing individual program areas without attention to the larger problems can achieve only incidental and haphazard improvements.[5]

PRESENT STATUS OF INSTITUTIONS

According to the 1971 census of juvenile detention and correctional facilities, there were 722 such institutions at that time. The administration of these institutions was found to be about equally divided between state and local governments. Detention centers are operated mostly by local governments, and correctional facilities by state governments. On June 30, 1971, these facilities held 57,329 individuals: 44,140 males and 13,099 females (see Table 8–1).[6]

In the temporary care facilities, among first commitments there were four males to every female. Among recommitments, the ratio was twelve to one. Of the types of temporary care detention facilities, detention centers and shelters were described in Chapter 5. Diagnostic centers and the correctional facilities are described below.

TABLE 8-1[1] Number of Juvenile Facilities and Number of Children Held on June 30, 1971

Type of facility	Number of facilities	Number of children held	Percentage of total children	Average length of stay
ALL FACILITIES IN THE UNITED STATES	722	57,239	100.00	Not calculated
ALL TEMPORARY CARE FACILITIES				14 days
Detention centers	303	11,748	20.52	11 days
Shelters	18	363	0.64	20 days
Reception or diagnostic centers	17	2,486	4.34	51 days
ALL CORRECTIONAL FACILITIES				7.8 months
Training schools	192	35,931	62.77	8.7 months
Ranches, forestry camps	114	5,666	9.90	6.6 months
Halfway houses and group homes	78	1,045	1.83	7.2 months

[1] Adapted from U.S. Department of Justice, Law Enforcement Assistance Administration, *Children in Custody: A Report on the Juvenile Detention and Correctional Facility Census of 1971*, U.S. Government Printing Office, Washington, D.C., 1974.

Reception and Diagnostic Centers

These centers handle mostly adjudicated delinquents; they are almost all operated by state governments. The staff members administer tests, collect social history data, and prescribe treatment. In states that do not have reception or diagnostic centers, many correctional facilities have their own reception or classification units where new arrivals are screened for assignment to treatment and educational programs.[7]

Training Schools

Known by different names, the training school is the most prevalent type of juvenile correctional facility. It is generally the largest of all juvenile facilities. Each state has separate institutions for boys and girls, and there are a few coeducational training schools. Because separate boys' and girls' schools provide an unnatural and repressive environment to the adolescent residents, many administrators seem to favor coeducational institutions. The training schools receive a wide variety of youths. However, those involved in felonies and other serious offenses are more likely to be sent to these schools for the protection of society and for their own protection and treatment.

Girls' training schools give rise to several types of romantic undercurrents—homosexual alliances between girls, heterosexual fantasies, and endless jealousies. Girls do not form gangs outside, and they do not generally form cliques inside the institution. Instead, they tend to cling closely to best friends. It has been observed that institutionalized girls painfully tattooed the names of their most intimate girlfriends on their wrists. A girl would then skin off the name with a razor when she had to seek a new girlfriend upon release of the old friend.

The main theme is lovemaking. Relationships are intense. In Arohota Borstal (Australia), the girls used a curious collection of names for each other. The names symbolized certain qualities of the relationships among them. Among the names were Rebel, Cobra, Tiger, Dagger (probably aggressive), Hubby, Wifey, Sister, Baby, Daughter, Cousy (kinship), Darl, Special Darl, Lovely (endearment), Sailor Boy, Bicycle, Mattress, Tel-Star, Big One, and Sloppy Chops (some kind of personal intimate relationship).[8] Much goes on beneath the surface and is therefore not visible to staff members in girls' communities. The staff members have to sense the internal dynamics of the community from occasional outbursts, fits of tears, and the cries and wails of the girls.

The girls who are sent to the institutions generally come from seriously disorganized family backgrounds. They thus present serious treatment and rehabilitation problems. Proportionately more girls than boys have drug problems and venereal diseases. In addition, they are burdened with out-of-wedlock pregnancies, illegitimate children, and a host of similar problems which complicate their rehabilitation.

Though not all girls' institutions are the same, some of the training schools are somewhat punitively regimented. They use punishment cells for very minor infractions of the rules.

Ranches and Forestry Camps

These camplike institutions are used generally for boys, and very rarely for girls. They are usually located in rural settings, and often permit greater freedom of movement than the training schools. It was once felt that a juvenile delinquent from an urban area would benefit from exposure to a rural environment. This is no longer held to be so. However, the greater community contact and less restrictive daily routine of these facilities are presently thought to be more beneficial for many juveniles than the strict custody of the training school.[9] At many places, children are transferred from training schools to forestry camps once they have received the maximum benefit from the school.

Halfway Houses and Group Homes

Halfway houses and group homes are the least physically restrictive of the correctional facilities. They are often found in urban areas, where such facilities are sorely needed for a large variety of problems. Existing institutions, such as drug abuse centers, mental health clinics, institutions for emotionally disturbed children, and homes for runaways are often full to capacity, with waiting lists for new clients. Some of these clients can be placed in halfway houses during their waiting period. Halfway houses and group homes are also suitable for those children who neither fit well in a foster home nor would benefit from being sent to a training school.

One group home can offer good care for eight to ten children under the supervision of two adults. Keller and Alper contend: "Permitting close association with others of their own age, the group situation is often easier for the adolescent to live with than placement in a foster home by himself would be."[10] Speaking about the particular suitability of group homes for some children, Fink et al. say: "Some of the children may have had such severe experiences in their own homes as not to be able to move into the closeness of a foster home nor to risk being lost in the institutional group."[11] Because these residential centers are located in the heart of the community, the juveniles can make good use of community resources.

> The growing belief that the correctional process should contain a maximum of interaction between the juvenile and his community has produced support for their establishment. A majority of such facilities are located in residential neighborhoods in converted private dwellings. Halfway houses and group homes generally allow their residents to leave the facility daily for attendance at school or work. This controlled exposure to the community is often supplemented by individual and group counseling. An individual may be committed directly to these facilities by the juvenile court or may be required to earn transfer by his behavior in a more secure setting.[12]

Distinct patterns are apparent in the geographic dispersion of different types of facilities. Halfway houses and group homes are most prevalent in more urbanized, highly industrial areas, notably the New York region. These types of facilities are virtually nonexistent in more agriculturally oriented and less urbanized sections of the country.

THE INMATES

Seventy percent of the females and 23 percent of the males in juvenile institutions are being held for offenses for which only juveniles can be charged, such as truancy and curfew violations. (It is a pity that 70 percent of the girls are considered dangerous to themselves or to society). Girls have a far lower rate of recommitment than boys, even though fewer girls are released on aftercare supervision. Releases to aftercare or parole comprise 71 percent of the discharges of children of both sexes.[13]

Half the male adjudicated delinquents are guilty of felonies, whereas only 8 percent of the female delinquents are confined for these offenses. The least common violations are drug offenses: Six percent of both the male and female adjudicants are held on this account.[14] The average length of stay of inmates in juvenile correction facilities in the year 1971 was about 7.8 months. The states which kept juveniles in these institutions for the shortest period of time were Oregon (4.8 months), Arizona (5.0 months), and Oklahoma and Kentucky (5.5 months each). The states which kept juveniles for the longest period were Wyoming (17.5 months), Kansas (14.5 months), and Texas (11.3 months).

There is no clear-cut geographical pattern as to the length of stay in training schools. Generally speaking, Western states (Oregon, Arizona) had the shortest institutional stay. Mountain states (Colorado, Utah, Wyoming) required their juveniles to stay longest in correctional facilities. There was no consistent relationship between the average length of stay and the per capita operating expenditure incurred in these institutions. The average per capita operating expenditure in the United States was $6989 in 1971. The Southern states in region IV (Alabama, Florida, Georgia, Kentucky, Mississippi, North Carolina, South Carolina, Tennessee) had the lowest per capita expenditure.[15]

WORKING PHILOSOPHY

According to the Task Force Report on Corrections, the early "school of industry" or "reformatory" sought chiefly to teach the difference between right and wrong. Today, the old method is being increasingly questioned. Working philosophies now are moving in new directions, primarily for two reasons. First, about half the individuals released from juvenile training facilities can be expected to be reincarcerated. Second, the experts agree that if treatment is to produce lasting change, it must touch upon the personal reasons for delinquency. The new approach must concern itself with the meaning of delinquent behavior *to the youngster*. The Task Force Report on Corrections goes on to say:

> Therefore, according to this view, the function of a training facility is to help a minor look honestly at his own attitudes and see to what degree they create difficulties in the sense that "as ye sow so shall ye reap." Having seen this, a minor then has a personal reference point for change that is connected with his own perception of "good"; he can arrive at personally responsible behavior because he feels this personal connection.[16]

So the institution is to create conditions which help youngsters understand their behavior and bring about genuine changes. Youngsters are to be trusted in situations requiring responsible and honest behavior, even at the risk of their escape from custody. The public, which has incarcerated the children for secure custody, is upset by escapes. Thus, the superintendent is obliged to wind up the project in youth training and revert to merely operating the institution smoothly. The superintendent begins to "play it safe" and take no chances with the children.

Another practice which diverts training schools from their primary task is the varied intake. Training schools become a dumping ground for many youths who do not belong in the schools. The court may commit youngsters to training schools when their primary need is a foster home. It may commit youngsters whose involvement in trouble is primarily situational rather than deep-seated, and who could be handled more efficiently under community supervision. The schools are also obliged to take in children who are mentally retarded or psychiatrically disturbed and for whom there is no room in the institutions appropriate to their needs.[17]

TREATMENT PROGRAMS

Ideally, a treatment program should be a coordinated effort on the part of all departments in the training school: clinical, educational, technical, and administrative services. Staff members must act as a team, playing their roles with a unity of purpose. This is easier said than done. Staff members differ widely in their views on correctional strategies and in their disciplinary orientations. The superintendent must be a person of exceptional ability in the area of human relationships to lead the entire staff in the proper direction. The following are some of the components of treatment programs, that must be coordinated to achieve the desired results.

Group Living

The primary characteristic of any child care institution is that the children are cared for in groups. Group living in a training school cottage, along with 15 to 20 other children, has advantages and disadvantages. Some of the basic needs of all children are protection, security, recognition, love, and a sense of achievement.[18] Many delinquents are deprived of these essentials, and the group can provide some of them. Group living also teaches fellowship, a sense of sharing, and a spirit of comradeship.

One of the chief disadvantages is that some individuals are lost in the group. Some children are too shy to participate in the group; they are lonely, or they stay out of the group. On the other hand, some are quick to assume leadership and bully other children in the group. The cottage parents must know what is happening in the group. Because of the nature of their job, they must have an exceptional understanding of children and of group dynamics.

> [The cottage staff] must possess a capacity to relate to children and a flexibility in adapting to new situations. They must be able, for example, to tolerate deviant behavior without condoning it or repressing it in a punitive manner. Other personal qualifications should include: emotional maturity and stability, ability to take hostility without reacting in a hostile manner, alertness, and sensitivity to group situations.[19]

It has been suggested that *group workers* can make useful contributions in the planning and development of the cottage life program. They have special skills in planning group composition, designing group living to support individual treatment, and creating an awareness of the impact of group pathology on treatment goals.[20]

Group Therapy Therapeutic procedures known as *group therapy* or *guided group interaction* make use of the group as an instrument of behavior change in the participants. In the initial sessions, the participants generally discuss their day-by-day problems of institutional life. Later on, the discussions move on to preparation for handling "life outside." The youngsters are helped to understand themselves as they compare their own reactions with those of others trying to resolve similar problems.[21]

Psychological and Psychiatric Services

A clinically trained psychologist administers diagnostic tests, interprets significant findings, attends case conferences, and conducts both individual and group therapy sessions. The psychologist can also be helpful in the selection of personnel and the inservice training of staff. The services of a psychiatrist are much more costly and, accordingly, more difficult to obtain. A psychiatrist can handle a few cases of severe psychiatric disturbance, make referrals to other specialists, and be consulted in overall program planning.[22] While all seventeen reception and diagnostic centers had full-time psychiatrists, only 10 of 192 training schools in the United States had full-time psychiatrists in 1971.[23]

Casework Services

Caseworkers (or social workers) have a key role in the treatment process. They gather significant information on the youngsters for the initial case conference and help in planning treatment programs for individuals. They maintain continuing contact with their clients and their clients' families. They attend to their clients' changing needs. They update the students' (inmates') records with progress reports received from different staff members. They also serve as liaison between the children and the outside world.

The Children's Bureau suggests that a caseworker should not be assigned more than thirty students as a full case load.[24] Because of the professional nature of the work, a caseworker should have a graduate degree from an accredited school of social work.

Religious services and counseling "are regarded by many as being on an equal plane with other effective treatment factors."[25] The well-trained chaplain plays an important role as a member of the treatment team. The chaplain should have special training and experience in the behavioral sciences, such as social work, psychology, or sociology.

Educational Program

The educational program in a training school is similar to the program of the public schools outside the institution. Students can transfer from one to the other easily. Training-school teachers must be capable of teaching remedial courses and specialized topics. Training schools encourage hobby programs and creative arts under the supervision of a classroom teacher. In a training school in Canada, the boys made a full-length film on "A Day in a Boys' Village."

Students are also introduced to a few trades, depending on their interest and the marketability of the skills involved. However, many leave the training school before their trade courses are completed. Recreational programs are provided (1) as an outlet for youthful energies, (2) as a valuable medium for teaching children how to use their leisure time, and (3) as an opportunity for healthy participation with other youths. The students are given a fair range of choices in both individual and group recreation.

Availability of Services

The 1967 Task Force Report on Corrections alleged that services which were shown as being available "on paper" were not always available "in practice." For example, medical and dental services were reportedly available in 96 percent of the state-operated juvenile institutions. However, budgetary considerations determined whether they were actually available. There were wide variations in the quality of professional services available at these state-operated juvenile institutions. Because of low salaries, there is a large turnover in the professional staff. The Task Force on Corrections concluded that the services were inadequate to meet the needs of the inmates and as such, needed vast improvement.[26]

In its 1973 report, *Corrections*, the National Advisory Commission on Criminal Justice Standards and Goals did not speak much about training schools. It remained silent on standards for training schools but, instead, emphasized community corrections.[27] The commission wanted to banish these institutions, except for the confinement of dangerous youths. A subsequent report says:

> While detailed national data are not presently available, it is safe to say that many more youngsters are put on probation or diverted at intake from the juvenile court into community programs than are incarcerated. Many authorities in juvenile corrections argue that, by and large, incarceration of juvenile delinquents has not proved to be a workable correctional strategy. Some maintain that most juvenile correctional institutions do more harm than good. Others argue, however, that sometimes juvenile delinquents must be incarcerated for both their own protection and that of the community.[28]

LINKS WITH THE COMMUNITY

A training school cannot afford to be isolated from the rest of the community. In the interest of reintegrating its students into the community, the school should maintain two-way communications with the community. Students should be referred as necessary to outside agencies, such as drug abuse centers, child guidance clinics, children's aid societies, employment agencies, family planning centers, and welfare departments. Depending on the degree of trust established between the staff and the students, the latter should be given some responsibility for attending public schools, churches, or training programs without supervision. They may also be sent home on furlough, allowed to attend movies, or sent to YMCA or YWCA summer camps.

Similarly, interested citizens should be allowed to interact with the youngsters through various activities. The volunteers should be well screened and briefed. Some training schools have used volunteers effectively as "sponsors" of individual children. In this "big brother" or "big sister" type of relationship, the adult should be willing to give service on a long-term basis. People from all walks of life are usually willing to volunteer.

> Their offers of help are usually in the form of donations, but frequently, too, in the form of some kind of service. Each offer must be dealt with on an individual basis, keeping in mind what is best for the children and at the same time retaining community understanding and support and recognizing that some volunteers can be excellent interpreters of the school. If

offers of service are accepted then the superintendent and the volunteers should explore together the conditions surrounding the service to be given.[29]

THE INMATE IN A TOTAL INSTITUTION

The inmate society is subjected to the severely damaging effects of institutionalization. The inmate's world is shrunk to a small campus, where all the activities of daily life—working, playing, and sleeping—are confined to one place. These activities are conducted according to a tight schedule, in the immediate company of a large number of other persons who are all required to do the same thing together.[30]

Goffman calls correctional institutions "total" institutions. The inmates are subjected to constant supervision and surveillance. This leads to hostile stereotypes: the staff often sees the inmates as bitter, secretive, and untrustworthy; the inmates often see the staff as high-handed and mean.[31] Work is unrewarding, devoid of all incentives, and boring. The training school may not train youngsters at all for life outside the institution. It may, on the other hand, untrain them and disable them somewhat, relative to daily life on the outside.[32]

In a custodial institution, the inmates are subjected to a process of *mortification of self*. They are asked to wear institutional clothes; they cannot wear their own clothes and have to part with their valuables. The boy cannot keep the length of hair he desires; the girl cannot dress the way she desires. The inmates suffer *personal defacement* and *personal disfigurement*.[33] They are no longer the beloved children of their families, but inmates in an impersonal world. They have been dispossessed of their previous roles.

The territory of the self is invaded: Their case histories contain several discreditable facts. They have to live with undesirable roommates. They are subject to search. They have no freedom of action.[34]

The inmates must adjust to all these deprivations. They seek various means of adjustment. To save their identity, they reject their rejectors rather than themselves. They make the institution their home (colonization). They seek stable sexual ties. They make friends (fraternalization). They become prostaff (conversion).[35]

None of the institutional activities prepares the inmates for their return to the larger society outside. In fact, they develop doubts about their ability to face the outside world. The disculturation and stigmatization resulting from confinement create several difficulties on their return to society.[36]

The deprivations inflicted by incarceration in large custodial institutions compels some inmates to resort to illicit means to fulfill their needs. The common misery brings them together. They close ranks against the staff, whom the inmates accuse of denying the fulfillment of their needs. Out of this antistaff cohesiveness emerge inmate leaders, who are very antisocial in their attitudes. These leaders try to win followers, amass power, and then use their power to meet illegitimate needs—their own and those of their adherents.

CUSTODIAL VERSUS TREATMENT INSTITUTIONS: DIFFERENTIAL IMPACT

As institutions differ in size, goals, and philosophy of treatment, so do they differ in their impact on the inmates. Street et al. thought that the belief system (delinquents are treatable or untreatable) and the institutional goals (custodial versus treatment) are the prime movers in the impact of treatment. "As the goals of organizations change under the impact of treatment concepts, staff attitudes, inmate orientations, and inmate leadership structures alter."[37] Street et al. present sets of beliefs which fall into three categories.

1. *Authority and Obedience* Inmates must learn to obey the authorities. The experience of incarceration and deprivation will make them change their deviant behavior.
2. *Learning and Socialization* Delinquents who have not learned good habits for lack of proper schooling can learn good habits if they are involved in a learning process—for example, academic and vocational programs. Those who were not well nurtured in a disorganized family should be socialized in the secure and supportive environment of a cottage parent system.
3. *Therapy* On account of deep-seated deviance, rehabilitation should take place through extensive changes in character and personality. The methods employed are individual, group, and milieu therapies.

Institutional Models

To parallel these belief systems, the researchers selected three organizational models, ranged along the custody-treatment continuum. The six institutions (three large and public, three small and private) corresponded to the following models, with two institutions in each category:

1. *Obedience/Conformity Model* The two custodial institutions used coercive methods.
2. *Reeducation/Development Model* The two institutions sent children to the community schools for academic and vocational training during the day.
3. *Treatment Model* The two therapy-oriented institutions used individual and group therapies to reconstitute the individuals.

The three sets of institutions were selected by the researchers to maximize differences in the goals and the strategies used to change inmates.[38] A comparative view of the characteristics of the three institutional categories is given in Table 8–2.

The most important finding obtained by this comparison is that the institutions differ in the damaging effects of total institutionalization. As the institutions become less depriving, more democratic, and more treatment oriented, the inmate groups become less opposed to the staff, more favorable to the staff, and more receptive to treatment technologies. A noteworthy observation is that inmate background attributes did not account for this variation.[39] The variations in impact on the inmates are the result of institutional goals and staff attitudes toward the control and treatment of their wards.

Street et al. also point to the self-fulfilling prophecies of the respective staffs. For example, the staff of the obedience/conformity institutions perceived their inmates negatively and tried to suppress them; the inmates reacted disruptively. In contrast, the staffs at the treatment institutions were not overly concerned about inmates' threats to institutional stability; they found that such threats usually did not come to fruition.[40] So staff attitudes are important; output depends on input.

TABLE 8-2 Institutions and Their Properties: A Comparative View

Dimension	Obedience/conformity institutions	Reeducation/development institutions	Treatment institutions
Assumptions	Inmates would learn to conform out of fear of the consequences	Inmates possess resources that could be drawn upon and developed	Deviance could be corrected only by a thoroughgoing reorientation and reconstitution of the inmate
Strategy to change people	Demanded compliance and submission	Sought moderate changes through training for a gainful career	Sought broad changes; altered personalities, improved interpersonal relations
Staff attitudes	Staff used coercive methods; staff pessimistic of inmate change	Used reeducative methods; staff optimistic of inmate change	Used more differentiated and voluntaristic methods; staff optimistic of inmate change
Authority	Cottage staff had most authority	Balanced distribution of authority	Clinicians had most authority
Coordination	Executive's firm direction of all phases of staff performance	Some coordination	Coordination of relatively autonomous subordinates
Routine	Tasks routinized	Some nonroutinized programs	Nonroutinized programming
Decision making	Decisions made about inmates without any personal consideration	Some personal consideration	Decisions made about inmates with their consent and personal input
Voluntaryism	Negative toward voluntaryism	Positive toward voluntaryism	Positive toward voluntaryism
STAFF PERSPECTIVE Relationship	Staff members perceived staff-inmate understanding as difficult	Staff members perceived staff-inmate understanding as possible and helpful	Staff members firmly believed in staff-inmate understanding as a key factor in treatment
Discipline	Discipline emphasized	Balance between discipline and permissiveness	Permissiveness emphasized
INMATES' INFORMAL SYSTEM Perspective	Inmates perceived the institution and staff negatively	Inmates' perception fairly positive	Inmates perceived the institution and staff positively
Inmate organization	Because of high deprivations, inmates tended to organize themselves cohesively to procure legitimate and illegitimate items of value	Group formation tended to be more after the pattern of treatment institutions	Inmates tended to organize more voluntarily around friendship patterns; inmate friendships were not antistaff, and the groups tended to be prostaff
Leadership	Inmate leadership highly involved in illicit and secret activities; inmate leaders tended to gather power by controlling illicit rewards; leaders presented solidary opposition to staff	The leaders were a good influence for the inmates; they were not antistaff in any way	Inmate leadership was positive and constructive in its outlook; there was no need for the leaders to gather power, as there was no quest for illicit rewards; leaders were prepared to act along with the staff

THE THERAPEUTIC COMMUNITY

The therapeutic community has been defined as a school for living: It trains the residents of an institution for adjustment to social life and work conditions outside the institution. It has also been called a school for personality growth: It prepares clients for better participation in the life of the community.[41] The therapeutic community puts emphasis on free communication between staff and inmates and on healthy democratization designed to help each other in the community. It is essential for a therapeutic community to recognize its goal clearly. Once there is agreement on the goal, the entire community strives collectively toward that goal.

The essentials of a therapeutic community may be grouped into two processes: The first is therapeutizing the environment of the institution. The second is generating programs for the residents for the (1) fulfillment of roles of responsibility, (2) expression of their creativity, and (3) encouragement of achievement.

Therapeutizing the Environment

The total institutions, having several structural and functional problems, exercise a destructive influence on their wards or residents. Those who are admitted to these institutions on account of some social, emotional, or character problem are further burdened with the problem of living in a closed institution. The problems of the residents, instead of being solved, become compounded. So, it is logical to first reduce the damaging effects of a total institution. Some suggestions are given below:

1. *Reduce Impersonality* Give very personal attention to the problems presented by the residents and the staff.
2. *Reduce Deprivations* The deprivations inflicted by total institutions are many. Not all of them can be eliminated; at best, some can be reduced somewhat. The quality of life can be improved by fewer restrictions, more amenities, better care, and progressive programs.
3. *Recognize Institutional Problems* Total institutions are beset with the usual problems: escapes, assaults, power struggles, group rivalries, group jealousies, conflicts, and hostility toward the staff. The institutional staff should give equal, fair, and firm

treatment to all parties and factions; develop rational social controls; promote healthy interaction between different reconcilable groups (and keep apart those groups that are deadly antagonists); seek participation of the group members in most decisions; and discourage bad practices early, before they become popular. The institutional community should give security to insecure members, recognition for good work, and rewards for good conduct.

4. *Normalize Life* Life in the institution should approximate life in the open community. The helping institution cannot help very much in an artificial and abnormal atmosphere.

Training for Responsible Roles

If we expect inmates to behave responsibly once they are outside the institution, we must entrust them with roles of responsibility. They should be allowed to form activity groups: hobby, drama, athletic, music, and art groups, for example. The staff should tap the creative potential of the inmates. Residents should be afforded all possible opportunities for social contact with employment services, firms, farms, factories, and aftercare agencies. In group counseling sessions, guest speakers should be invited to talk on problems affecting youth. In his famous study, *Cottage Six*, Polsky says:

> In short, the staff must help to motivate the boys toward goals, democratically pursued, which are realistic and meaningful: develop skills and positive attitudes toward work, overcome fears toward girls and sex, learn the meaning of cooperation, discover the joy of play, form a realistic orientation toward their families and cultivate a sense of personal identity. However, utopian as these ideals may sound, it is important for the staff to be clear about the goals each cottage should strive for.[42]

Some experimental communities, such as the Detroit Pioneer House, Highfields, and the Provo experiment, have come to be known as classic in the juvenile literature. There must be some other illuminating examples of therapeutic communities, both in America and abroad, which have remained unknown.

EFFECTIVENESS OF INSTITUTIONAL PROGRAMS

Lipton et al. have analyzed several studies and have come up with the following findings with regard to the effectiveness of different institutional practices. It should be noted that even though a program helps inmates adjust in the institution, it may or may not be of help in postrelease adjustment.

Individual Psychotherapy

Boys, 15 to 17 years of age, in two California institutions were given individual psychotherapy. These boys did not differ from untreated boys on measures of institutional adjustment. Individual therapy also showed minimal impact on postinstitutional behavior.[43]

Group Treatment

Various forms of group treatment, especially when used in combination with community meetings or individual counseling, improve institutional adjustment. Small-group counseling showed better results when the youthful offenders were matched with a counselor of similar personality characteristics, or when the boys were asked to select their own counselor after a 2-week get-acquainted period. In other words, group counseling programs fare better if the participating inmates feel comfortable with the counselor.[44] Also, participants with a high maturity level show a more favorable impact than do those with a low maturity level.[45]

The studies also indicated that group counseling administered to *newly admitted* youthful offenders does improve institutional adjustment. To be more gainful, group counseling should be started *early* during the incarceration rather than late; and it should be administered by professional therapists.[46] It has been pointed out by Lipton et al. that the skills required to get along in an institution may not be the same as those required to get along in the community. "Those responsible for the operation of custodial institutions may have to choose between programs that assist in maintaining institutional order and those that have impact upon post-institutional performance of offenders."[47]

It is also important to remember that each institution has its own potential. When a program is introduced in several institutions, its "impact on inmates' institutional adjustment and post-release behavior may differ dramatically from institution to institution."[48] This finding has a very important implication: The outcome (success or failure) of a program is a property of the institution rather than of the program itself. Every institution has to find its own way in making a program work; it may learn, however, from the successes and failures of other institutions.

Milieu Therapy

Milieu therapy improves the institutional adjustment of juvenile, youthful, or adult offenders. It improves staff-inmate relationships, and places inmate leadership in the hands of "rule followers" and not "rule violators." Milieu therapy may produce a "cool" institution, but Lipton et al. require further evidence to determine "whether institutional adjustment of this sort benefits the offender outside the institution."[49] It is difficult to determine how long the benefits of milieu therapy last—more so when the inmates move back to their communities, which are more crime-provoking than therapeutic.

Other Programs

In the matter of *educational programs* in the institutions, the attitudes of teachers and peers toward the student's education were more important than the instructional content. The teacher's sincere concern, personal interest, and dynamic instruction are very vital to an inmate's educational achievement. Similarly, the supportive influence of peers is very helpful. In one of the studies, "when the teacher was allowed to develop a more tightly knit, mutually supportive peer group with his boys, significant improvements in educational achievements were obtained."[50] This was accomplished before they could develop a united antichange front.

While educational programs undoubtedly add to the personal equipment of the inmate, ex-offenders need the active help of many persons in the community to regain their place in society.

> Regular academic instruction is simply not sufficient to overcome the enormous environmental and social obstacles that interfere with the reentry of "ex-offenders" into the com-

munity. Such problems as the response to ex-offenders by employers, by the police, by unions, and even by their own families cannot be overcome by simply improving the educational level of the ex-offenders.[51]

The *drug abusers* have not been easy to treat. Most correctional workers have used group methods with an expectation that the participants can help each other. It has been suggested that users of different drugs have different subcultures, and that workers should understand the differences in the subcultural patterns. Lipton et al. say

> The study points to the need to distinguish various subcultural patterns in drug use—for example, recreational use of marijuana, subcultures focused on opiates, chronic drunkenness offenders, skid row heavy drinking, religious use of psilocybin, addiction to medically useful "dangerous drugs," and so forth. Omnibus drug programs that view all drug abuse as similar are not likely to even gain access to drug users especially if such programs do not accurately portray the differential effects of various drugs.[52]

Furthermore, group methods can be more effective with addicts when they make themselves accessible for treatment and are motivated to improve.[53]

SUMMARY

Juvenile institutions trace their origin to the house of refuge, first founded in 1825. The early superintendents of these houses were very harsh disciplinarians. Repressive discipline was considered good for the incarcerated children and good for society. While the superintendents called for still more authority to handle the children, reformers protested that the children were treated in the same way as the worst criminals in large penitentiaries.

With the introduction of industry and education in these institutions, the houses of refuge came to be known as industrial schools or training schools. Most are single-sex institutions, although there are some coeducational institutions as well.

Recently, there has been a growing disenchantment with these institutions. Many experts want to discontinue their use, and retain only a few for dangerous and violent youths. It appears that these institutions were overused for the detention of children who did not belong in custodial institutions: 70 percent of the girls and 23 percent of the boys had committed only juvenile offenses, such as truancy and curfew violations.

Many training schools are located in isolated areas. Some youths are now transferred to halfway houses or group homes which are located in urban centers; other children are sent to forestry camps and ranches for varied experiences.

The moralistic approach has been replaced by an insightful approach: youngsters are helped to take an honest look at themselves. The training of students involves living in groups, with group discussions and group therapy. Individual services are available through casework and psychological and psychiatric services. The average student stays in the training school for a period of 8 months. During this time, the students can take part in educational, vocational, recreational, and religious programs.

A total institution is very depriving for the inmates, and damaging to their self-image. The inmates become antistaff. A training school which is custodial in its orientation actually untrains youngsters for outside life. On the other hand treatment-oriented institutions, which use therapeutic and voluntaristic methods, generate positive attitudes in inmates. The inmates are prostaff and can be involved in very constructive activities. A therapeutic community makes an all-out effort to bring about positive changes in its inmates. To rise to the status of a therapeutic community, an institution must rid itself of all destructive and harmful influences and institute programs for training in responsibility.

Evaluating the effectiveness of institutional programs, Lipton et al. found that group counseling was more effective if the youths feel more comfortable with their counselor and if they began to participate in group counseling early—soon after their admission to the institution. Students who score higher on the maturity scale profit more from group therapy. Just as inmates differ in their willingness to participate and profit from a program, so do institutions differ in their potential for making the treatment a success. In educational programs, the teacher's real concern and personal interest and the supportive influence of peers are very beneficial.

Discussion Questions

1. If 70 percent of the girls confined in juvenile institutions are status offenders (runaways, incorrigibles, etc.), do you favor the phasing out of training schools for girls?
2. What are the differences between institutional communities for boys and those for girls?
3. What classifications of juvenile offenders would you recommend for transfer to ranches and/or forestry camps?
4. How would you design a volunteers' program for a juvenile institution?
5. What kind of program do you recommend for the training of cottage parents?
6. What are the advantages of using group counseling in institutions?

Glossary

Casework The mode of operation of the social workers. Consists of investigation, diagnosis, and counseling of individuals and families to help them improve personal and community relationships.

Cottage Parents The employees of juvenile institutions who live with the children in the cottage and take care of them day and night. They act as parents, guides, and counselors.

Disculturation According to Erving Goffman, inmates of a total institution go through a process of untraining which renders them incapable of managing certain features of daily life on the outside, if and when they are released. This process is known as disculturation.

Group Therapy Any form of treatment in which several persons work together, with a therapist, to help effect a cure or solve a problem for themselves and the others.

Group Worker A person who has the skills to facilitate growth of individuals through various group activities.

Maturity Level The degree to which a person has achieved adulthood, socially and emotionally.

Mental Retardation Any less-than-normal intellectual development.

Milieu Therapy A treatment designed for maladjusted persons, involving substantial changes in the person's immediate environment or life circumstances.

Voluntaristic Methods The methods employed by volunteers, both individually and collectively, to help the offending and maladjusted persons resettle in the community.

Voluntaryism Involvement of interested citizens who volunteer their services to public and private agencies to help solve the difficult problems of crime and criminals.

Footnotes

[1] National Advisory Commission on Criminal Justice Standards and Goals, *Corrections,* U.S. Government Printing Office, Washington, D.C., 1973, p. 350.

[2] National Advisory Commission on Criminal Justice Standards and Goals, p. 351.

[3] David J. Rothman, *The Discovery of the Asylum,* Little, Brown, Boston, 1971, pp. 212–232.

[4] David J. Rothman, p. 258.

[5] National Advisory Commission on Criminal Justice Standards and Goals, p. 352.

[6] U.S. Department of Justice, Law Enforcement Assistance Administration, *Children in Custody: A Report on the Juvenile Detention and Correctional Facility Census of 1971,* U.S. Government Printing Office, Washington, D.C., 1974, p. 1.

[7] U.S. Department of Justice, p. 5.

[8] A. J. W. Taylor, "The Significance of 'Darls' and 'Special Relationships' for Borstal Girls," *British Journal of Criminology,* vol. 5, no. 4, pp. 406–409, October 1965.

[9] U.S. Department of Justice, p. 6.

[10] Oliver J. Keller and Benedict S. Alper, *Halfway Houses: Community Centered Correction and Treatment,* Heath, Lexington, Mass., 1970, p. 90.

[11] Arthur E. Fink et al., *The Field of Social Work*, 5th ed., Holt, New York, 1968, p. 193.

[12] U.S. Department of Justice, p. 6.

[13] U.S. Department of Justice, pp. 6–9.

[14] U.S. Department of Justice, pp. 6, 8.

[15] U.S. Department of Justice, pp. 54–55.

[16] President's Commission on Crime, *Task Force Report: Corrections*, U.S. Government Printing Office, Washington, D.C., 1967, p. 142.

[17] President's Commission on Crime, p. 143.

[18] U.S. Department of Health, Education, and Welfare, *Institutions Serving Delinquent Children: Guides and Goals*, Children's Bureau Publication 360–1957, U.S. Government Printing Office, Washington, D.C., p. 41.

[19] U.S. Department of Health, Education, and Welfare, p. 45.

[20] U.S. Department of Health, Education, and Welfare, p. 54.

[21] U.S. Department of Health, Education, and Welfare, p. 55.

[22] U.S. Department of Health, Education, and Welfare, p. 57.

[23] U.S. Department of Justice, p. 18.

[24] U.S. Department of Health, Education, and Welfare, p. 52.

[25] U.S. Department of Health, Education, and Welfare, p. 62.

[26] President's Commission on Crime, p. 144.

[27] National Advisory Commission on Criminal Justice Standards and Goals, p. 352.

[28] U.S. Department of Justice, p. 6.

[29] U.S. Department of Health, Education, and Welfare, p. 77.

[30] Erving Goffman, "On the Characteristics of the Total Institutions: The Inmate World," in Donald R. Cressey, editor, *The Prison, Studies in Institutional Organization and Change*, Holt, New York, 1961, p. 17.

[31] Erving Goffman, p. 18.

[32] Erving Goffman, p. 23.

[33] Erving Goffman, p. 28.

[34] Erving Goffman, p. 44.

[35] Erving Goffman, pp. 54–59.

[36] Erving Goffman, pp. 65–66.

[37] David Street et al., *Organization for Treatment: A Comparative Study of Institutions for Delinquents*, Free Press, New York, 1966, p. vii (foreword by Morris Janowitz).

[38] David Street, pp. 21–25.

[39] David Street, p. 249.

[40] David Street, p. 251.

[41] Marshall Edelson, *Sociotherapy and Psychotherapy,* University of Chicago Press, Chicago, 1970, p. 170.

[42] Howard W. Polsky, *Cottage Six,* Russell Sage Foundation, New York, 1962, p. 177.

[43] Douglas Lipton et al., *The Effectiveness of Correctional Treatment,* Praeger, New York, 1975, p. 307.

[44] Douglas Lipton et al., p. 311.

[45] Douglas Lipton et al., pp. 312–313.

[46] Douglas Lipton et al., p. 314.

[47] Douglas Lipton et al., pp. 315–316.

[48] Douglas Lipton et al., p. 325.

[49] Douglas Lipton et al., p. 324.

[50] Douglas Lipton et al., p. 361.

[51] Douglas Lipton et al., p. 363.

[52] Douglas Lipton et al., p. 388.

[53] Douglas Lipton et al., p. 389.

Community Corrections

Community corrections is not entirely a new movement. As far back as the 1840s, John Augustus was supervising offenders in the community; however, the idea was not generally accepted until the middle of this century. Both juvenile and adult corrections remained separate from the community for about 150 years. When overreliance on institutions continued to produce disastrous results for both prisoners and administrators, the latter had to think of alternatives to confinement. This led to the rise of several residential and nonresidential programs in the community.

In the juvenile field, a major breakthrough came from the President's Commission on Crime in 1967. They proposed a new coordinating agency called the *youth services bureau*. For effective reintegration of youth into the community, citizens must become deeply involved with community-based corrections. The juvenile programs need a great number of volunteers. Such issues are discussed in this chapter.

COMMUNITY-BASED CORRECTIONS: AN ALTERNATIVE TO CONFINEMENT

According to the National Advisory Commission on Criminal Justice Standards and Goals, the term *community-based corrections* includes all correctional activities that take place in the community. The community base must be an alternative to the confinement of an offender at any point in the correctional process.[1] The juvenile offender can be diverted to such an alternative at several points during the long journey from prearrest to parole.

Every police department seeks available sources in the community for deterring or diverting delinquent behavior. The juvenile court relies heavily on community-based alternatives; probation is one of the most often used programs. The juvenile correctional system makes use of several residential and nonresidential programs in the community. Correctional workers, if they are community oriented, can easily make use of resources that are provided to citizens in general—health, education, counseling, and employment services.

The Juvenile Justice and Delinquency Prevention Act of 1974 gives the following picture of the community corrections.

> The term "community based" facility, program or service means a small, open group home or other suitable place located near the juvenile's home or family and programs of community supervision and service which maintain community and consumer participation in the planning operation, and evaluation of their programs which may include, but are not limited to, medical, educational, vocational, social, and psychological guidance, training, counseling, alcoholism treatment, drug treatment, and other rehabilitative services.[2]

Some major advantages of community-based corrections are:

1. Nondangerous offenders can be treated more profitably in the community with minimum disruption of their lives.
2. Community-based programs are more restorative and rehabilitative in nature.
3. These programs are much less expensive than incarceration in the institutions.
4. Although the success rate of community-based programs (in terms of the clients' staying out of trouble with the law) is not significantly higher than the success rate resulting from incarceration in the institutions, the success of the former is not any lower than that of the latter.

> The most rigorous research designs generally have elicited the finding that offenders eligible for supervision in the community in lieu of institutionalization do *as well* in the community as they do in prison or training school. When intervening variables are controlled, recidivism rates appear to be about the same.[3]

A large number of offenders who are candidates for incarceration may instead be retained in the community as safely, as effectively, and at much less expense.

5. The deterrence studies hold some surprises for those who consider incarceration as more deterrent than community-based programs. Available studies suggest strongly that jurisdictions making extensive use of probation instead of prison do not experience increased recidivism. Similarly, studies of confinement length do not establish that longer prison terms result in decreased recidivism. Most likely, community-based programs are as deterrent as prisons. Simply being under official jurisdiction constitutes a punitive experience for nearly all offenders.[4]

6. The elimination of incarceration does not eliminate control. The use of control and surveillance is basic to a sound community corrections system.

YOUTH SERVICES BUREAU[5]

The youth services bureau (YSB) is expected to become the most influential agency in coordinating community services pertinent to the needs of youth. The juvenile courts have been the fulcrum of the juvenile justice system since the turn of the century. Youth services bureaus are likely to play a similarly important role outside the judicial system in the community in the years to come.

The idea of the youth services bureau originated with the President's Commission on Crime in 1967. The Task Force on Juvenile Delinquency and Youth Crime recommended that communities establish youth services bureaus, if possible, in comprehensive neighborhood community centers. It was suggested that these centers and bureaus be close to where the youngsters live, so that they could walk in whenever they needed a service. Youngsters could ask for help on their own, or be referred by their family, school, or church. The police and the courts were also to make use of these bureaus when indicated.

The commission envisaged that referral to the bureau and acceptance of the bureau's services would be voluntary. The commission did not intend that the bureaus have any coercive power; they were to be free of all the dangers and disadvantages of coercive power. However, the bureaus were to have the authority to refer to the courts within a brief length of time—30 to 60 days—those with whom they could not deal effectively. The YSBs were expected to handle a large number of youths. There might well be some who needed an authoritative approach and would have to be processed through the courts. Some YSB clients might be "trouble-making" and "acting out" youths, in the words of the Task Force on Juvenile Delinquency and Youth Crime.

A national census in 1972 identified 150 youth services bureaus. Since then, many more bureaus have been established in the United States, with the help of federal funds. The principal goal of the bureaus is to provide and coordinate programs for young people.

The Bureau's Goals

At the present time, youth services bureaus have at least five goals. These are:

1. Diversion
2. Providing services to youths
3. Coordination of both individual cases and programs for young people
4. Modification of systems of services for youth
5. Involvement of youth in decision making and the development of individual responsibility[6]

Diversion

Diversion is no longer a matter of grace or leniency; it has become indispensable. The juvenile justice system simply cannot handle all the cases referred to it.[9] According to a 1970 estimate, the police made 4 million contacts with youths during that year. Two million of these contacts resulted in arrests, and over a million of the arrests resulted in referral to the juvenile courts. Of the cases referred to juvenile courts throughout the nation, nearly 500,000 were handled judicially. Thus, roughly, one out of eight police contacts resulted in a court appearance.[7] Today, no one denies the necessity of diversion; the important thing is to develop criteria and guidelines for diversion. There is, at present, a movement to exclude status offenders from the juvenile courts and divert them to the youth services bureaus exclusively. It has also been proposed that the police and court intake units exhaust all possible diversionary avenues before referring a juvenile to the courts. These strategies increase the importance of diversion. Diversionary avenues are expected to expand with the growth of youth services bureaus.

It is desired that the YSBs be free of the influence of criminal justice agencies. An independent bureau is likely to have better relationships with its clients. However, the most successful bureaus maintain close communications with the justice agencies, without compromising their independence. In several communities, the YSB staff has participated in ride-along programs with police patrol officers, often for several evenings. This type of experience increases the sensitivity of YSB staffs to the problems of law enforcement officers in working with juveniles and their families.[8] Juvenile justice agencies should drop judicial proceedings against any youth who has been referred to a YSB. This allows the bureau freedom in the nonjudicial handling of the youth.

Providing Services for Youth

There has always been some distance, both geographical and social, between the youth and the social agencies in a community. Many social agencies are located a considerable distance from the habitat of the youth who need them most; the agencies thus seem inaccessible. When social services are not within easy reach of youths, the youths tend to care less about making use of these services. Both parties are somewhat suspicious of each other.

To the youngsters, the agencies seem too impersonal, and somewhat alien to their subculture. The youths do not accept social services unless these services are approved by their peers. To the agencies, many of the delinquents seem hard to reach. The agencies are then inclined to systematically exclude troublemaking youth from participation. The YSBs introduce youngsters to the appropriate agencies, and even purchase their services if costs are involved.

There has been some controversy as to whether a YSB should develop and provide services itself, or function principally as an information and referral service. One set of standards for youth services bureaus states explicitly that a bureau should only organize the delivery of services to children and their families. Another question concerns whether or not a self-referred youth should be provided services without the permission of his or her parents. The majority opinion favors providing services to youths in their best interest without parental permission.

In order to encourage self-referrals, the bureaus have made their services accessible to young people through convenient

250 Juvenile Delinquency

locations and hours, by instituting hotlines and drop-in centers, and through the activities of outreach workers. Bureaus are being located near schools and near business and commercial areas frequented by young people. The hotlines are being operated by sympathetic interns who are usually college students.

YSBs arrange individual and family counseling, with systematic follow-up and case conferences, in complete confidentiality. Group programs include new approaches to youth-police relations, parental education, group activities, and group counseling. Group homes and crisis centers are also operated under the auspices of YSBs. The Youth Advocacy Program in South Bend, Indiana, contracts for a street academy, an alternative school program for dropouts from the public schools.[9] Youth services bureaus are trying to undo the harm done to dropouts, before it is too late. If a conventional school has driven these youths to the streets, then a YSB provides a different kind of small academy for them on the street.

Coordination of Cases and Programs

One important function of YSBs is to coordinate centrally all community services for young people (see Figure 2). This coordination must necessarily be undertaken at two levels: (1) case coordination, and (2) program coordination. On the individual case level, services to youth have often been fragmented and duplicated. "Youth workers have more frequently been responsible only for the content of their endeavors rather than for both their content and consequences."[10] Case conferences can improve the consistency of approach and integration of services. Programs can best be coordinated by:

1. Making a directory of all the programs available in a certain area
2. Identifying duplications and gaps in available services
3. Eliminating unnecessary duplication and filling gaps
4. Bringing together the different agencies for discussions on matters of mutual interest

The directory of services should be updated frequently.

System Modification and Youth Development

The YSB system can be modified by periodically evaluating services and making necessary changes in the whole system or in subsystems. Youth services bureaus greatly encourage the involvement of youth in planning and administering the bureaus' programs.

> Developing youth responsibility for delinquency prevention, modifying existing services, and providing alternative services are all closely interrelated, if one accepts the premises that the recipients of services have useful opinions and creative ideas about the services, and that increasing their input into the planning of services is valuable.[11]

Youth services bureaus make extensive use of volunteers, both professional and nonprofessional. The most powerful resource of the bureaus is the youths themselves: Youths who come to the bureaus seeking service frequently become deliverers of service. The YSB is a place where young people can serve as well as be served.[12]

RESIDENTIAL CENTERS

Community-based corrections requires some residential centers for a large variety of offenders for diverse reasons. Known by different names, these residential centers fall in the following categories: group homes, halfway houses, work-release centers, study-release centers, drug abuse centers, and crisis centers.

Six to ten young people usually live in a group home. The home is owned or rented by agencies and staffed by employed "parents" or counselors. They are supplemented with necessary professional services, obtained mostly through existing community resources.[13]

Halfway houses have several functions: They serve as work-release centers; study-release centers; centers for the preparation of inmates for release to the community; hostels for probationers; temporary shelters for probationers; and temporary shelters for parolees, runaways, and inmate patients who visit psychiatrists or other specialists on an outpatient basis. Juvenile offend-

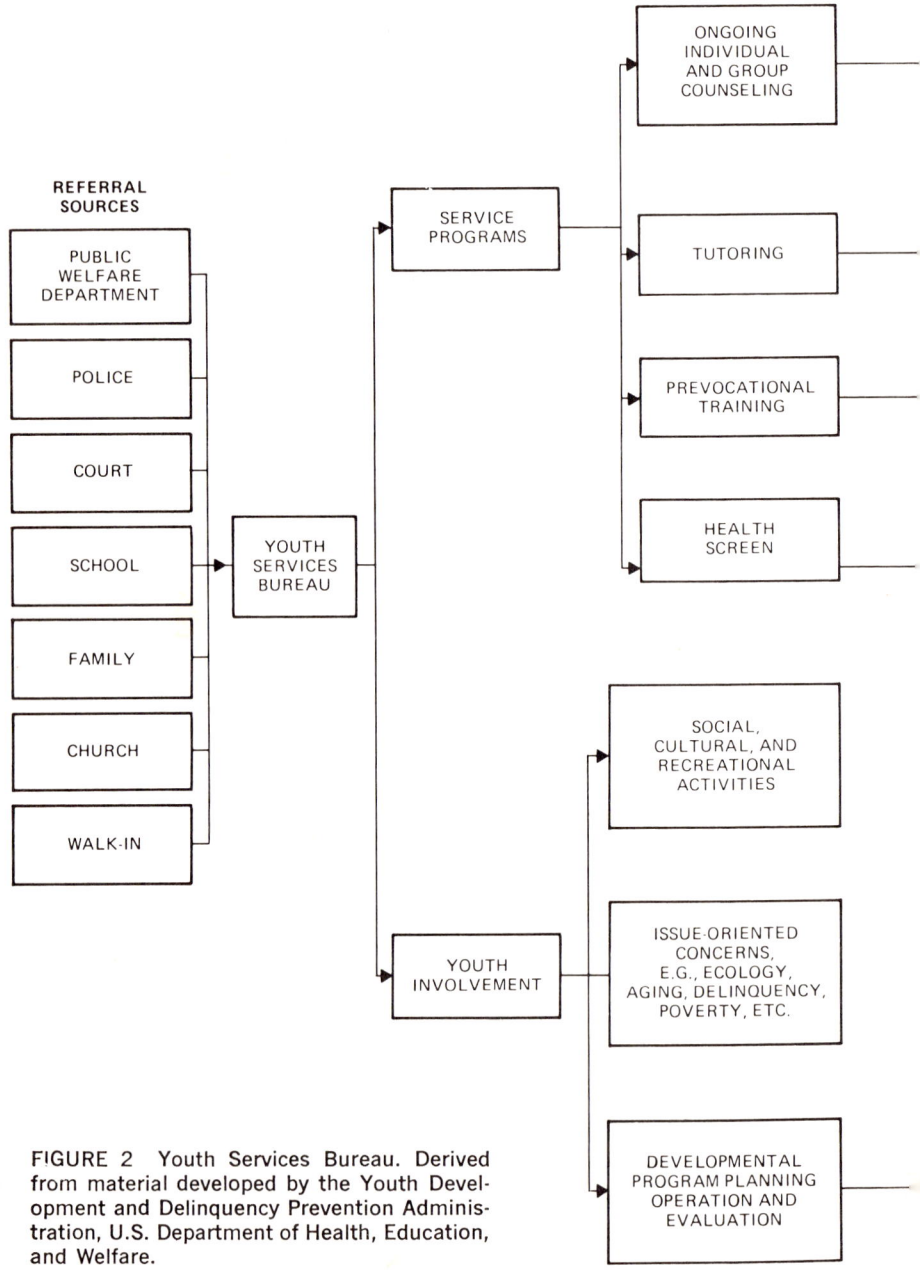

FIGURE 2 Youth Services Bureau. Derived from material developed by the Youth Development and Delinquency Prevention Administration, U.S. Department of Health, Education, and Welfare.

YOUTH SERVICES SYSTEM

- FAMILY COUNSELING → INDEPENDENT HOUSING LOCATED
- INDIVIDUAL COUNSELING → UTILIZE INDIVIDUAL AS COUNSEL AIDE → PERMANENT VOLUNTEER

- G.E.D.* PREPARATION → AWARD OF G.E.D.* → ADMITTANCE TO COLLEGE

- VOCATIONAL TRAINING → JOB DEVELOPMENT AND PLACEMENT → JOB UPGRADING

- TATTOO REMOVAL
- PSYCHIATRIC AND PSYCHOLOGICAL TESTING
- EYE CHECK / DENTAL CHECK

*GENERAL EDUCATION DIPLOMA

- RUNAWAYS → EMERGENCY SHELTER
- HOT LINE CRISIS CENTER
- YOUTH-TO-YOUTH ADVOCACY
- DRUG ABUSE → SCHOOL DRUG INFORMATION PROGRAM

ers can be admitted to halfway houses by direct commitment or by transfer.

Drug abuse centers serve both inpatients and outpatients. Crisis centers serve a large variety of juvenile offenders in diverse emergencies. While these centers provide shelter, board, lodging, and counseling to their residents, the latter are encouraged to retain their contacts with the community. The centers provide transport for residents to their places of work, schools, clinics, shopping centers, churches, drug abuse centers, detoxification centers, and recreational centers. Those who are under partial custody are encouraged to visit their families on home leave or furlough. Families are invited to the centers and are involved in family counseling programs.

Volunteers work with the youths, both on a one-to-one basis and on a group basis. Volunteers visit the youths at the halfway houses and take them on outings. They provide a variety of services ranging from genuine friendship to professional therapy. Some centers are coeducational; they provide a healthy interaction between the sexes. Single-sex centers arrange social get-togethers for this purpose. A halfway house can be arranged as a therapeutic community if the staff so desires.

These community treatment centers are operated by federal, state, local, and private agencies. Some of the private centers are supported by churches. According to the National Advisory Commission on Criminal Justice Standards and Goals, "the popularity of the 'community correctional center' concept in recent years has led to a bandwagon effect with rapid growth of a wide variety of programs." Broadly speaking, residential centers serve the following purposes:

1. Act as an alternative to incarceration in secure, isolated institutions. Centers can provide custody, protection and even temporary removal without inflicting the usual damage of a closed correctional institution.
2. Assist, through graduated release, the reentry of offenders into the community on their way out of the institution.
3. Provide, in the community, study, training, or work which is not available in an isolated training school.
4. Provide temporary shelter to a juvenile probationer or parolee who has been rendered homeless for some reason.
5. Make available to the juvenile offender some special commu-

nity services which are not easily available in a training school, such as special medical, surgical, dental, or psychiatric care.

6. Provide intensive treatment, such as individual, group, and family counseling, to juvenile offenders, either as inpatients or outpatients.

7. Serve as a "restitution" house where offenders live while working to earn funds to compensate victims.

Residential centers occupy an important place in corrections. They represent a kind of mixture of institutional and community-based programs. These centers are more successful with some offenders than with others. In terms of recidivism, older youthful offenders (aged 16 to 21) seem to succeed better after being released from such less restrictive institutions, particularly when they do not identify with the criminal world.[14]

Residential Milieu Therapy: The Highfields[15]

Of the several experiments in residential milieu therapy, the Highfields experiment stands out as a classic. Boys adjudicated by the courts were randomly distributed between Highfields (the experimental group) and a reformatory (the control group). The Highfields boys worked in the community during the day and were bused back to the center in the evening. The Highfields was a small residential center that could accommodate twenty boys at a time. The usual stay at the center was about 3 months. The center was operated administratively by two or three people.

Group sessions, supervised by a trained therapist, were held five evenings a week. During their group meetings, the participants used a method known as "guided group interaction." Guided group interaction focuses on here-and-now interpersonal interactions, rather than on internal processes. Intense discussion revolves around the current problems and experiences of the group members.

The research addressed itself to measuring the effect of the Highfields experiment on (1) recidivism, (2) expressed attitudes toward families and law and order, and (3) the basic personality structure. The boys released through Highfields showed a lower rate of recidivism than those given reformatory releases. However, the Highfields treatment did not bring about any significant change in their attitudes or in their personality characteristics.

(It should be noted that black boys showed greater success with the experiment than white boys.) In sum, residential centers seem to have a different impact on different types of offenders.

The Highfields study was followed by two similar studies in New Jersey, known as the Essexfields and Collegefields.[16]

Silverlake Experiment[17]

Another comprehensive study evaluating the impact of a community-based residential center is known as the Silverlake experiment. An experimental group and a control group were chosen from the inmate population of Boys Republic, situated in Los Angeles County. The experimental boys, aged 15 to 17, were lodged in a large house on the outskirts of downtown Los Angeles. The total number of boys at any one time never exceeded twenty; the size of the staff was also small. An experienced person, a bachelor, was hired as the director of the Silverlake experiment; he resided at the house. The program included a daily group meeting, attendance at school, some housekeeping chores, and tutorial activities. The daily meetings of boys were aimed at problem solving, using guided group interaction. The boys played ball in the evening and were allowed weekend visits home. The program remained in operation for a period of 32 months.

The experiment proved the following points in favor of community-based corrections: Treatment of delinquents in an open center presented little danger to the community. The rate of recidivism in the experimental group was about the same as in the institutional group. The operating costs of the open center were far lower than those of the larger institution.[18]

With correctional institutions located in isolated areas, the community and the corrections facilities have not gotten to know each other very well. Now, whenever a juvenile center is located near a community, the residents become suspicious and fearful of the center and its inmates. Silverlake had similar experiences; the neighborhood was not pleased with the presence of the boys. Even though the boys did not bother them, "the boys did not look right" to their neighbors. Public schools were reluctant to enroll Silverlake boys. Even the families of the Silverlake youths were negative about the experiment.

Normally, the police do not view such an experiment favorably. However, this experiment had a great supporter in the captain of the Juvenile Bureau of the Los Angeles Police. He came out to a citizens' meeting to testify that there had been no increase in crime in the neighborhood. This is an indication that better communication between residential centers and the community is very desirable.[19]

Runaways from open centers can, at times, present problems to the staff. In the Silverlake experiment, runaways rose to 37 percent in the experimental group. The identification of the escape risks has always been a dilemma for corrections workers. At Silverlake, boys with a background of serious automobile and family-related offenses, low self-concept, and a tendency to be autistic proved a higher escape risk.[20]

While examining the runaway phenomenon, Empey and Lubeck made a very valuable observation—that there may not be a uniform set of personal and social variables that will predict running away, unless organizational characteristics are held constant.[21] When the organizational characteristics are changed, predictors made up of personal and social variables undergo a change in predictive capacity. This concept will be clear from the following illustration:

At the approximate midpoint of the study, the Silverlake staff was confronted with a high runaway rate. Expecting a serious reaction from the community, the staff imposed strong negative sanctions against runaways. Runaways were arbitrarily transferred from Silverlake to another institution for incarceration. A comparison of presanction and postsanction personal and social variables yielded interesting results. Before the runaway sanctions, peer influence was a propelling force behind the runaways; it declined after the sanction. Conversely, personality factors which were weak predictors before the sanction became more prominent after the sanction. In other words, the imposition of stringent sanctions deterred certain types of individuals from running but, at the same time, stirred the anxiety of other boys.[22]

Thus, personal and social variables alone are not very effective predictors in corrections. These variables become more accurate as predictors in the context of organizational characteristics.

NONRESIDENTIAL PROGRAMS

Structured correctional programs which supervise a substantial part of an offender's day but do not include live-in requirements are another community-based necessity. The clients are persons who need more intensive services than probation usually can offer, yet are not in need of institutionalization. School and counseling programs, day treatment centers with vocational training, and guided group interaction programs are among the treatment modes used, many with related services to families.[23]

Provo Experiment[24]

A classic example of a nonresidential program is the Provo experiment. The program was begun at Pinehills, Utah; it was designed to help habitual and persistent delinquents between the ages of 14 and 18 years. The experiment was based on the sociological premise that these habitual offenders were the active members of a delinquent social system; and, as such, they would experience personal change if their group (the gang) changed its shared values and points of view. The group should, accordingly, be the active change agent. The group should play a major role in helping its members solve their problems and make basic decisions affecting the participating members. It was also recognized that the project needed the community's active support for reintegration of the delinquent boys.

The experiment included only repeater offenders. After the adjudication of each boy's case, the judge decided either to place the boy on probation or incarcerate him in a training school. Boys for the experimental group were chosen randomly from these two groups. The subjects in the experimental group were thus compared with two other groups—the probation group and the training school group.

The boys were exposed to the program for periods ranging from 6 to 9 months. The subjects in the experimental group lived in their own homes. Some went to school, while others were employed in a paid city work program. On Saturdays, all the boys worked. Late in the afternoon of each day, the boys left school or work, went to Pinehills, and attended a group meeting. These sessions were patterned after the technique of guided group interaction, emphasizing the idea that only through a group and its processes can a boy work out his problems. The group was powerful in the sense that it decided when each boy was ready to be released. These boys knew each other well, and it was difficult for them to hide their past activities or to fake improvement. Each boy had to confess all his delinquent acts and then analyze his feeling and attitudes in so doing. The group also had the authority to recommend to the court the transfer of a member to the state training school.

From a peer point of view, this procedure had three main goals:

1. To question the utility of a life devoted to delinquency
2. To suggest alternative behavior
3. To provide recognition for a youngster's personal reformation and willingness to reform others[25]

The experimental group showed a more favorable evaluation, for both the short term and the long term. The experimental group had a mean arrest rate of 0.60, against 1.82 for the controls.[26] Six months after release, the experimental group showed a success rate of 84 percent, the probation group 77 percent, and the incarcerated group 42 percent. Furthermore, the most serious offenses were committed by escapees from incarceration, and not by the experimental subjects who never left the community.

The Provo experiment demonstrated that serious offenders can be treated in the community without posing unnecessary danger. However, a similar experiment, known as the Los Angeles Community Delinquency Control Project, did not show very encouraging results for the community-based group. Boys who succeed in one program may not succeed in another, and vice versa. Just as individuals differ, programs differ in their organization, setting, and content. The Los Angeles city boys may have had more difficulty in adjusting to their urban milieu than the Provo rural boys had.

Empey advises the proper matching of personal and organizational factors.[27] Comparing the residential (Silverlake experiment) and nonresidential (Provo experiment) programs, he found that the nonresidential program yields more desirable results.[28] Moreover, "the experimental community program seemed to have a more lasting impact on those assigned to it than did the incarceration control program."[29] According to Empey, just as local communities, families, and schools are likely to vary, correctional programs will have to vary in the way they operate.

A monograph prepared by the National Institute of Mental Health describes some *attendance centers* or *daycare centers* where boys were sent under court order for intensive treatment. The boys were compelled to attend a course of academic and vocational training, followed by group counseling at the day-care center. They returned to their homes in the evening, but were required to bring their parents with them at least one night during each week for family therapy sessions.

Girls aged 14 to 17 who failed to adjust adequately on probation were referred to another center by their probation officers. Entry to the program was voluntary. The program was aimed at instilling a sense of responsibility and self-esteem in the girls. Weekly meetings of parents at the center were intended to strengthen family ties.[30]

One common ingredient in all drug abuse programs is some form of group therapy. Daytop Village in New York treated heroin addicts who were on probation. Program elements included reality therapy on a group basis, social meetings with members of the outside community, marathon encounters, parents' group meetings, vocational guidance, a graduated plan for return to the community, and periodic testing for the use of narcotics.[31] In a Honolulu study, glue sniffers were compared with marijuana users, with the following findings:

> The inhalant users more often come from economically and culturally deprived backgrounds; their parents more typically explain the drug use in terms of conditions external to the child. The "deprivation" in the life of the marijuana users is more interpersonal. Parents of marijuana users tend to see the cause of their child's drug use as within their offspring and thus under his control. . . . Group treatment appears especially important for inhalant users since they are highly peer-group oriented.[32]

Exemplary Projects[33]

More recently, a few nonresidential programs have qualified as exemplary projects. These projects have passed the rigorous screening conducted by the Law Enforcement Assistance Administration and have succeeded in reducing crime. Brief descriptions follow.

Community-based Adolescent Diversion Project, Champaign-Urbana, Illinois In these two adjacent communities, the university and the criminal justice system have joined forces in a successful new approach to helping juveniles in trouble. Youngsters who have contacts with the police that would normally lead to arrest are referred instead to the project. The youths thus bypass the juvenile court and the prosecutor.

Undergraduates at the University of Illinois fill volunteer roles in the project for academic credit in psychology. The student counselors are trained and supervised by experienced psychologists as part of their ongoing course activities. They are graded on their work with project clients.

Each youngster is assigned to a student volunteer for a 4½-month period. After assessing the youngster's problems and needs, the counselor develops a program for the client, using one of two innovative techniques:

- The youngster may sign a contract with his or her parent and the project. The contract spells out specific obligations to be fulfilled. The contract helps to instill responsibility, and gradual achievement of the provisions enhances the youngster's self-confidence.
- The counselor may use the child advocacy approach, introducing the youngster to educational, welfare, health, mental health, and vocational resources in the community and encouraging their use.

The project's diversion power is evident in the following comparisons between the seventy-three participants and a control group:

Number of Police Contacts per Juvenile (academic year 1974–75)		
Group	One year prior to project	During project
Participants	2.21	0.46
Control group	2.25	2.25

601 Juvenile Diversion Project, Sacramento, California The 601 project of the Sacramento Probation Department provides short-term family crisis counseling in place of juvenile court processing for status offenders, truants, runaways, and unmanageable youngsters. Youths and their families meet with 601-project counselors, usually within 2 hours of referral, to work out the delinquency problem together. If a youth cannot reasonably return home at once, temporary accommodations elsewhere are sought, with the consent of both parents and child.

The original 601 program (the name derives from the relevant section of the California Penal Code) has been expanded to include certain cases of criminal conduct, such as petty theft and possession of drugs. The basis for this expansion lies in the project's first-year record:

	Project cases	Control cases
Petitions filed	3.7%	19.8%
Repeat offenses (within 1 year)	46.3	54.2
Juvenile hall detention	13.9	69.4
Average detention time, nights	0.5	4.6
Average case handling time, hours	14.2	23.7
Average case cost	$284	$526

Providence Educational Center (PEC), St. Louis, Missouri The Center, funded by the Law Enforcement Assistance Administration (LEAA) under its Impact City Program, diverts delinquent boys from training school incarceration. Through an intensive education and counseling program, which allows most boys to remain in their homes, PEC has cut case costs and lowered recidivism rates.

Teams of professionally trained counselors, educators, and social workers devise an individual program for each child. A boy "graduates" when he has achieved the eighth-grade reading level required for high school admission in St. Louis and/or has demonstrated adequate social functioning—usually 9 months after referral. PEC can accommodate seventy-five boys.

PEC provides enriched, intensive education not available in other juvenile institutions. It does so at a greatly reduced per-child cost, and with a markedly lower rate of recidivism. Its impact can be seen in the following statistics:

Comparative Costs of St. Louis Area Juvenile Treatment Institutions

Treatment center	Cost per child
Providence Educational Center	$ 3,309
Missouri Hills Home for Boys	6,800
Boys Town of Missouri	6,700
Missouri State Training School	11,000
	Comparative recidivism rate, %
Providence Educational Center	28.1
Probation	65–70
Residential institutions	50

INTERACTION BETWEEN CORRECTIONS AND COMMUNITY: A TWO-WAY PROCESS

The problem of delinquency is too monumental to be solved by a handful of people in the juvenile justice system. It is the problem of everyone, and the entire community should be involved in its solution. The most important of the social institutions that are vitally concerned with the treatment of delinquents are (1) the family, (2) the school, (3) the church, and (4) the work world. These are the institutions with whom the delinquent's relationship is somewhat spoiled.

Just as there are parent-teacher associations, there is a need for parent-counselor associations. All families that are affected directly or indirectly by juvenile delinquency should give active cooperation to correctional agencies. Schools are already concerned with juvenile justice agencies, but they have a tremendous responsibility to involve themselves actively in preventive, corrective, and remedial work. The schools should have very strong links with youth services bureaus. The church has already evidenced its interest in youth by establishing several church-supported juvenile services. There is room to widen and upgrade these services. American business, with all its economic power, can be of great assistance in the rehabilitation of young offenders. Business people should take the initiative in opening doors to jobs for ex-offenders by:

- Providing postrelease and prerelease employment opportunities in meaningful positions
- Giving appropriate guidance to correctional administrators regarding job trends and anticipated employment openings
- Mobilizing business and public support for improved industrial and vocational training programs in institutions
- Providing volunteer management expertise to advise on the curriculum and equipment needed for realistic training
- Informing the membership of business associations about the manpower resources available from correctional institutions[34]

America has historically dealt with crime and delinquency problems locally. For this reason, it is imperative for local jurisdictions to marshal all the resources within their area. The community has the responsibility of making policies and then implementing them. Lay citizens should function in task forces or study groups and serve in a general advisory role. Advisory bodies should have broad representation and should include members of minorities, ex-offenders, women, and special community interest groups.[35]

Voluntary associations of private citizens with shared concerns already exist. They are known by different names, such as prisoners' aid societies, the John Howard Society, discharged offenders' society, Hope, and New Life. An outstanding voluntary association is the National Council on Crime and Delinquency, which has local chapters in almost every state. This organization has played a very active role in helping to get new laws legislated and in educating interested citizens' groups in matters pertaining to crime and delinquency.

In direct service roles, thousands of Americans are involved as volunteers. An active and involved citizens' group can:

- Mobilize public and legislative support for diversified treatment services and alternatives to incarceration
- Stimulate the development of detoxification centers to divert alcoholic offenders from the correctional system and into facilities with medical services
- Support the establishment of halfway houses and undertake programs to educate the community to the need for these facilities
- Organize volunteers to participate in tutoring programs for offenders
- Initiate a volunteer probation aid program to provide troubled youths with adult guidance and with assistance in schoolwork and in finding jobs
- Initiate a similar program to provide, for those in institutions, periodic contacts with people from the community who can listen to their problems, advise them, and even develop special programs to take institutionalized offenders into their homes and into the community on a well-organized basis[36]

If the interaction between the community and corrections is to be a two-way process, then correctional clients and correctional workers should contribute to the community. What can youthful offenders do for the community? We have noted that delinquent girls often express a strong desire for involvement in altruistic activities. They should be given an opportunity to volunteer for such activities. The author recalls how the thirty-seven inmates of a reform school in India helped to pave the streets of a host community on whose land they were camping for ten days. In an Illinois reformatory, a few inmates staged a variety show every week for the recreation of retarded children. On another occasion, training school inmates volunteered to donate blood in response to an emergency call from an area hospital. In an area hit by a natural disaster, the youthful residents of a halfway house were the first to rush immediate relief to the victims of the disaster.

There are numerous examples of this type. One could think of several projects in which correctional clients could be engaged to render service to their community. This kind of mutual help not only aids in breaking the usual resistance of the community to offenders, but brings about better understanding between the two.

Juvenile workers, and particularly administrators, can expect more cooperation from the community if they keep the public informed of their activities and of the impact of different projects on youth and the community. In corrections, public relations departments are generally not very effective in keeping the public informed. New correctional experiments meet with both successes and failures. To win public confidence, corrections should share its strengths and its weaknesses. The National Advisory Commission on Criminal Justice Standards and Goals advises:

> The information program should go beyond the usual press releases and occasional public hearings. Corrections must assume an educational role, a change agent role. . . . The change agent model should include massive public education efforts through the communications media and intensive educational-organizational efforts with many subcommittees —ethnic, racial, and special interest groups—for support of general community corrections and specific projects.[37]

VOLUNTEERS

There is a growing and pressing need for volunteers at all levels of the juvenile justice system. Every year, more and more agencies are adopting volunteer programs, but not all the programs are well managed. In some states, laws require the use of volunteers; those states have gained a bit more experience with volunteers. Unless an agency is fully prepared to organize and accept a volunteer program, the program remains ineffective and tends to fade out.

Unfortunately, some agencies and staff members have mixed feelings about the use of volunteers; they see them as a threat and an interference. Volunteers are inspired by a certain enthusiasm, missionary zeal, and helping spirit. If their enthusiasm is not fully matched by the staff, it begins to weaken. A recent survey concludes that "only a distinct minority of programs can claim to be rendering regular volunteer service to a majority of offenders."[38] So there is plenty of room for expansion and consolidation.

Volunteers' Profile

Volunteers perform a variety of tasks, mostly involving direct contact with offenders. Their top preference is for those tasks which emphasize continuous regular contact with offenders. This would include the areas of counseling, tutoring, recreation, visitation, contribution of materials, religious programs, entertainment, job placement, arts and crafts, assisting offender self-help groups, and prerelease preparation.[39] Volunteers also help with clerical and other administrative duties; medical doctors, nurses, psychologists, social workers, and lawyers render professional services.

What kind of people volunteer for corrections work? Largely, volunteers come from the source or sources that are tapped: a church, a university, a professional organization, a union. In one jurisdiction, a majority of volunteers may come from a church; another jurisdiction may have mostly college students as its volunteers. It depends on where volunteers are recruited and on who is available at a particular time or place. A widespread appeal will attract volunteers from all walks of life and socioeconomic levels.

An exemplary project on volunteer probation counselors in Lincoln, Nebraska, claimed to draw volunteers from all sectors of the community: blue-collar workers, professors, housewives, plumbers, attorneys, college students, and retirees.

> [The volunteers] ranged in age from 18 to 69 years, with the average being 27 years. About 60 percent were men, and about 60 percent of the volunteers were married. Thirty-nine

percent had previous counseling experience, formal training, or work experience with other community service agencies, sometimes in a volunteer role. . . . About 70 percent of [them] agree to be reassigned.[40]

In a study of probation volunteers in New Hampshire, the author found that about 40 percent of them were professionals (social workers, teachers, attorneys, managers, and sales representatives). The second largest group was students. In small towns, they were all selected by the local probation officers, which augured well for good teamwork.

Why do volunteers volunteer? The most frequent answers are generally like the following:

- "I wanted the knowledge and experience."
- "I enjoy being with people."
- "I wanted these youngsters to have some of the advantages I have had."
- "I wanted an opportunity to use skills which I possess."[41]

The Task Force on Corrections asserts that volunteers can be very successful with youthful delinquents. The delinquents generally respond favorably to a volunteer who can fill the role of the model which is lacking in their lives.[42]

SUMMARY

After years of isolation in institutions, corrections has moved into the heart of the community, where problems are expected to be solved more realistically. If offenders are to be prepared for a law-abiding life in society, the preparation should take place in the community. Following the recommendation of the President's Commission on Crime (1967), several jurisdictions are developing *youth services bureaus* to handle troubled and troublesome young people outside the criminal system. At present, youth services are fragmented, uncoordinated, and, therefore, ineffective. The bureaus will serve as brokers between youths and the social agencies, will buy services for youths when needed, and will follow up to assess the impact of the services.

To be effective, youth services must be meaningful to the youth. The bureaus are youth oriented; youngsters can walk in, request services, make their own decisions, and even volunteer their services to help others. Youths can be referred to YSBs by parents, schools, police, and the courts. However, the acceptance of a service is entirely voluntary.

The YSBs perform a very timely service in a society where there has been too much reliance on an overcrowded juvenile justice system. According to the President's Commission on Crime (1967), "about 40 percent of all male children now living in the United States will be arrested for a non-traffic offense during their lives."[43] Such a large number of youth cannot and should not be dealt with within the icy orbit of the juvenile justice system. Perhaps a large number of status offenders could be handled by youth services bureaus without any reference to the justice system. Much depends on what we make of the YSB. Any new organization can fall into a rut if we do not use it prudently.

Community-based treatment includes both residential and nonresidential programs. *Residential centers* serve several functions: work release, study release, graduated release, probation hostel, transitional lodge, and port of entry to the community. These centers serve youths at different stages of their correctional journey, and for diverse purposes. There are several residential programs, but the two classic examples are the Highfields experiment and the Silverlake experiment. Both used guided group interaction and work experience in the community.

One lesson learned from both experiments was that residential programs are more beneficial to some types of offenders than to others. Therefore, candidates for residential programs should be screened carefully. Also, the behavior of the inmates is tied completely to the organizational characteristics of the residential center: Organizational changes in the Silverlake center brought about significant changes in runaway patterns.

Nonresidential programs are generally conducted at an attendance center, during the day or in the evening, but do not include live-in requirements. Programs may consist of intensive educational, vocational, and counseling programs. Guided group interaction has been a popular form of therapy for use with peer groups, particularly drug abusers. The famous Provo experiment was based on the sociological premise that persistent offenders were generally active members of a delinquent social system. Personal change in an individual member can come only through his or her reference group. The boys participating in the experiment questioned each other intensely and helped prepare each other for law-abiding behavior. Provo and several other recent experiments seem to have been successful.

Corrections and the *community* need to work with each other closely. The family, school, and church should close ranks with corrections to start special remedial, tutorial, recreational, and counseling programs for youngsters in trouble. Both the concerned citizen and the professional person should serve on task forces to solve correctional problems. The experts should be invited to assume advisory roles. There should be proper representation of minorities on these task forces. The involved citizen should help to create new laws which are suitable to present changing needs, help provide new agencies, and help recruit volunteers.

To fight public apathy, both adult and juvenile corrections should become involved in public relations work very actively. The public should be informed and educated about youth problems and the needs of corrections agencies. Improved communication with the community will attract more and better volunteers to juvenile corrections.

Discussion Questions

1. Assume you are an administrator of community corrections, and you plan to set up a halfway house in a neighborhood. The residents of the neighborhood are strongly opposed to the proposed halfway house. How can you educate the community concerning your proposal? What reasoning would you use in support of your halfway house?
2. A group home can become a total institution in the hands of a security oriented staff. What steps would you take to guard against such a development?
3. Training school officials are generally institution oriented, and probation officers are mostly court oriented. How can we improve their orientation to the community?
4. Describe some of the youth services in your community.
5. A youth services bureau desires to develop some services of its own. What should those services entail?
6. Discuss the nature of the relationship between youth services bureaus and the social service agencies to whom they will refer youths. Do you anticipate some conflict between the two? Why?

7. How would you recruit suitable volunteers to help the residents of a group home?
8. How does guided group interaction change the behavior of participants?

Glossary

Autistic Tending to think and react in terms of the satisfaction of needs or the fulfillment of desires at the expense of realistic behavior.

Control Group In an investigation, subjects that are as similar as possible to the experimental group, and are exposed to the same conditions except for the variable or treatment being studied.

Deterrent A restraining factor.

Experimental Group In an investigation, subjects who are exposed to the variable or treatment being studied and whose reactions will indicate the influence of the variable or treatment.

Furlough A short, authorized leave of absence; in corrections, usually granted so that an inmate may visit his or her home.

Hotline A telephone service which gives information, free advice, first aid, and preliminary counseling to the caller.

Study-Release Center A center for juvenile or adult offenders which allows them to go out to school for study.

Work-Release Center A residential center from where the juvenile or adult offenders go out to work in the community during the day and participate in various programs offered at the center at other hours.

Footnotes

[1] National Advisory Commission on Criminal Justice Standards and Goals, *Corrections*, U.S. Government Printing Office, Washington, D.C., 1973, p. 222.

[2] *Public Law 93–415*, sec. 103(1), 93d Cong., S. 821, September 7, 1974.

Community Corrections 271

[3] National Institute of Mental Health, *Community Based Correctional Programs: Models and Practices*, U.S. Government Printing Office, Washington, D.C., 1971, p. 33.

[4] National Advisory Commission on Criminal Justice Standards and Goals, p. 224.

[5] President's Commission on Crime, *Task Force Report: Juvenile Delinquency and Youth Crime*, U.S. Government Printing Office, Washington, D.C., 1967, pp. 19–21; and National Advisory Commission on Criminal Justice Standards and Goals, *Community Crime Prevention*, U.S. Government Printing Office, Washington, D.C., 1973, pp. 51–69.

[6] National Advisory Commission on Criminal Justice Standards and Goals, *Community Crime Prevention*, U.S. Government Printing Office, Washington, D.C., 1973, p. 57.

[7] National Advisory Commission on Criminal Justice Standards and Goals, p. 57.

[8] National Advisory Commission on Criminal Justice Standards and Goals, p. 61.

[9] National Advisory Commission on Criminal Justice Standards and Goals, p. 66.

[10] National Advisory Commission on Criminal Justice Standards and Goals, p. 67.

[11] National Advisory Commission on Criminal Justice Standards and Goals, p. 69.

[12] U.S. Department of Health, Education, and Welfare, *The Challenge of Youth Service Bureaus*, U.S. Government Printing Office, Washington, D.C., 1973, p. 14.

[13] National Advisory Commission on Criminal Justice Standards and Goals, *Corrections*, p. 233 (also see chap. 8).

[14] Douglas Lipton et al., *The Effectiveness of Correctional Treatment*, Praeger, New York, 1975, p. 88.

[15] H. Ashley Weeks, *Youthful Offenders at Highfields*, University of Michigan Press, Ann Arbor, 1958, pp. 1–5, 7–10, 20–24, 108–128.

[16] Albert Elias and Paul Pilnick, "The Essexfields Group Rehabilitation Project for Youthful Offenders," in *Corrections in the Community*, Monograph 4, Corrections Board, Sacramento, Calif., 1964; and Saul Pilnick et al., *Collegefields: From Delinquency to Freedom*, report to the Juvenile Delinquency and Youth Development Office on Collegefields Group Educational Center, Newark State College, Newark, N.J., 1967.

[17] LaMar T. Empey and Steven G. Lubeck, *The Silverlake Experiment*, Aldine, Chicago, 1971.

[18] LaMar T. Empey and Steven G. Lubeck, p. 307.

[19] LaMar T. Empey and Steven G. Lubeck, pp. 161–185.

272 Juvenile Delinquency

[20] LaMar T. Empey and Steven G. Lubeck, p. 226.

[21] LaMar T. Empey and Steven G. Lubeck, p. 217.

[22] LaMar T. Empey and Steven G. Lubeck, p. 221.

[23] National Advisory Commission on Criminal Justice Standards and Goals, *Corrections*, p. 232.

[24] LaMar T. Empey, *The Provo Experiment, Evaluating Community Control of Delinquency*, Lexington Books, Lexington, Mass., 1972.

[25] LaMar T. Empey, p. 10.

[26] LaMar T. Empey, p. 83.

[27] LaMar T. Empey, p. 89.

[28] LaMar T. Empey, p. 93.

[29] LaMar T. Empey, p. 223.

[30] National Institute of Mental Health, pp. 14–16.

[31] National Institute of Mental Health, *Correctional Treatment in Community Settings*, U.S. Government Printing Office, Washington, D.C., 1972, p. 37.

[32] National Institute of Mental Health, p. 39.

[33] U.S. Department of Justice, National Institute of Law Enforcement and Criminal Justice, *Exemplary Projects*, U.S. Government Printing Office, Washington, D.C., 1976.

[34] Chamber of Commerce of the United States, *Marshalling Citizen Power to Modernize Corrections*, Washington, D.C., 1972, p. 16.

[35] National Advisory Commission on Criminal Justice Standards and Goals, *Corrections*, p. 228.

[36] Chamber of Commerce of the United States, pp. 17–18.

[37] National Advisory Commission on Criminal Justice Standards and Goals, *Corrections*, p. 231.

[38] U.S. Department of Justice, *Guidelines and Standards for the Use of Volunteers in Correctional Programs* (prepared by Ivan H. Scheier et al.), Law Enforcement Assistance Administration, Washington, D.C., 1972, p. 15.

[39] U.S. Department of Justice, p. 16.

[40] U.S. Department of Justice, Law Enforcement Assistance Administration, *The Volunteer Probation Counselor Program*, U.S. Government Printing Office, Washington, D.C., 1975, p. 9.

[41] U.S. Department of Justice, *Guidelines and Standards for the Use of Volunteers in Correctional Programs*, p. 101.

[42] President's Commission on Crime, *Task Force Report: Corrections*, U.S. Government Printing Office, Washington, D.C., 1967, p. 104.

[43] President's Commission on Crime, *The Challenge of Crime in a Free Society*, U.S. Government Printing Office, Washington, D.C., 1967, p. v.

Delinquency Prevention

In many societies, relatively little attention is given to the prevention of delinquency and crime. The juvenile justice and criminal justice systems are so occupied with apprehended offenders that they have little time for prevention work. In fact, the criminal justice system deals with crime mostly after it has happened; rarely does it consider prevention as a part of the job. Very few jurisdictions have a department that deals directly with the prevention of delinquency, although there may be several agencies working to prevent delinquency and crime indirectly or incidentally.

Most theorists and practitioners deal with the prevention of delinquency from a sociological perspective. Their "target is not the delinquent, nor the individual person who commits it, but the framework inside of which the delinquent career is initiated, nurtured, and confirmed."[1] The National Advisory Commission on Criminal Justice Standards and Goals works on the same premise: Delinquents are alienated from the community, and the causes of their alienation are located in the community and its social institutions. The commission leans heavily on the community for prevention and has even titled its report *Communtiy Crime Prevention.*

THE ASSUMPTIONS[2]

The report of the National Advisory Commission on Criminal Justice Standards and Goals is based on three major assumptions:

1. Citizen apathy and indifference contribute to the spread of delinquency and crime.
2. Delinquency and crime rates are influenced by the activities of private and public agencies.

3. Community crime prevention efforts would benefit existing institutions and agencies that are organized for purposes other than crime prevention.

Elaborating on these assumptions, the report comments: "This country has preferred in large part to ignore the frustration and rage that produce crime and instead has developed a ponderous bureaucracy to deal with symptoms, rather than the problem itself."[3] The commission strongly urges the worried citizenry to translate its indignation into active participation in crime control.

Based on the second assumption, a major theme of the report is the more efficient and responsive delivery of general services—education, manpower development, recreation—and social services, including drug abuse treatment and prevention programs. Better delivery of such services should reduce the feelings of alienation of many citizens, especially the poor and the minorities.

Agencies outside the criminal justice system have a very vital role in the prevention of delinquency and crime. Participation in crime prevention activities will benefit these social agencies in the discharging and fulfilling their primary duties. To illustrate, employers who sponsor drug education or treatment programs for their employees advance their own economic interests and lessen the dangers of drug abuse in the community. School-sponsored job counseling and referral services can reduce the number of dropouts and reduce the incidence of classroom disruption and delinquency. Similarly, a governmental organization which purges itself of corruption not only improves its efficiency but also its integrity, and it sets an example of honesty for the public. According to Grünhut, "the state which claims the right of punishment must uphold superior values which the [offender] can reasonably be expected to acknowledge."[4]

Based on the assumptions, the commission

1. Recommends extensive citizen action
2. Advocates responsiveness in the delivery of services
3. Presents youth services bureaus as a model for the delivery of social services
4. Urges practical programs for crime prevention
5. Asks for integrity in government, with special reference to combating official corruption and organized crime

A glance through Table 10–1 will bring the different prevention plans and programs into better focus. The descriptions that fol-

TABLE 10-1 Plan for Community Crime Prevention

Citizen action	Delivery of services	Practical programs
Citizen participation, individual and collective	Ways to reduce alienation, frustration, and estrangement	Programs for drug prevention
Attacking crime's infrastructure: improving opportunities for education, employment, recreation, and counseling	Upgrading municipal services	Programs for employment
	Providing access to government services	Programs for education
Citizen action within the criminal justice system	Setting up grievance mechanisms	Programs for recreation
	Involving the community in governmental processes	Programs for religion
	Youth services bureaus: coordinating the delivery of services	

low are brief, but the effort involved in the prevention of delinquency is colossal.

CITIZEN ACTION

Crime prevention is the business of every institution and of every citizen. Some authorities advocate that neighborhoods receive government financial and technical assistance to spur citizen involvement. Other authorities insist that the funding of delinquency prevention projects should be contingent upon community involvement. A major hurdle to community involvement has been the lack of information about the many different crime prevention activities now in existence.

Citizen Participation at the Individual and Collective Levels

There are countless ways in which an individual citizen can contribute to crime prevention. The citizen can

- Be vigilant so as to detect and then report criminal activity
- Boycott criminal activities such as the gambling which finances organized crime
- Take steps to guard his or her property and that of neighbors
- Volunteer to work with the police, juvenile court, and corrections agencies.

At the collective level, citizens can band together to form crime prevention societies. The residents of a neighborhood can volunteer to provide additional street patrols to reinforce police efforts. Tenants can take turns to guard their apartment complex according to a mutually agreeable schedule. In one burglary-ridden depressed ghetto, for example, residents and store owners got together and forced the local fences out of business. The burglaries stopped, almost completely.[5] Such communities should be applauded.

Attacking Crime's Infrastructure

Citizens can prevent crime by focusing their attention on social factors that lead to crime, for example, unemployment, poor education, and lack of recreational opportunities. Because we shall discuss these subjects later in the chapter in greater detail, this section only outlines some opportunities for citizen action.

Education Many citizens are involved in encouraging school dropouts to complete their education. Some volunteer groups tutor students on a one-to-one basis. Other groups provide alternative educational opportunities, such as street academies and vocational programs. Individuals also assist schools in counseling youth on drug use, pregnancy, family relations, employment, and various forms of social behavior. The establishment of scholarship funds is yet another area for citizen action.[6]

Employment Business people and others are working to place disadvantaged youths in summer jobs and in part-time jobs during the school year. The National Alliance of Businessmen's JOBS program is the largest program of this type. Citizens' groups are promoting "hire first, train later" programs. In such programs, an applicant undergoes a 2-week orientation program prior to being placed with an employer who agrees to provide on-the-job training and other support.[7]

Recreation Citizens' organizations are active in financing or operating summer camps for disadvantaged children. The Fresh Air Fund in New York City has provided free summer vacations for an estimated 18,000 children. Big Brothers regularly take youths to sporting, entertainment, and cultural events. Big Sisters also counsel youths. Some groups have financed youth centers or spearheaded drives for parks and other municipal recreational facilities.[8]

Counseling and Treatment Citizens counsel and advise youths with a wide array of problems and within a variety of organizational frameworks. According to the National Advisory Commission on Criminal Justice Standards and Goals report for 1973, there are over 300 hotlines, manned mostly by volunteers. Counseling might occur in the setting of a local YMCA, which refers persons with serious problems to community agencies. Or, citizens might volunteer at counseling centers designed to develop better and more secure relationships between children and parents. Others work at clinics to assist professionals who treat drug- or alcohol-related cases.[9]

Citizen Action within the Criminal Justice System

We have already discussed the role of the citizen in the activities of the police, courts, and corrections agencies. There is, in fact, no end to what citizens can do for these three arms of the criminal justice system. Citizens' organizations can sponsor areawide campaigns to educate the public about various projects that assist the police in investigation, patrol work, street lighting, and police-community relations. Citizens can work with the courts on a wide spectrum of jobs ranging from office work to probation duties. In the area of corrections, most volunteers like to counsel, although there is scope for a large variety of citizen help. The Big Brothers, and then the Big Sisters were organized for this purpose. But the most noble example is the Block Mothers, who keep their doors open to any child who is in trouble. Their doors are marked with a pair of clasped hands.

DELIVERY OF GOVERNMENT AND SOCIAL SERVICES

The National Advisory Commission on Criminal Justice Standards and Goals makes the very somber point that citizen alienation is on the increase. A survey by Harris, released in 1972, confirmed the fact that levels of alienation increased in 1 year from 40 percent to 47 percent among those surveyed.[10] A team of researchers at the Institute for Social Research has identified some of the forces that move certain individuals to violence. They believe that individuals are more likely to resort to violence when they are alienated, when they perceive themselves as members of a group that has less access than other groups to valued resources, and when they experience a substantial increase in expectation.[11] The National Commission on the Causes and Prevention of Violence blamed the estrangement between ghetto residents and social and political institutions as contributing to criminal conduct. The commission also called for immediate reordering of our national priorities.

The way in which we can make the greatest progress toward reducing violence in America is by taking the actions necessary to improve the conditions of family and community life for all who live in our cities, and especially for the poor who are concentrated in the ghetto slums.[12]

The National Commission on the Causes and Prevention of Violence makes a strong plea for reconstruction of urban life. The report, *Community Crime Prevention*, notes that citizens will view government in a more positive light if the following things are done promptly:

- Municipal services are upgraded.
- Methods of access to government services are improved.
- The citizen complaint and grievance mechanism is improved.
- Citizen involvement in governmental process is increased.[13]

Upgrading Municipal Services

Municipal services in ghetto areas are inadequate. Ghetto residents live with the fact that city governments do not pave, repair, clean, and light the streets and sidewalks in their neighborhoods as systematically as they do in more affluent areas. Ghetto residents daily witness assaults, gang fights, narcotics traffic, gambling, and vicious vandalism in their neighborhoods. They find that the police fail to respond quickly to calls for help in stopping these crimes. Every day, these citizens experience losses of life, liberty, and property—losses that are more serious and more widespread than those that occur in higher-income neighborhoods. Moreover, the quality of education in ghetto areas remains deficient, retarding human development and limiting employment opportunities.[14]

The commission recommends strongly that resources be allocated to each neighborhood of the city or county on the basis of *need*. The full range of fire services, police services, public transportation, and sanitation services should be provided. Similarly, public recreation facilities, street lighting, and medical services should be provided according to the size of the land area, density and nature of the population, and need.

Access to Government Services

In many places, services are located quite far from the people for whom they are intended. People who need the services then have difficulty in making use of them. The commission recommends that the physical distance be reduced by decentralizing services and establishing multiservice centers and "little city halls."

Many ghetto dwellers do not know about services which are available, or they are too apathetic to ask for these services. This apathy seems to be a universal phenomenon. In India, there are millions of farmers who own only four to five acres of land. With such a small landholding, it is very difficult for an individual farmer to buy seeds, fertilizer, or insecticides. The government of India and the state governments have opened outlets where the farmers can get these supplies on credit and can ask for certain free services. The author has observed that the small farmers scarcely use these agencies. The small farmer either does not know or does not care for the service. However, the relatively big farmers are always ready to exploit the available services. The government should, therefore, disseminate information systematically through the effective use of media—specifically, cable television—and through personal contact.

Grievance Mechanisms

Governments should set up grievance mechanisms to consider public complaints, and hold public hearings at convenient places. The services of mediators should be utilized when necessary. The commission recommends that a central complaint and information office be established wherever local governments and agencies provide diverse services to populations of 100,000 or more. In small communities, at least one full- or part-time employee should be appointed to provide complaint and information services.[15]

Community Involvement in Governmental Processes

Perhaps the most effective way of dealing with the alienation and frustration of underprivileged communities is to involve them in governmental processes. This can be done by inviting them to participate in town meetings, and by ensuring citizen representation in neighborhood councils, community development corporations, multiservice centers, and little city halls. Such participation is beneficial to both the citizens and the government. The citizens share in making the decisions that affect them, and the government benefits from the expertise of the participating citizens. Both profit from the mutual confidence and cooperation.

The commission has also recommended the establishment of two levels of local government—one extending throughout the metropolitan area, and the other serving local communities in the form of neighborhood governments. Under such a system, some functions should be shared and others divided. The neighborhood governments should be sensitive to the needs of their citizens and flexible in terms of procedures. They should attempt to respond quickly to neighborhood requests and complaints.[16]

YOUTH SERVICES BUREAUS

We discussed youth services bureaus in the previous chapter. The 1967 President's Commission on Crime and the 1973 National Advisory Commission on Criminal Justice Standards and Goals relied heavily on the YSB as an all-purpose tool for delinquency prevention and youth development. In delivering services to youth, the bureaus play a major role as coordinators, brokers, and even buyers of services.

Youth services bureaus are generally independent, locally operated agencies. They involve a large number of community people, particularly youths, in the solution of youth problems.[17] Although the relationship between the YSB and the youth is voluntary, the bureaus are advised to provide their services to youth aggressively. This should include the use of hotlines and outreach or street workers whenever appropriate.[18]

PRACTICAL PROGRAMS FOR DELINQUENCY PREVENTION

In its report, *Community Crime Prevention*, the National Advisory Commission on Criminal Justice Standards and Goals addresses itself to some of the most baffling problems connected with delinquency and suggests practical programs as solutions. The problems are drug abuse, insufficient employment, inadequate education, lack of healthy recreation, and lack of leadership by the church. The commission has also recommended programs for the reduction of criminal opportunity, including improved security for homes, and street lighting for high delinquency areas. However, in this chapter we discuss only those areas which are of immediate importance to youth development.

PROGRAMS FOR DRUG ABUSE TREATMENT AND PREVENTION

The commission believes it is important to set up *drug treatment* programs for addicts being processed by the criminal justice system. Such treatment should be made available early in the criminal justice process. In addition, the commission proposes that comprehensive drug abuse *prevention programs* should be developed by communities. It suggests that children be informed about drugs at an early age by parents and teachers. Peer-group influence also should be utilized in prevention strategies.

Drug Users and Their Experiences

There are a variety of drug users, with different degrees of involvement. The great majority of marihuana users do not move on to heroin addiction. The commission stresses the importance of these two facts in rational drug treatment and prevention programs. The types of drug users are:

1. *Experimental User*   Is curious about drugs and uses them to test their effects on different activities.
2. *Social or Recreational User*   Uses drugs occasionally at a party, to socialize with friends.
3. *Seeker*   Drugs play a significant role in this user's life. The user necessarily spends a lot of time and money in obtaining drugs. Despite heavy and regular use, the addict may still remain functional and able to meet primary social and physical needs.
4. *Self-medicating User*   Uses legally distributed tranquilizers or stimulants as a habitual response to boredom, loneliness, frustration, and stress. Both the self-medicator and the seeker may often use drugs as a kind of self-therapy.
5. *Dysfunctional Drug User*   Drugs begin to dominate the life of this user. The process of securing and using them interferes with essential activities.

There are, thus, varying commitments to drug usage. The commission points out that "heavy involvement with drugs depends more upon the person than upon the drug itself, since any changes in mood, behavior, and emotion will be experienced as pleasurable or alarming, depending on psychological or social needs."[19] A stable personality may experiment with drugs without total involvement, but an unstable personality may be totally consumed by drugs. The user's subjective expectations, the surroundings, and the presence of friends also affect the response to drugs. And, because each user is different, there is a need for different types of drug treatment and prevention programs.

A Comprehensive Approach to Treatment

To meet a variety of social and psychological needs, both of individuals and of groups, the commission suggests several ingredients for a comprehensive treatment program. The following is a brief description of these subsystems.

1. *Multimodality Treatment System* The system should have central intake and diagnostic units to receive patients referred by the criminal justice system and by other sources. Centralized programs would help meet each individual's physical and psychological needs by referring the individual to the particular treatment program best equipped to handle him or her while alleviating the drug problem; helping the individual avoid criminal activities; and ultimately removing the individual from drug use altogether, if possible.[20]

2. *Compulsory Treatment* The commission does not subscribe to the element of compulsion in drug treatment, but agrees that court orders may be necessary in some cases.

3. *Crisis Intervention and Emergency Treatment* This form of treatment may be located either in a hospital or in a community clinic. Its functions would include emergency medical aid and psychological services, such as hotline telephone help and various types of counseling. It would handle cases of "bad trips," overdoses, toxic drug reactions, and transient psychotic episodes. Selected centers could provide services to runaways and persons suffering from venereal diseases.[21]

4. *Methadone Maintenance* Every jurisdiction which has a substantial heroin addict population should arrange to have a methadone maintenance treatment program. This treatment has helped some patients, despite many relapses.

5. *Therapeutic Community Program* Groups of former addicts would enter the therapeutic community for abstention and emotional growth. Residents would be expected to remain in therapeutic communities for extended periods of time, ranging from 18 months to 2 years or more. During this period, they would participate in group encounters promoting free expression of feeling. Violation of community norms could lead to sharp reprimands, the silent treatment, and even banishment. Those who do well in helping their peers and helping themselves would start assuming responsible roles in the community. Some might be appointed to the permanent staff and assume rehabilitative functions. Synanon and Delancey Street are outstanding examples of existing therapeutic communities.

6. *Residential Programs* Closed residential facilities should provide a therapeutic environment for patients who are acting out in the community and need a period of compulsory institutionalization to be helped. There, addicts could live free of their drug use with the help of constraints, including locked doors. *Open* residential facilities could combine the advantages of a closed center with some services available in the community. Halfway houses would provide lodging and supportive services for residents who are making the transition from a structured institutional setting to living in the open community.[22]

7. *Use of Ex-Addicts* All the programs listed above should make abundant use of ex-addicts who have the ability to counsel others.

Drug Abuse Prevention Programming

The commission regrets that previous prevention efforts did not make use of the available facts, and prevention agencies used scare tactics to frighten the public. There were better informed persons among the public, particularly drug users who contradicted statements made by the prevention agencies. This imparted a hysterical quality to prevention efforts and often rendered them ineffective.[23] The commission accordingly advises that communities must renounce prevailing mistruths and base prevention programs on available facts.

> It is likely that only a small proportion, approximately one percent or less of the 13- through 30-year old population group, is involved in heavy, dysfunctional drug use. A larger proportion, perhaps 22 to 24 percent, is engaged in active drug seeking behavior and demonstrates regular drug-taking patterns. The remaining three-fourths are most likely either nonusers, self-medicating users, or social-recreational drug users. Prevention, therefore, must address the predominant group. In short, the great task of drug prevention is to guard against the individual's movement from occasional to serious dysfunctional use.[24]

Current Prevention Strategies Presently, prevention efforts are directed toward personality development and the influence of family and peers. The commission advocates the development of family-life curricula in schools to enhance self-understanding, intrafamily relationships, and the role of the family in society. Educational emphasis should be on the development of essential skills: intrapersonal skills, interpersonal skills, and coping skills.

> Specifically, drug abuse experts now recognize that it is often necessary to equip youngsters to deal more effectively with life, so they will not resort to dysfunctional drug use. The burden for accomplishing this rests primarily with families and schools. There is need, therefore, to focus on increasing parental child-rearing effectiveness through various kinds of counseling. Where parents themselves have problems, these should be addressed as early as possible, before youngsters have begun school.[25]

PROGRAMS FOR EMPLOYMENT

To prevent delinquency and crime through employment, the commission wants to direct programs mainly toward *inner-city youth*, particularly youths from minorities. For these youths—both delinquent and nondelinquent—the employment situation is not a very happy one. For every offender with an employment problem, there are many nonoffenders with equally serious problems. Many nonoffenders have motivational problems, few skills, educational deficiencies, and limited opportunities.

Youths in their late teens seem to go through a period in which they test and then leave the labor market. When they are hard pressed for money, they take a low-wage job. If the job does not interest them, they quit to get some experience on the street. Street life represents leisure; at times, it offers opportunities to earn illicit income. According to a Harlem study, at least two out of five 18- to 24-year-olds in Harlem have some form of illegal income. Many of these youths are arrested. It has been estimated that between 50 and 90 percent of all inner-city males have a serious encounter with the law before they reach the age of 25. Arrest records often rule out legitimate employment.[26]

Inner-city children are generally not well educated. However, a high school diploma does not seem to increase their chances for employment; their minority status operates against them. And, if they have an arrest on their record, employer prejudice is increased greatly. Every time they are turned down, they return to the street. "The availability and attractiveness of employment opportunities are a major factor governing commitment to street life versus the straight life."[27] The urban slum areas are characterized by low income, high unemployment, family instability, and the greatest population density. Improving the socioeconomic conditions of inner-city youth seems to be the logical way to combat delinquency.

The Target Groups

The commission identifies three groups in the population who are high crime risks and who therefore require concentrated attention. Their economic problems arise from both personal disabilities and unequal opportunities.

The first group includes many parolees, probationers, and previous offenders. Their employment problems were generally severe before their encounters with the law; these problems are aggravated by having a criminal record. This group also includes low-income inner-city youth for whom street life, work, and crime are mixed together, making contact with the law almost inevitable.

The second group is made up of individuals addicted to drugs or suffering from emotional problems that lead them into crime. They are trapped in a vicious cycle of alienation, drugs, delinquency, lack of job skills, and unemployment.

The third group is made up of actual and potential delinquents who can be assisted by measures designed to change the economic climate of American cities. In this group are individuals who are the products of an environment that condones and sometimes rewards criminal behavior. Unless this environment is changed, a continuous stream of offenders will be produced. To reverse this pattern requires across-the board upgrading of opportunities for those left out of America's economic, social, and political mainstream.

To meet the needs of these three groups, the commission suggests the following three approaches:

1. Help individuals who come from specific groups with severe economic problems and high rates of crime.
2. Help those whose economic difficulties are compounded by drug involvement or similar deviancies.
3. Work to improve the economic system that generates subcultures of crime.[28]

The Employment Problems of Offenders

The rate of employment of offenders is lower than that of nonoffenders of all ages, both before incarceration and after release. In 1964, a study was made of the postrelease work experiences of federal prisoners. Fewer than three-fifths of the people sampled were employed full time, as compared to four-fifths of the male civilian labor force.[29] At the height of the economic boom in 1969, more than 25 percent of the nonwhite 16- to 19-year-olds living in the inner city were unemployed.[30]

There is abundant documentation of the relationship between the availability of jobs and the level of criminal activity. Glaser and Rice found that property crimes by adults vary directly with the level of unemployment.[31] Fleischer's complex statistical analysis estimated that for every 1 percent increase in unemployment, there is a 0.5 percent increase in the rate of delinquency.[32]

The commission concludes that a cause-and-effect relationship cannot be proved. However, it is clear that the reduction of unemployment would have a significant impact on criminal conduct.[33]

In the past two decades, several industries have moved from the inner cities to the suburbs. This trend has further aggravated the already acute problem of youth employment. Under these circumstances, crime becomes a way of life in central cities; for many inner-city residents, it represents the only available way of life.

Overcoming the Employment Problems of High Risk Potential Offenders

The National Advisory Commission on Criminal Justice Standards and Goals would place emphasis on the preparation of youths for the world of work.

Compulsory education laws created part of the problem. Dropouts frequently are delinquent, but their delinquency invariably begins when they are in school. Rather than force youngsters to endure school failure and frustration, the school should provide a more meaningful education in relation to the probable career objectives of the student.[34]

Combating Discrimination The Commission notes with regret that "to date, antidiscrimination efforts have had little impact on minority youths. The problems of teen-age workers have gone all but unnoticed." Minority youths are hired last, fired first, paid least, and given the most unattractive jobs. Government policy, private leadership, and minority-group activism should combine to reduce discrimination.[35]

Expansion of Job Opportunities for Youth The Manpower Development and Training Act (MDTA) provides vocational training in some skills for which there is a demonstrated demand. In 1972 and 1973, about 33 percent of the MDTA program enrollees were 16 to 21 year old blacks. The Job Corps often provides room and board, basic education, and other inclusive services to youths aged 16 to 21 years. Follow-up studies suggest that the employment prospects of enrollees did not improve considerably, as compared to the control group. The commission makes the following recommendations to expand job opportunities:

1. That employers and unions accelerate efforts to expand job opportunities for economically and educationally disadvantaged youths
2. That each community broaden its after-school and summer employment programs for youth, including the 14- and 15-year-olds who may have been excluded from such programs in the past
3. That public employment programs be created to provide more rewarding and promising jobs for ex-offenders and others traditionally shut out of the job market[36]

PROGRAMS FOR EDUCATION

Ideally, one would look toward the schools as a powerful and postive socializing agent in preventing delinquency. In actual practice, however, the school system has generated delinquency. This delinquency has resulted, at least partly, from the failure and frustration that go with schooling.

[The American educational system] has not seen itself as part of a process providing differential experiences for people maturing into adults. As a consequence, it has found little need to look at itself as an instrument which would contribute to either the prevention or production of crime. The conclusion of the Commission is that we are doing very little in the schools as a direct, intentional effort to discourage young people from criminal careers. However, there is a strong suggestion that some of the basic conditions of schools . . . actually create the animosities, frustrations, and despair that lead people eventually to violence.[37]

In the schools, there is an overemphasis on achievement and competition. This works to the detriment of children from disadvantaged groups. For some children, it leads to a sense of failure, despair, hopelessness, and hostility.

Parents' Participation

It is quite common for parents and teachers to blame each other for the misconduct of young students. Teachers complain that the parents have not socialized their children well for learning. Parents accuse the teachers of apathy and inattention. According to the commission report, "differences in early childhood learning are caused by different home environments and are not overcome by normal schooling." The report goes on to assert that "variations in what children learn in school depend largely on what they bring to school, not on variations in what schools offer them."[38]

What can the schools do to reshape the child's early environment? The commission suggests that parents and teachers should get together to work jointly with the children. "Little that the schools do can be effective, and a great deal of what they do can be aborted if the home cannot be reconstituted to accommodate the school, or the school remade to acknowledge the preeminent influence of parents."[39]

The commission advocates the use of parents as teachers. But the parents need two types of training. First, parents should be taught the techniques, activities, and skills they need to use the ordinary household environment and routine as a constructive learning setting. Second, parents should be trained to help their children with school-related assignments.

Parents can organize a wide variety of activities to assist and reinforce the efforts of the schools in the development of youngsters. Tutorial pools, homework houses, special home courses (for example, foreign languages), and craft classes are obvious examples of such backup assistance.[40]

Reality-based Curricula

It is now increasingly obvious to many youths that much of what is taught in school is not relevant to life outside the school building. That is, it does not prepare them to find a job that will satisfy them. A substantial part of our school curriculum is geared to preparing students to enter college, yet a large number of students do not enter college. To make education more relevant and meaningful to youth, the educational system should ensure career preparation for every student. Career education involves learning goals that relate education to the world of work. It also involves the opportunity to explore and be trained in special subjects leading toward a particular career or career pattern (career requiring similar skills). Some procedures that would help achieve these goals are:

1. Awareness, through experience, observation, and study, in kindergarten through grade 6, of the total range of occupations and careers
2. Exploration of selected occupational clusters (manufacturing occupations, health occupations, personal service occupations, and homemaking-related occupations, for example) in the junior high school
3. Specialization in a single occupational cluster or a single occupation in grades 10 and 11
4. Use of community business, industrial, and professional facilities, as well as the school, for career education purposes
5. Provision of work-study programs, internships, and on-the-job training
6. Enrichment of academic subjects—communication, the arts, math, and science—through exploration of their relevance to occupations and careers
7. Acceptance by the school of responsibility for students after they leave, to assist them in the next move upward, or to reenroll them for more preparation[41]

Supportive Services

The present role of the school counselor is not as effective as the role the commission suggests. The commission recommends that the schools provide programs for more effective supportive services—health, legal placement, counseling, and guidance. Counselors must be the coordinators of tutorial assistance programs, parent involvement strategies, peer-group contacts, and university specialty services. They must be dedicated to helping students cope with the systems in which they live.

Counselors could serve as mediators between students and the community, and between students and teachers. They could act as surrogate parents, advocates, and expediters. To extend the range of school services, counselors should also use and help train parents, peers, neighborhood aides, and paraprofessionals. The delivery of these supportive services may be such a monumental task that the commission saw fit to recommend the hiring of a coordinator of services.

PROGRAMS FOR RECREATION

Whether recreation in itself can prevent crime and delinquency is open to debate. The 1967 President's Commission on Crime surveyed a number of studies. The commission concluded that "these studies neither demonstrated in any conclusive fashion that recreation prevented delinquency nor were they able to demonstrate conclusively that recreation was without value in delinquency prevention." It further stated that "it would appear that certain types of recreational opportunities may deter youngsters from delinquency, but this effect is largely dependent on the nature of the activity and cannot be attributed to recreation as an entity."[42] A major consideration is the therapeutic value of recreational activity.

No one would claim recreation as a cure for all kinds of delinquency. However, recreational activities can provide healthful excitement to youngsters and perhaps divert them from pathological excitement. When a 16 year old youth was asked why he murdered a storekeeper, his cold answer was that "there was nothing else to do." We also know that many of Thrasher's 1313 gangs in Chicago started as play groups. Miller found that excitement and fun seeking are of focal concern to the lower class, and particularly their youth. Cohen contends that gang boys are impulsive hedonists who may start serious acts of vandalism to seek fun and excitement.

All of this indicates the necessity of recreational programs for all youth, and particularly for potential delinquents residing in slums. The National Advisory Commission recommends that recreation be recognized as an *integral* part of an intervention strategy aimed at preventing delinquency; it should not be given a minor role. Other recommendations made by the commission are as follows:

1. Municipal recreation programs should assume responsibility for all youth in the community, emphasizing outreach services involving roving recreation workers in order to recruit youths who might otherwise not be reached and for whom recreation may provide a deterrent to delinquency.
2. Counseling services should be made available either as a part of the recreation program or on a referral basis to allied agencies in the community.
3. Individual needs rather than mass group programs should be considered in recreation planning.
4. Decision making, planning, and organization for recreation services should be shared with those for whom the programs are intended.
5. Parents should be encouraged to participate in leisure activities with their children.
6. Continual evaluation to determine whether youth are being diverted from delinquent acts should be a part of all recreational programs.[43]

PROGRAMS FOR RELIGION

Religious organizations regularly respond to crises in our society. The spiritual centers of the nation can become part of a massive new effort to reduce and prevent crime. According to the Yearbook of American Churches, there are more than 322,000 churches, synagogues, and temples in the United States, with inclusive memberships of more than 128 million persons.

Order within a society depends not only on the enforcement of its laws, but also upon voluntary adherence to the moral and social principles underlying the laws. Adherence helps create a climate of confidence that makes social order possible. A high rate of crime creates a low level of confidence in society. The religious community can address itself to the erosion of trust between persons, in institutions, and in government. The church can urge the faithful to assume responsibility for crime prevention. It can promote empathy rather than apathy.

The National Council on Crime and Delinquency is endeavoring to recruit a million citizens concerned about crime for participation in volunteer programs. The religious community can help support such involvement by publicizing and promoting it to its congregations.[44] The commission recommends that congregations use their buildings, facilities, and equipment for community programs, especially those directed toward the young.

CRITIQUE

Although there are a few direct references to the family in the various programs, the National Advisory Commission on Criminal Justice Standards and Goals report does not suggest separate programs for the family. It could be that the commission, with its focus on the community, reckoned the family as part of the community. The American family in the inner city has been greatly emaciated. It needs counseling in several areas, particularly in the matter of children's problems. For this, we may need several scores of family counseling clinics. Our hope is that youth services bureaus will provide a variety of services to troubled youths and their families.

SUMMARY

Delinquency prevention efforts are aimed at the community, and the community must participate fully in these efforts. A rapidly growing industrial society raises the expectations of all persons, but cannot meet the growing expectations of its entire population. Ghetto dwellers and inner-city youth feel alienated and neglected. Society can integrate them only through the intensive and extensive efforts of social institutions—family, school, work world, and health agency. The criminal justice system is limited in what it can do toward prevention; the real battle will be fought in the community, by several public and private agencies and more so by the citizens themselves.

The National Advisory Commission urges responsiveness in the delivery of services and expects that newly created youth services bureaus will actively coordinate these services. Citizens should participate in combating crime at the individual and collective levels, policy making and active levels, and professional, paraprofessional, and nonprofessional levels. Citizens have several roles in community prevention efforts: advisory, supportive, supervisory, and voluntary. Citizens can help prevent crime both from within and from outside the criminal justice system.

The delivery of municipal services should be improved in deteriorated areas. These municipal services include, among others, fire service, public transportation, street lighting, sanitation, and health services. Government services should be located close to slum areas to be within easy reach of needy citizens.

The commission suggests several practical programs for the prevention of delinquency and crime. For *drug abuse* prevention, the commission proposes that mistruths about drugs and drug users be dispelled. Because of the differences among drug users and their experiences, the commission recommends a multifaceted treatment system. This comprehensive approach to treatment includes crisis intervention, compulsory treatment, methadone maintenance, and residential programs using therapeutic and group counseling. Extensive community education on drugs, involving users' friends and families, ex-addicts, and volunteers, should be undertaken.

To combat *unemployment,* the commission suggests that certain target groups be identified. The groups include people whose economic problems arise from personal disabilities (lack of training and experience) or unequal opportunities (lack of jobs because of low status and criminal records). These people have been driven to the streets, and the only way to bring them back to the mainstream of society is to train them and provide them with jobs.

Educational programs, which are supposed to socialize and train youths, have alienated many of them. The commission recommends that parents participate in educational activities at the elementary and junior high school levels. It advises the schools to change their curricula toward career education and to increase the scope of their counseling and supportive services.

Recreational programs are essential, not only for healthy growth, but also to divert youngsters from vandalism. However, recreational activities should be supplemented with appropriate forms of counseling.

Finally, religious organizations can add greatly to prevention efforts by setting the proper moral and spiritual tone and by mustering citizens' help.

Discussion Questions

1. Can you recall any particular citizens' effort to reduce the incidence of burglary? What strategy was employed? How successful was the prevention effort?
2. Design a project to prevent vandalism in your area. How would you muster some citizen help?
3. Describe some of the citizens' committees involved in the prevention of delinquency in your area.
4. How would you design a drug education program for your community?
5. How have Synanon and Delancey Street helped the drug addict?
6. What are some of the mistruths about drug addicts?
7. What can we do to divert youth from the "street life" to the "straight life"?
8. What conditions in the schools (both physical and curricular) would you like to change?
9. How will you attract members of gangs to supervised recreational activities?

Glossary

Alienation A feeling of estrangement and separation from one's society.

Big Brothers An organization of men who, under the professional supervision of trained social workers, volunteer guidance through friendship on an individual basis to boys in "father-absent" homes.

Big Sisters An organization of women who volunteer casework services to predelinquent, delinquent, and neglected children and their families.

Delancey Street A private organization founded by an ex-convict which has provided several residential centers to former convicts and drug addicts. The ex-convicts and addicts come to these centers voluntarily to seek help. Among other things, the program includes self-analysis, peer analysis, and support. Delancey Street also makes loans to its residents to help them resettle in life.

Ombudsman Agent or representative public official appointed to deal with individual complaints against government acts.

Paraprofessional A worker who has working knowledge and practical training in a profession but does not have a professional degree. The paraprofessional assists the professional substantially.

Footnotes

[1] Joseph D. Lohman in his foreword to William E. Amos and Charles F. Wellford, *Delinquency Prevention*, Prentice-Hall, Englewood Cliffs, N.J. 1967, p. xv.

[2] National Advisory Commission on Criminal Justice Standards and Goals, *Community Crime Prevention*, U.S. Government Printing Office, Washington, D.C., 1973, p. 1. The rest of this chapter is largely a summary of the commission report, which is the most updated and comprehensive document on crime prevention.

[3] National Advisory Commission on Criminal Justice Standards and Goals, p. 2.

[4] Max Grünhut, *Penal Reform: A Comparative Study*, Clarendon Press, Oxford, 1948, p. 3.

[5] National Advisory Commission on Criminal Justice Standards and Goals, p. 10.

[6] National Advisory Commission on Criminal Justice Standards and Goals, p. 12.

[7] National Advisory Commission on Criminal Justice Standards and Goals, p. 12.

[8] National Advisory Commission on Criminal Justice Standards and Goals, p. 12.

[9] National Advisory Commission on Criminal Justice Standards and Goals, p. 12.

[10] Louis Harris, "Feelings of Alienation Up Sharply in Past Year," *1972 Chicago Tribune*, New York News Syndicate, Inc., in National Advisory Commission on Criminal Justice Standards and Goals, p. 34.

[11] Monica Blumenthal and others, *Justifying Violence: Attitudes of American Men*, Institute of Social Research, University of Michigan Press, 1972, p. 10.

296 Juvenile Delinquency

[12] National Commission on the Causes and Prevention of Violence, *To Establish Justice, To Insure Domestic Tranquility*, 1969, pp. xxi, xxii, in National Advisory Commission on Criminal Justice Standards and Goals, p. 34.

[13] National Advisory Commission on Criminal Justice Standards and Goals, p. 34.

[14] National Advisory Commission on Criminal Justice Standards and Goals, p. 35.

[15] National Advisory Commission on Criminal Justice Standards and Goals, p. 50.

[16] National Advisory Commission on Criminal Justice Standards and Goals, p. 49.

[17] National Advisory Commission on Criminal Justice Standards and Goals, p. 72.

[18] National Advisory Commission on Criminal Justice Standards and Goals, p. 74.

[19] National Advisory Commission on Criminal Justice Standards and Goals, p. 87.

[20] National Advisory Commission on Criminal Justice Standards and Goals, p. 92.

[21] National Advisory Commission on Criminal Justice Standards and Goals, pp. 91–92.

[22] National Advisory Commission on Criminal Justice Standards and Goals, p. 99.

[23] National Advisory Commission on Criminal Justice Standards and Goals, p. 89.

[24] National Advisory Commission on Criminal Justice Standards and Goals, pp. 105–106.

[25] National Advisory Commission on Criminal Justice Standards and Goals, p. 107.

[26] National Advisory Commission on Criminal Justice Standards and Goals, p. 114.

[27] National Advisory Commission on Criminal Justice Standards and Goals, p. 114.

[28] National Advisory Commission on Criminal Justice Standards and Goals, p. 112.

[29] National Advisory Commission on Criminal Justice Standards and Goals, p. 113.

[30] National Advisory Commission on Criminal Justice Standards and Goals, p. 115.

[31] Daniel Glaser and Kenneth Rice, "Crime, Age and Unemployment," *American Sociological Review,* vol. 24, pp. 679–686, October 1959, in National Advisory Commission on Criminal Justice Standards and Goals, p. 114.

[32] Belton M. Fleischer, "The Effect of Unemployment on Delinquent Behavior," *Journal of Political Economics,* vol. 61, pp. 543–555, National Advisory Commission on Criminal Justice Standards and Goals, p. 114.

[33] National Advisory Commission on Criminal Justice Standards and Goals, p. 114.

[34] National Advisory Commission on Criminal Justice Standards and Goals, p. 120.

[35] National Advisory Commission on Criminal Justice Standards and Goals, p. 121.

[36] National Advisory Commission on Criminal Justice Standards and Goals, pp. 124, 126, 131.

[37] National Advisory Commission on Criminal Justice Standards and Goals, p. 140.

[38] James S. Coleman, *Equality of Educational Opportunity,* 1966; Central Advisory Council for Education, *Children and Their Primary School,* Her Majesty's Stationery Office, London, 1967; and Bart Barnes, *The Washington Post,* September 7, 1972, in National Advisory Commission on Criminal Justice Standards and Goals, p. 143.

[39] National Advisory Commission on Criminal Justice Standards and Goals, p. 143.

[40] National Advisory Commission on Criminal Justice Standards and Goals, p. 144.

[41] National Advisory Commission on Criminal Justice Standards and Goals, p. 160.

[42] President's Commission on Crime, *Task Force Report: Juvenile Delinquency and Youth Crime,* U.S. Government Printing Office, Washington, D.C., 1967, p. 334, in National Advisory Commission on Criminal Justice Standards and Goals, p. 175.

[43] National Advisory Commission on Criminal Justice Standards and Goals, p. 182.

[44] National Advisory Commission on Criminal Justice Standards and Goals, pp. 183–86.

11 Final Impressions

In the end, a few impressions stand out. Juvenile delinquency constitutes an enormous problem. Its enormity can be reduced somewhat by the exclusion of status offenders from the juvenile justice system. The societies in which juvenile delinquency is less of a problem than it is in America are those societies that do not drag their children to police, courts, and juvenile institutions for minor infractions. Intervention by the justice system stigmatizes and antagonizes youths and places them on the criminal track. New legislation heralds a national approach in which community-based programs will be extended, research encouraged, and training provided to both employees and volunteers of all juvenile justice agencies. There are also some new trends in treatment. Americans are moving toward self-help group treatment. The treatment method may vary, but it is essentially a process of self correction through the intervention of peers—for example, former addicts and delinquents.

STATUS OFFENDERS

There is a strong feeling among many commissions and some legislators that status offenders (incorrigibles, truants, runaways) should not be dealt with by the juvenile justice system. Such behavior is a warning signal of some dysfunction in the home, school, or peer group. It can be handled better by the family and by educational and welfare groups than by the justice system. Perhaps status offenders could be served better by youth services bureaus than by the police and courts.

The decriminalization of status offenders would not only relieve the overcrowded juvenile system, but would also save children from the consequences of a criminal trial. It is not uncommon to hear a child protest that he or she did not do any wrong, but only ran away from alcoholic parents. Such a child should not be in court at all, though the child's family should be advised to seek counseling. In the famous Provo experiment, the incarceration of status offenders was associated with an increase in delinquency.[1]

Those who oppose this separation of status offenders contend that some status offenders commit delinquent acts as well as status offenses. However, such youths could be handled by the juvenile justice system for their delinquent acts, without extending the system's jurisdiction to *all* status offenders. It seems necessary and logical that status offenders will, in the future, be excluded from the jurisdiction of the juvenile justice system; they will be diverted to youth services bureaus and other social service agencies.

INAPPROPRIATE INTERVENTION

Many believe that the United States has overreacted to the delinquency of its youth. This exaggerated reaction has added to the problem. Our juvenile laws are very broad in their coverage. Indiscriminately used, the laws can lead to serious interventions in the lives of our youth. One sensible solution to this problem is to narrow the scope of our laws and refrain from unnecessary intervention. We have to increase our tolerance to the different life-styles of our youth. Schur asserts emphatically: *"Leave kids alone wherever possible.* In rethinking the delinquency problem, he suggests radical nonintervention as the basic injunction for public policy.[2]

Schur analyzes three forms of reaction to delinquency. The first form of reaction blames the *individual* for his or her delinquency. Adherents to this school of thought focus treatment on the individual, using therapy in training schools. The second group assumes that delinquency is concentrated in the *lower class* and is the product of delinquent subcultures. This group makes the community the target of improvement. The third school of thought reckons crime as a product of *exaggerated reaction* to delinquent behavior on the part of the legal system. According to Schur, delinquents are shaped by contingencies of legal processing.

> Contingencies significantly shape delinquency rates and in large measure determine which specific individuals reach the various stages in the juvenile justice system.... [There-

fore] the primary target for delinquency policy should be neither the individual nor the local community setting, but rather the delinquency-defining processes themselves.[3]

All of this favors the decriminalization of status offenses and certain victimless offenses. Diversion should be an essential procedure at all levels of juvenile justice. The police should condone a good part of juvenile behavior; the courts should be more concerned with dispensing justice; and corrections should lean heavily toward community-based programs. In other words, if intervention is necessary, it should be benign, restorative, corrective, and rehabilitative in nature.

FEDERAL EFFORTS: NEW LEGISLATION

Although the problems of juvenile delinquency must be solved locally, federal assistance is needed, in terms of both funds and technical know-how. Federal efforts date as far back as 1912, when the Children's Bureau was created by Congress. The Children's Bureau was organized to investigate all matters pertaining to the welfare of children, with special reference to infant mortality, accidents, dangerous occupations, desertion, juvenile courts, and juvenile institutions. Other landmarks in federal involvement are as follows:

1950 Midcentury White House Conference on Children and Youth. Considered methods for strengthening the juvenile justice system.
1968 Juvenile Delinquency Prevention and Control Act. Assigned to the U.S. Department of Health, Education, and Welfare (HEW) the responsibility for developing a national approach to the problems of juvenile delinquency.
1968 Omnibus Crime Control and Safe Streets Act. Authorized the funding of delinquency control and prevention programs.
1974 Juvenile Justice and Delinquency Prevention Act. Provided, for the first time, a comprehensive, unified national program for dealing with delinquency prevention and control.

The Juvenile Justice and Delinquency Prevention Act of 1974 transferred the main responsibility for preventing delinquency to the Law Enforcement Assistance Administration of the U.S. Department of Justice. The problem of runaway youth remained with HEW. The highlights of the 1974 act are, briefly:[4]

1. The purpose of the act is to provide technical assistance and training programs for all staff and volunteers and to establish a centralized research effort.

2. A National Advisory Committee for Juvenile Justice and Delinquency Prevention was established. The committee has twenty-one members, one-third of them below 26 years of age.

3. The act provides funds to states for alternatives to juvenile detention and for diverse community-based programs. Efforts will be made to strengthen the family unit so that the juvenile may remain at home. The act promises incentives to those units of local government which undertake to reduce the rate of incarceration of youths in secure institutions.

4. The act urges good employment conditions for workers, with rights to pensions, collective bargaining, and training/retraining programs.

5. The act established a National Institute for Juvenile Justice and Delinquency Prevention. Its purpose is to provide a coordinating center for the collection, preparation, and dissemination of useful data regarding the treatment and control of juvenile offenders. Another purpose of the Institute is to provide training for public and private employees. The Institute is authorized to

a. Conduct, encourage, and coordinate research

b. Encourage the development of demonstration projects

c. Provide for the evaluation of all juvenile delinquency programs funded under the act

d. Develop seminars, workshops, and training teams

WORK FORCE

People are the most effective resource for helping other people. To handle juveniles, we need people with ability, devotion, and training in police departments, the courts, and corrections jobs. Several commissions have suggested that police officers have a minimum of 1 year of college education. By 1983, every police candidate will be required to have at least a bachelor's degree. Similarly, about 30 percent of the juvenile judges who do not have law degrees must upgrade their education. While all juvenile justice workers need training, there is an added dilemma for these workers—the ambiguity in their roles.

> People who work in corrections—the public which employs them—are uncertain as to whether the system is supposed to punish lawbreakers or to rehabilitate them, to protect society

or to change social conditions, or to do some or all of these things under varying circumstances. Employees who disagree among themselves as to what their roles should be are unlikely to perform well or to find satisfaction in their work.[5]

Because of the nature of its clientele, juvenile corrections work is already attracting workers of both sexes who are young and interested in working with other youths. What is needed is more emphasis on the recruiting of workers from minority groups. Another important resource is that of volunteers, including ex-offenders (who can serve as success models) and inner-city residents.

If good workers are to be recruited and retained, they must be paid well. Fringe benefits and working conditions must be improved. A well qualified staff pays off in the long run. Staff members should do all they can to improve their image, both among themselves and among the public. With the shift of emphasis to community corrections, juvenile corrections workers should also transfer their orientation from the institution to the community.

Today's juvenile staffers should be effective community workers. They should cultivate useful relationships with helping agencies in the community. They should disseminate information to all those who ask for it and to those whose cooperation is sought. If citizens' involvement is required, they must put some effort into the matter of educating the community.

Staff Education

In the United States, community colleges and universities have started educational programs ranging from associate degree programs to master's or doctor's degree programs. They are partially financed by Law Enforcement Educational Program (LEEP) funds. Many of these programs are as yet anemic and need strengthening. The curricula for these programs are not yet standardized; faculties come from varying backgrounds and experience, and they teach what they like. It is expected that, with the availability of more funds and better faculty, these programs will become more relevant to inservice and preservice candidates.

The colleges should develop a set of core courses and optional tracks for specialization: administration, management of juvenile institutions, counseling and treatment, and community-based corrections. Juvenile agencies should make contractual agreements with educational institutions to offer both degree courses and special courses. Courses could be offered at the community agencies themselves. This would make it convenient for inservice students to attend. It would also provide an original and practical setting for preservice students. These "community courses" might be credited as resident courses as opposed to extension courses. There would be some library facilities at the community site; about one-fourth of the classes should be held on the college campus, to enable students to consult the larger university library and make use of other academic resources.

Campus students should, in turn, visit the community agencies. Community agencies should be approved for the training of preservice interns. This would promote a healthy exchange between the "town" and "gown." The benefits are mutual: The interns and the agencies have a lot to share with each other. Interns are mostly young persons with whom juveniles find it easy to communicate.

Volunteers are another group with diverse abilities; they can provide excellent links with the community. If an agency uses volunteers, it should have proper procedures for recruiting, training, and utilizing them.

Practical, or field, training is an essential part of the curriculum and should make up about one-fourth of the total. The National Advisory Commission on Criminal Justice Standards and Goals emphasizes *intergroup relations* and an understanding of the "lifestyles common among offenders." Most juvenile and adult offenders are somewhat deficient in maintaining interpersonal relationships. Correctional workers should thus develop the skills needed to sensitize their clients in this area of human relationships. The area could be highlighted in special seminars, symposia, and workshops. Short courses could be offered on topics of special interest, such as status offenders, intake procedures, family counseling, police-juvenile relations, court procedures, and drug programs.

National Institutes

At this writing, at least three national institutes are in different stages of development. The National Institute of Law Enforcement and Criminal Justice has supported many new antidelinquency projects, encouraged research studies, and published their results. Some of these projects have been judged to be exemplary projects.

Recent federal legislation (1974) established a National Institute for Juvenile Justice and Delinquency Prevention, as described earlier in this chapter. There is also the National Institute of Corrections, which serves as a clearinghouse for information on crime and corrections, provides consultant services, funds training programs, and coordinates correctional research. Before the institute was created, these functions were not being satisfactorily fulfilled on a national basis.

TREATMENT TRENDS

To a layman, treating or correcting an offender does not seem to be a difficult job. However, many of the methods employed in the past have been either totally inefficient or, at best, partially effective. The high rate of recidivism is testimony to the inefficiency of the treatment methods.

Historically, American society has emphasized various treatment philosophies at different times, starting with a great reliance on *direct punishment* in the eighteenth century. The nineteenth century founders of the house of refuge placed great emphasis on *discipline;* the designers of the Pennsylvania penitentiary system had great faith in the *penitence* of offenders in solitary cells. Late in the nineteenth century, *educational* and *vocational* programs were introduced; around the turn of the century, *counseling* was administered on a limited basis. With the advent of Freudian psychoanalysis, correctional counseling was somewhat influenced by neo-Freudian theories, but soon there were a host of other competing schools of thought.

There were very few therapists working with delinquents. Those who did work in juvenile institutions and agencies varied greatly in their approaches. Each therapist had his or her own form of therapy. Similarly, the people directing institutions or agencies followed their own notions about the treatment of delinquents, to the exclusion of all other treatments. It should be noted that all these treatment methods were aimed at *individual reform;* scarcely any attention was paid to *societal reform.* Only scant attention was paid to the family—whatever little assistance was given to a family in trouble came mostly in the form of welfare funds.

As a result of several socioeconomic and subcultural pressures, the ability of the family to socialize and contain its youth was weakened. The task of corrections became more and more difficult. Many of the important functions of the natural family were taken over by foster families, juvenile institutions, and other private and public social agencies. These characteristics are typical of a fast-moving industrial society. Necessary though these arrangements are, they remain, at best, a poor substitute for the normal family.

After World War II, another form of therapy, known as *group therapy, group counseling,* or *guided group interaction,* became popular. It was first used in institutions, to a limited degree, and has now spread to community-based programs. Participants in these group sessions generally have the same kinds of problems; they help each other face the realities of their personal and social problems. Guided group interaction has been used in several experimental communities, such as the Highfields, Provo, and Silverlake experiments. The results were encouraging. However, in adult corrections, while group counseling does result in some improvement in the behavior of prison inmates, there is no carryover effect during parole.

Despite these initial findings, guided group interaction (with some variations) is being practiced widely with a variety of youth groups, particularly with alcoholics and drug addicts. Some of the ingredients of this form of treatment are a *commitment* to the group, a *willingness* to be cured, and an *active participation* in the treatment process. It is a self-help process with the positive reinforcement of one's peers. An important goal in the therapy procedure is fostering a sense of *responsibility* in the client. Glasser's Reality Therapy, which has been used extensively with delinquent groups, also emphasizes responsibility.

It is noteworthy that, in the middle of the last century, individual penitence in the silence of a segregated cell was considered appropriate by the Pennsylvania penitentiary system. Today, an active participation in group counseling, aided by family therapy and other community integration processes, is considered appropriate correctional procedure.

It is true that guided group interaction or group counseling has not proven to be of help to all types of offenders. However, no single treatment can make that claim. The essence of classification of juvenile offenders lies in screening, sorting, and then matching different types of offenders with different forms of treatment. According to a survey of studies in 1966, the offenders who benefited most from group methods were fairly normal in intelligence, free from psychological disturbances, relatively older youths, and in the middle of the extroversion-introversion scale.[6] These youths generally adjust easily to peer groups.

Successful therapy cannot be conducted in a vacuum—it must be supported by family, peers, school, church, community, and a fair system of justice.

Footnotes

[1] LaMar T. Empey et al., *The Provo Experiment,* Lexington Books, Lexington, Mass., 1972, p. 253.

[2] Edwin M. Schur, *Radical Nonintervention, Rethinking the Delinquency Problem,* Prentice-Hall, Englewood Cliffs, N.J., 1973, p. 155.

[3] Edwin M. Schur, p. 154.

[4] *Public Law 93–415,* 93rd Cong., S. 821, September 7, 1974.

[5] National Advisory Commission on Criminal Justice Standards and Goals, *Corrections,* U.S. Government Printing Office, Washington, D.C., 1973, p. 464.

[6] William R. Arnold and Bill Stiles, "A Summary of Increasing Group Methods in Correctional Institutions," *International Journal of Group Psychotherapy,* vol. 22, pp. 87–89, January 1972.

Appendix

AGENCIES CONCERNED WITH JUVENILE SERVICES

National

Law Enforcement Assistance Administration (LEAA)
U.S. Department of Justice
633 Indiana Ave., N. W.
Washington, D.C. 20531

From 1968 to 1975, the Law Enforcement Assistance Administration (LEAA) has awarded more than $4 billion to state and local governments to improve systems of police, courts, and corrections, and also to combat juvenile delinquency. LEAA has also started several programs for crime reduction.

At LEAA, research is conducted by the National Institute of Law Enforcement and Criminal Justice (NILECJ) and the National Institute for Juvenile Justice and Delinquency Prevention (NIJJDP). (NIJJDP concentrates its attention on youth crime and on the problems of juvenile justice.)

If you need information and literature on any aspect of crime and delinquency, you may write to the following LEAA agency:

National Criminal Justice Reference Service (NCJRS)
P. O. Box 24036, S. W. Post Office
Washington, D.C. 20024

NCJRS prepares reference materials covering all aspects of law enforcement and criminal justice. Its computer-assisted data base includes books and publications as well as bibliographic material and an abstract of each item in the system. NCJRS has arrangements to acquire international material through the UN Clearinghouse in Rome, Italy.

If you need grants or loans to improve your educational status, apply to the colleges and universities in your area which have been awarded Law Enforcement Education Program (LEEP) funds. Some of these colleges and universities also fund internship programs.

LEAA operates through ten regional offices located in (1) Boston, (2) New York, (3) Philadelphia, (4) Atlanta, (5) Chicago, (6) Dallas, (7) Kansas City, (8) Denver, (9) San Francisco, and (10) Seattle. (The numbers signify the number of the region.)

There are state planning agencies (SPA) funded by LEAA that are known by such different names as the Crime Commission, Governor's Planning Committee, and Agency to Reduce Crime.

There are private national organizations which have played an important role in the prevention of delinquency. Some of these are as follows:

National Council on Crime and Delinquency (NCCD)
411 Hackensack Avenue
Hackensack, New Jersey 07601

NCCD has chapters in almost all states. This organization works with different citizens' groups to create public opinion on important issues of crime and delinquency. Working through legislatures, NCCD has historically shown a great interest in updating criminal laws and penal codes. In order to promote sound practices in criminal and juvenile justice systems, NCCD has designed several model acts which propose minimum standards for police, courts, jails, prisons, probation, and parole. NCCD has an extensive list of publications, including a journal of its own and an abstract on crime and delinquency literature.

American Correctional Association (ACA)
4321 Hartwick Road, Suite L-208
College Park, Maryland 20740

Founded in 1870, ACA's objective is to improve correctional standards, including the selection of personnel. ACA publishes an annual *Directory of State and Federal Correctional Institutions* (both adult and juvenile) in the United States, Canada, and the United Kingdom. The association has a number of other publications.

State and Local

At the state and local levels the juvenile services are administered as follows:

Administrative Breakdown of Juvenile Services by Number of States and Territories (U.S.) (October 1975)

Parent agency	Juvenile detention	Juvenile probation	Juvenile institutions	Juvenile aftercare
Local	43	26	0	4
State (D. C., Territories)	8	8	50	47
State-local	2	19	0	2

The broad pattern is that juvenile detention is managed mostly by local agencies; probation is divided between the local and state agencies; the juvenile institutions and aftercare are the responsibility of the state. The state departments administering juvenile services are known by different names:

Department of Correction
Department of Health and Mental Hygiene
Department of Health and Social Services
Department of Health and Welfare
Department of Human Resources
Department of Institutions
Department of Offender Rehabilitation
Department of Social and Rehabilitation Services
Department of Youth Services

In a few states, juvenile services are administered by the Youth Division of the Department of Correction, but the general pattern is to have a separate department for juvenile services.

DIRECTORIES

For detailed information on juvenile probation and aftercare agencies as well as juvenile correctional institutions, you may consult the following directories:

Directory of Juvenile and Adult Correctional Departments, Institutions, Agencies and Parole Authorities. (United States, Canada, and the United Kingdom.) Available from ACA. Issued yearly.

Criminal Justice Agencies. Directories for all ten regions are prepared by the U.S. Department of Justice. Available from LEAA.

VISITS

Visits to juvenile agencies or institutions can be arranged by writing to the administrators of these agencies. The superintendents of training schools generally welcome visitors so long as the visitors do not disrupt the school routine.

VOLUNTEER WORK

If you want to volunteer your services to work with delinquent youth, you may apply to the Volunteers in Correction (VIC) or Volunteers in Probation (VIP). Their addresses may be obtained from the phone directory or from one of the juvenile agencies.

EMPLOYMENT

Check with local and state agencies. Write to the Personnel Department.

ABSTRACTS, JOURNALS, AND REPORTS

In order to help you research papers, essays, and theses on any aspect of crime and delinquency, a partial listing of abstracts, journals, and national commission reports follows:

Abstracts

Abstracts on Criminology and Penology
Crime and Delinquency Abstracts
Crime and Delinquency Literature
International Bibliography on Crime and Delinquency
Psychological Abstracts
Social Science Abstracts
Sociological Abstracts

Journals

American Journal of Correction
American Journal of Psychology
American Journal of Sociology
British Journal of Criminology
British Journal of Delinquency
Canadian Journal of Criminology and Corrections

Crime and Delinquency
Criminology
Federal Probation
International Journal of Criminology and Penology
*International Journal of Offender Therapy and Comparative
   Criminology*
Journal of Correctional Education
Journal of Criminal Law, Criminology and Police Science
Journal of Criminal Psychopathology
Journal of Social Issues
Social Case Work
Social Forces
Social Problems
Social Work

National Commission Reports

National Advisory Commission on Criminal Justice Standards and Goals

A National Strategy to Reduce Crime, 1973
Criminal Justice System, 1973
Police, 1973
Courts, 1973
Community Crime Prevention, 1973
Standards and Goals for Juvenile Justice, 1973
   (Juvenile Delinquency Interdepartmental Council)

President's Commission on Law Enforcement and Administration of Justice
The Challenge of Crime in a Free Society, 1967
Task Force Reports:
   Corrections, 1967
   Crime and Its Impact—An Assessment, 1967
   Juvenile Delinquency and Youth Crime, 1967
   Narcotics and Drug Abuse, 1967
   The Courts, 1967
   The Police, 1967

President's Committee on Juvenile Delinquency and Youth Crime
Counter-attack on Delinquency, 1964
Juvenile Gangs, Gilbert Geis, 1965
Training for New Careers, 1965

National Commission on the Causes and Prevention of Violence
To Establish Justice, to Insure Domestic Tranquility, 1969
Task Force Reports:
  Violence in America, 1969
  Law and Order Reconsidered, 1969
  Crimes of Violence, Vols. 11 to 13, 1969

Index

Adams, William T., 94
Affluence, delinquency and, 22–24
Age limits of delinquency, 3–4
　raising and lowering of, 4
Aggravated assault, 116
　drinking and, 117
　homicidal threat in, 116–117
　victim-offender relationship in, 116
Aichhorn, August, 45–46
Allen, Donald E., 93–94
Alper, Benedict S., 224
Amir, Menachem, 113, 115
Anomie, 34–35
Armstrong, Clairette P., 125
Arnold, William R., 201–203, 307
Arrests
　for different offenses, 9–10
　by race, 10
　by sex, 18
　trends in, 16
Attitudes toward children, 5
　among American colonists, 5
　fear of the offender and, 1
　socioeconomic changes and, 5
Augustus, John, 7, 188–189
Australia, institutions for girls in, 223
Authority offenders, 106
　(*See also* Status offenders)
Auto thief, 122

Balistrieri, James, 122
Ball, J. C., 94
Barker, Gordon H., 94
Becker, Howard S., 61
Bell, Daniel, 38
Best interest of the child, juvenile court acting in, 161
"Beyond control" youth, 125
Black, Susan, 121
Blum, Richard H., 87
Body types, ectomorph, endomorph, and mesomorph, 43
Bohlke, Robert H., 78

Burglars, 120–121
Butler, Edgar W., 94

Carey, James T., 89
Caseload size, 195–196
　effect of, on parole agents, 206
Caseworkers, 228
Causation theories:
　conflict approach, 34, 40–42
　cultural approach, 34, 38
　psychoanalytical approach, 44
　subcultural approach, 34, 37, 39
　three loci, classified in terms of 33
Cavan, Ruth S., 52
Chein, Isidor, 87
Children's Bureau, 2, 228
Citizens, involvement of, 263–264
Citizens' advisory committees, 144–146
　communication with minorities through, 144
Civil commitment, 199–200
　as unproductive disposition, 200
Class conflict, 42
Classification of delinquents, 105
Clinard, Marshall B., 76, 105
Cloward, Richard A., 35–36, 82
Cohen, Albert C., 39–40, 291
Community-based corrections, 245
Community crime prevention:
　access to government services for, 278–279
　assumptions about, 273–274
　attacking crime's infrastructure for, 276
　citizen action for, 274–275
　citizen participation for, 275
　delivery of services for, 274–277
　practical programs for, 274, 280
　role of agencies outside criminal justice system in, 274

316 Juvenile Delinquency

Community crime prevention (*Cont.*):
  role of youth services bureaus in, 280
  setting up grievance mechanism for, 279
  upgrading municipal services for, 278
Conflict of group interests, 41
Conklin, John E., 119
Consent decree, 165
Containment theory, 58–59
  inner and outer containment, 58
  pressures, pulls, and pushes, 58–59
Correctional experiments, evaluating, 207
Cortes, Juan B., 43
Cressey, Donald R., 56
Culture conflict, 40
  insulation of Asian immigrants against, 40–41
Curtis, George C., 108
Custodial versus treatment institutions, 232
  influence of belief system in, 232
  influence of institutional goals, 232
  institutional models, 233
  institutional properties, 234
  self-fulfilling prophecies of the staff, 233

David, Pedro R., 121
Daytop Village in New York, 260
Delinquency prevention, 273–294
  citizen action, 275–277
  government and social services, 277–280
  programs for (*see* Programs)
  youth services bureaus, 247–251, 280, 300
  (*See also* Community crime prevention)

Delinquent conduct:
  delinquent ego and, 46
  failure of ego functions and, 46
  legal definition of, 2–3
  as a product of exaggerated legal reaction, 300
  as a solution of conflicts, 46–47
Delinquent expression, diversity of, 71
  peer-oriented group activities, 71
Delinquent solution versus neurotic solution, 47
Delinquent subculture, status seeking as, 39–40
Delinquents, subterranean values of, 50
Dependency cases, 3
Detention centers, 146–149, 222
Deviance, primary and secondary, 62
Dinitz, Simon, 49
Diversion, juvenile, 199–200, 248
  favorable and unfavorable factors of, 212–213
  intake services and, 163
Drug abuse and addiction, 85–90
  effectiveness of programs for, 239
  prevention programs for (*see* Programs, for drug abuse treatment and prevention)
  relationship of, to delinquency, 87–88
Durkheim, Emile, 34, 35

Educational programs for juvenile inmates, 238
  favorable conditions for, 238
Empey, LaMar T., 259, 300
England, Ralph W., 76–77
Esselstyn, T. C., 126
Evaluating correctional experiments, 207
Exemplary projects, 260–262
Experimental communities, 236

Index 317

Family, benign influence of, in India and Japan, 208–209
Family court, 178
Family discipline, Orientals and, 40–41
Family functioning and delinquency, 52
  impairment of parental roles, 204
Family life and delinquency, 52
Family therapy, 204
Fannin, Leon F., 76
Federal legislation:
  Juvenile Delinquency Prevention and Control Act of 1968, 8
  Juvenile Justice and Delinquency Prevention Act of 1974, 8, 301–302
  Omnibus Crime Control and Safe Streets Act of 1968, 301
Felice, Marianne, 93
Female delinquency, 18, 90–95
  increase in violent crime, property crime, prostitution, and drug law violations, 18
Female delinquent(s), 90–95
  as altruist, 90
  and clinging to the institution, 95
  home life of, 93–94
  increases in the offenses of, 190
  marital difficulties of, 92
  recidivism rate of, 94–95
  sense of guilt and low self-image of, 92
  sexual difficulties and loneliness of, 92
  and sexual themes, 91
Female inmates:
  recommitment rate of, 225
  as status offenders, 225
Ferdinand, Theodore N., 52
Ferracuti, Franco, 109–110
Finestone, Harold, 87

Forcible rapists, 113
  characteristics and history of, 113
  of minors versus adults, 114
  (*See also* Rape)
Forestry camps as correctional facilities, 222, 223

Gangs:
  in Asian countries, 83
  ganging process and control in, 79–80
  girls in, 80
  in India, 83
  interstitial element in, 79
  leader of, 81
  levels of membership in, 80–82
  as a near group, 81
  in Paris, 83
  as products of community, 82
  sexual activity in, 80
  social identity and social support in, 79
  in the Soviet Union, 84–85
  and status seeking, 39
  struggle for existence in, 80
  territorial claims of, 82
  and violence, 83–84
Gatti, Florence M., 43
Gault case, 171–174
  rulings on: notice of charges, 173
    right to appellate review, 172
    right to confrontation and cross-examination, 174
    right to counsel, 173–174
    right to transcript of the proceedings, 172
Gebbard, Paul H., 114
Geis, Gilbert, 84–85
Geographic distribution of delinquency, 11
  areas of high delinquency rate, 11, 16
Gibbons, Don C., 105
Gil, David G., 108
Glaser, Daniel, 57

318 Juvenile Delinquency

Glue sniffers versus marihuana users, 260
Glueck, Bernard C., 114
Glueck, Eleanor T., 43, 53–54, 91, 204
Glueck, Sheldon, 43, 53–54, 91, 204
Goffman, Erving, 231
Gough's Responsibility Scale, 49
Gough's Socialization Scale, 49
Green, Nancy B., 126
Grounding, 139
Group counseling, favorable impact of, 206
Group homes, 197, 222, 224
Group methods, best beneficiaries of, 306–307
Group therapy, 228
Group treatment, 237
  conditions for better results in, 237
Group worker, 227
Grünhut, Max, 274
Guided group interaction, 198, 228, 255
Guttmacher, Manfred, 112

Halfway houses, 222, 224, 251
  multifunctions of, 251
  as pre-release centers, temporary shelters, outpatient clinics, and detoxification centers, 254
Hall, Calvin S., 44
Help giver as help taker, 198
Highfields experiment in residential milieu therapy, 255–256
  effect on recidivism, 255
  differential impact on different offenders, 256
Hill, Mathew Davenport, 188
Homicide rate, national and international, 106–107
  (*See also* Murderers)
House of refuge, 6, 220
  from repression to custodianship, 220
  strict discipline in, 220

India, 24, 208–209, 265
  female delinquency in, low rate of, 209
  female judges in, 209
Informal probation, 164
Inmates helping the community, 264–265
Instincts, asocial, 43–44
Intake services and diversion, 163
Interactionist perspective, 61–63
Internal forces hampering juvenile court, 176
  faulty recording system, 176
  hurried trials, 177
  overload, 176
  the stigma, 177

Japan, 24, 208
  use of volunteers in, 197, 208
Juvenile aftercare, 200–201
Juvenile Aid Bureau (juvenile investigations unit), 140–141, 150–151
Juvenile court judges, education and training of, 178
Juvenile courts, 157–182
  acting in the best interest of the child, 161
  appeal, 168
  condemnation, incapacitation by, 166
  detention by, 168
  dissatisfaction with, 166
  external forces against, 174–175
  features of, 158
  inferior status of, 175
  jurisdiction of: over adoption, guardianship, and nonsupport, 162
    over delinquency, neglect, and dependency, 162
    over PINS, 159–160
  and juveniles' rights, 166
  as parens patriae, 159, 161
  philosophy of, 159
  privacy and confidentiality, 167

Juvenile courts (*Cont.*):
   protection of society by, 161
   right to notice, 169
   self incrimination, 167–168
   and stigmatization of trial, 166
   too many masters and too many demands, 175
   (*See also* Gault case; *Kent v. United States*)
Juvenile detention homes, 146–149
   assistance of volunteers in, 148
   regional facilities, 148
Juvenile institutions, 219–240
   boys' villages, boys' ranches, and girls' towns, 9, 223
   drift away from, 8–9
   history of, 220–221
   house of refuge (*see* House of refuge)
   industrial schools, 8
   reform schools, 8
   reliance on, 6
   training schools (*see* Training schools)
Juvenile probation, 187–214
   aftercare, 200–201
   functions and goals of, 187, 190–192
   history of, 188–189
   intake, social study, and supervision of, 190–191
   services: organization of, 192–193
      supporting, 197–199
   (*See also specific country*)
Juvenile standards:
   on apprehending, fingerprinting and photographing, 152
   on notification of youth's parents, 152
Juveniles:
   attitude of, toward the police, 138
   and citizen complaints, 136
   encounters of, with the police, 136

Keeping the public informed, 265
Keller, Oliver J., 224
Kent v. United States, 169–171
   opportunity for hearing and effective legal defense, 171
Konopka, Gisela, 92, 93
Kvaraceus, William, 78

Lamberti, Joseph W., 111–112
Lander, Barnard, 35
Larceny, 123
   involvement of females in, 123
   motivations for, 123
Latent and manifest delinquency, 45
Laws:
   concerning abortion, drugs, and morality, 41
   of imitation, 56–57
Learning criminal behavior:
   through differential association, 55–56
   through differential identification, 57
   through imitation, 56–57
Lemert, Edwin M., 62, 177
Lipton, Douglas, 206, 237, 238, 255
Local jail, 146–147
   annual inspection of, 147
Lombroso, Cesare, 111
Loss of friends and higher rate of parole failure, 201–202
Loss of status in the group leading to parole failure, 201–202
Lower class, the, focal concerns (values) of, 36–38
Lubeck, Steven G., 257

McCord, Joan, 52, 53, 95
McCord, William, 52, 53, 95
MacDonald, John M., 116–117
McKay, Henry D., 93
Mannheim, Hermann, 95
Manpower Development and Training Act (MDTA), 287

Marihuana, 88–90
    and aggression and violence, 89
    and users' attitudes toward society and sex, 89
    "drop-out" or "hang-loose" ethic, 89
Marihuana users versus glue sniffers, 260
Martin, John M., 73
Martinson, Robert, 206, 237, 255
Matza, David, 50
Merton, Robert K., 34, 35
Middle-class delinquency, 75
    of girls, 77
    theories of, 77–78
Middle-class delinquents, 75–76
    and the car, 75
    compared with lower-class delinquents, 76
    offenses of, 75
    self-concepts of, 76
    and techniques of delinquency, 76
Middle-class values, 39
Milieu therapy, 238, 255–257
Miller, Walter B., 36–37, 78, 290
Mind, the conscious and unconscious, 44
Mulvihill, Donald J., 107
Murderers, 106–113
    absent or indifferent fathers of, 111
    amnesia in, 112
    children and adolescents as, 108–109
    compared with their nonmurderer brothers, 111
    differentiation of, 110
    under 18 years old, 106
    families of, 110
    female, 106
    Negro, 106
    psychotic, 111
    stranger killers, 112
    sudden, 112
Murders:
    in the family, 108
    handguns used in, 109
    among spouses, 108

Murders (*Cont.*):
    and subculture of violence, 109
    victim precipitated, 109
    victim's role in, 109
Murphy, Patrick T., 177
Myerhoff, Barbara G., 75, 76
Myerhoff, Howard L., 75, 76

National Advisory Commission on Criminal Justice Standards and Goals, 276, 277
National Commission on the Causes and Prevention of Violence, 277, 278
National Council on Crime and Delinquency, 264
National institutes, 304–305
Neglect cases, age and incidence of, 3
Neglected minor, 160
Neurotics, 47–48
Nonreported delinquency, 21–22
Normandeau, André, 119
Nye, F. Ivan, 60–61

Offord, D. R., 93, 95
Ohlin, Lloyd E., 35–36, 82
Opiate users, 86
    and cohesiveness of family, 87
    social and personal characteristics of, 86
Opportunities, illegitimate and legitimate, 35–36
Organic psychoses and delinquency, 48

Palmer, Stuart, 110
Parens patriae, 159, 161, 169, 170
Parents of parolees, 203–204
    serial monogamy of, 203
Paris, gangs in, 83
Parolees, success and failure of, 201–205
Pennsylvania prison system, 220

Personal and social control, 60–61
  direct control, indirect control, and internalized control, 60
Personality system: id, ego, and superego, 44
Pickpockets, 24
Piliavin, Irving, 136
Police-community relations, 141, 145
  citizens' advisory committees, 144
  headquarters unit and precinct units, 142
  as a staff and a line function, 142
Police discretionary authority, 151
  written guidelines for, 151
Police disposition, 13, 137–140
  depending on youth's demeanor, 138
  and relations with community, 140
  use of youth services bureaus
Police officers:
  attitudes of, influenced by situational factors and personal background, 136
  childhood and career experiences of, 140
  encounters of, with juveniles, 135–136
  as faculty members, 143
  as guest speakers, 143
  and job satisfaction from helping people, 145
  skills of, in human relationship, 135
  as social workers, 145
Police programs for youth, 143–144
Polk, Kenneth, 54, 55
Polsky, Howard W., 236
Poor societies and delinquency, 24
  delinquent youth in India, 24, 25

Poor societies and delinquency (*Cont.*):
  illicit trafficking in women in Asia, 25
  pickpockets in South Asia, 24–25
Portune, Robert, 143–144
Power conflict, 42
Prevention of delinquency (*see* Delinquency prevention)
Probation (*see* Juvenile probation)
Probation officers, 187, 193–195
  as community worker, 198
  functions of, 165
  role of, 187
  service conditions of, 194–195
  training and qualifications of, 191, 193–194
Programs:
  for drug abuse treatment and prevention, 281–284
    ex-addicts as change agents, 283
    multimodality treatment system, 282
    residential, 283
    therapeutic community program, 282
    types of drug users, 281
  for education, 287–290
    participation by parents, 288
    reality-based curricular, 289
  for employment, 284–287
    combatting discrimination, 287
    expansion of job opportunities for youth, 287
    target groups, 285
  for recreation, 290–291
  for religion, 291–292
Providence Educational Center (PEC) in St. Louis, Missouri, 262
Provo experiment in nonresidential correctional programs, 258–259
Psychopathic characteristics, 96

Index 321

Psychotic states and delinquency, 48

Quality of supervision, 196
Quinney, Richard, 42, 105

Race and arrests, 10–11, 16
Ranches as correctional facilities, 222, 223
Rape, forcible, 113
    and alcohol, 113–114
    circumstances leading to, 115
    group rapes, 116
    incidence of, 113
    patterns of, 115
    victim of, 115
Ray, Isaac, 111
Reception or diagnostic centers, 222
Recidivist parolees, group adjustment of, 202–203
Reckless, Walter C., 38, 41–42, 49–50, 57, 58
Reckless's Self-concept Questionnaire, 49
Recruitment:
    of effective community workers, 303
    of minorities and ex-offenders as volunteers, 303–304
Redl, Fritz, 45–46
Referees, 195
Reiss, Albert J., 126–127
Reissman, Frank, 198
Riege, M. G., 93
Robbers, types of, 119
Robbery, 117–120
    accomplices in, 119
    fear of, 118
    and fear of strangers, 118
    juvenile versus adult, 119
Rosenberg, Bernard, 126
Rothman, David J., 5, 6, 220
Rubington, Earl, 62
Runaways, 123–125, 299
    age of, 123
    families of, 124

Runaways (*Cont.*):
    female, classification of, 124–126
    profile of, 124

Sandhu, Harjit S., 92, 93, 106
Savitz, Leonard D., 122
Schafer, Walter E., 54
Schilder, Paul, 111
School failure and delinquency, 54
Schur, Edwin M., 38, 300
Scott, Joseph W., 77
Self-factor, 49
Sellin, Thorsten, 40–41, 119
Sellin-Wolfgang seriousness-of-crime index, 119
Shaw, Clifford R., 93
Sheldon, William H., 43
Shelters, 146, 149, 222
Silverlake experiment in residential milieu therapy, 256–257
Silverstein, Harry, 126
Socialization, 45
    parent-child relationship, proper and improper, 45
Somerville, Dora B., 93
Soviet Union:
    commissions on juvenile affairs in, 209
    commitment of youths to labor colonies in, 210
Spergel, Irving, 82–83
Staff education:
    development of core courses, 303
    exchange between "town" and "gown," 304
    financed by LEEP (Law Enforcement Educational Program) funds, 303
Standards:
    on consent decree, 180–181
    on detention, 181
    on informal probation, 180
    on intake services, legislation on, 179

States:
  with lowest per capita operating expenditures, 225
  requiring longest and shortest stay in juvenile institutions, 225
Status offenders:
  increase in delinquency with incarceration of, 300
  removal of, from justice system, 299
  to be served by YSB, 300
  (*See also* Authority offenders)
Steinmetz, Suzanne K., 108
Stiles, Bill, 307
Straus, Murray A., 108
Street, David, 232, 233
Successful parolees, 204–205
Sutherland, Edwin H., 55–56
Sweden, 89, 210–212
  child welfare boards in, 210
  drunken drivers in, 211
  no juvenile courts in, 210
  probation hostels in, 212
Sykes, Gresham M., 50–51

Tappan, Paul W., 2
Tarde, Gabriel, 56–57
Taylor, A. J. W., 223
Temporary detention, 146–149
Therapeutic communities, 235–236
  definition of, 235
  generating programs for creativity, responsibility, and achievement, 235, 236
Thrasher, Frederic M., 78–81, 290
Toby, Jackson, 22–23, 27
Total institutions:
  adjustments to deprivations, 231
  effects of, 231–232
  leadership in, 232
Training schools, 220–223
  casework services in, 228
  the cottage staff in, 227

Training schools (*Cont.*):
  counseling and religious services in educational program in, 229, 238
  as dumping ground for youth, 226
  function of, 226
  for girls, 222–223
  group living in, 227
  group therapy in, 228
  length of stay at, 225
  life in, 231
  links with the community, 230
  psychological and psychiatric services in, 228
  recreational services in, 229
  staff-inmate relationship in, 231, 234
  as a total institution, 231
Treatment in the community, 5, 9
  during the 18th century, 5
  family responsibility for resocialization, 5
Treatment institutions, 232
  role of belief system and institutional goals, 232
Treatment philosophies, 220, 305
  direct punishment, penitence, training, and counseling, 305
  group therapy, 306
  individual reform and societal reform, 305
  ingredients of treatment, 306
  reality therapy, 306
Typology of delinquents, 105

Unsuccessful parolees, 205

Vandalism, 72–75
  five stages of, 74
  middle-class delinquents and, 75
Vandals, 73–74
  families of, 73

Vandals (*Cont.*):
   and railways, 73
   self-image of, 73, 74
   types of, 73
Vaz, Edmund W., 76, 77, 83
Vedder, Clyde B., 93
Victimization, 21
   of young persons, minorities, and poor people, 21
Vintner, Robert D., 175, 176
Violence:
   in the family, 108
   at the hands of strangers, 118
   as a norm, 109
Vold, George B., 41, 42
Volunteers, 264–267
   acceptance of, 265–266
   profile of, 266–267
   use of, in Japan, 197, 208

Wade, Andrew L., 74
Wattenberg, William W., 122
Weeks, H. Ashley, 255
Weinberg, Martin S., 62
Werthman, Carl, 136
White House Conferences on Children, 7, 301
White youth versus black youth, offenses of, 72
Wilks, Judith, 206, 237, 255
Wilson, Margaret S., 56–57
Wineman, David, 45–46
Wise, Nancy Barton, 77
Wolfgang, Marvin E., 109–110, 119

Yablonsky, Lewis, 81–84
Youth services bureaus (YSB), 247–251, 280, 300

HV 9104 .S3155

Sandhu, Harjit S.

Juvenile delinquency